THE STATE OF
BLACK AMERICA 1989

Published by **National Urban League, Inc.**

January 1989

THE STATE OF BLACK AMERICA 1989

Editor

Janet Dewart

Copyright © National Urban League, Inc., 1989
Library of Congress Catalog Number 77-647469
ISBN 0-914758-10-1

Price $19.00

The cover art is *"The Promise"* by Hughie Lee Smith. *"The Promise"* is the second in the *"Great Artists"* series of limited edition lithographs on black Americans created for the National Urban League through a donation from the House of Seagram.

National Urban League, Inc.

The Equal Opportunity Building ■ 500 East 62nd Street ■ New York, New York 10021

Founded in 1910, the National Urban League is the premier social service and civil rights organization in America. The League is a nonprofit, community-based agency headquartered in New York City, with 113 affiliates in 34 states and the District of Columbia. Its principal objective is to secure equal opportunity for blacks and other minorities.

TABLE OF CONTENTS

About The Authors

DR. JOHN O. CALMORE
Associate Professor
Loyola Law School

Professor Calmore is a distinguished scholar on housing and community development law at Loyola Law School. Previously, he was an associate professor at North Carolina Central University School of Law, where he taught civil rights, housing and community development law, and torts.

Before that, he was Staff Attorney, Western Center on Law and Poverty, where he was responsible for complex litigation and advocacy primarily in the areas of housing, welfare, and health; for state-wide task force coordination; for training of legal workers; and for general backup for attorneys throughout the state of California. John O. Calmore was also Staff Attorney, National Housing Law Project, and Staff Attorney, Western Center on Law and Poverty, in Los Angeles.

He has published numerous articles on fair housing including: "North Carolina's Retreat from Fair Housing: A Critical Examination of North Carolina Human Relations Council vs. Weaver Realty Company"; "National Housing Policies and Black America: Trends, Issues and Implications"; "Proving Housing Discrimination: Intent vs. Effect—The Search for the Proper Touchstone Continues"; and "Fair Housing and the Black Poor: An Advocacy Guide."

Professor Calmore has provided papers and testimony that were presented before the U.S. Commission on Civil Rights, and he is on the board of directors of numerous fair housing organizations.

Professor Calmore received his B.A. from Stanford University and his J.D. from Harvard Law School.

DR. PRICE M. COBBS
President
Pacific Management Systems

Dr. Price M. Cobbs is the President of Pacific Management Systems and the Chief Executive Officer of Cobbs, Inc. He co-authored with William Grier two books, *Black Rage* and *The Jesus Bag*. Both books are considered classics in understanding the inner-drives of black Americans. He has written and lectured extensively on the dynamics and effects of racism and has developed a clinical model to change attitudes and assumptions that arise from racial, ethnic, and value differences.

For the past 20 years he has been an internationally recognized management consultant to Fortune 500 companies, government agencies, and community projects. Most recently, he has conducted seminars at the United Nations headquarters in New York and for the city government of Oakland, California. In 1986, he was a speaker at the annual National Urban League Conference and was an invited Eminent Scholar at Norfolk State University, Norfolk, Virginia.

Dr. Cobbs is a Fellow of the American Psychiatric Association, a member of the Institute of Medicine of the National Academy of Sciences, Certified Consultants International, and a Life Member of the NAACP.

He received a B.A. from the University of California-Berkeley and his M.D. from Meharry Medical College in Nashville, Tennessee. He is currently an Assistant Clinical Professor of Psychiatry, University of California, San Francisco.

MARIAN WRIGHT EDELMAN
President
Children's Defense Fund

Marian Wright Edelman is a leading advocate for children in America. She is the author of *Families in Peril: An Agenda for Social Change* and is the founder and president of the Children's Defense Fund in Washington, D.C.

She earned her B.A. at Spelman College and her LL.B from Yale Law School. She also studied at the University of Geneva in Switzerland.

Mrs. Edelman was director of the Center for Law and Education, Harvard University. Prior to that, she was a Field Foundation Fellow and partner at the Washington Research Project of the Southern Center for Public Policy. Upon the completion of her law degree in 1963, she was the first black woman admitted to the bar in the state of Mississippi, where she practiced law during the height of the Civil Rights Movement. She then became a staff attorney to the NAACP Legal Defense and Educational Fund, Inc.

As president of the Children's Defense Fund, Mrs. Edelman has supervised numerous research and policy studies in defense of children including: poverty and children, adolescent pregnancy, teens and AIDS, education, young families, natality statistics, and maternal and child health.

Mrs. Edelman is chair of the board of Trustees of Spelman College; a member of the board of the Martin L ther King, Jr. Center; a board member of the Council on Foreign Relations; and a member of the board of the March of Dimes. She has won numerous awards and honorary degrees.

DR. LAWFORD L. GODDARD
Associate Director
Institute for the Advanced Study of Black Family Life and Culture, Inc.

Dr. Lawford Lawrence Goddard is a distinguished sociologist/demographer who received his doctoral degree from Stanford University with a minor in Education. He is currently Associate Director of Education and Training at the Institute for the Advanced Study of Black Family Life and Culture, Inc., in Oakland, California, and Senior Research Associate, Alcohol Scholar at the Charles R. Drew University of Medicine and Science, Los Angeles, California.

Dr. Goddard possesses a broad multi-disciplinary social science background, having studied extensively in the areas of sociology, demography, education, history, political economy, and cultural pluralism. As a sociologist interested in human development, Dr. Goddard is particularly concerned with such issues as health, adolescents, and the elderly. He has also studied mortality patterns, fertility values, and population redistribution as they relate to social change and impact on Third World communities and countries.

Dr. Goddard has studied and traveled extensively in the Caribbean and has conducted research on the political economy of migration and the process of economic development and population changes and their impact on the system of social stratification.

His most recent area of interest concerns strategies against substance abuse— education, motivation, manhood and responsibility training, and counseling.

DR. CHARLES V. HAMILTON
Wallace S. Sayre Professor of Government
Columbia University

Dr. Charles V. Hamilton is a distinguished political scientist who has studied black political power in America. Currently, he is the Wallace S. Sayre Professor of Government, Department of Political Science, at Columbia University. Previously, he taught at Albany State College, Tuskegee Institute, and at Rutgers, The State University of New Jersey campus at Newark.

He co-authored with Stokely Carmichael, *Black Power: The Politics of Liberation in America* and *The Bench and the Ballot: Southern Federal Judges and Black Voters*. He authored the *Black Preacher in America* and edited the *Black Experience in American Politics*. In 1982, he published the book, *American Government*. He has written numerous articles for *Ebony, Black World, New York Times Magazine, Black Scholar, Phylon*, and the *Journal of Negro Education*.

Dr. Hamilton earned his B.A. at Roosevelt University; J.D. at Loyola University School of Law; and his M.A. and Ph.D. at the University of Chicago. He has also been a Phi Beta Kappa Visiting Scholar Lecturer and a Visiting Scholar at Russell Sage Foundation.

DR. ROBERT B. HILL
Research Consultant

Dr. Robert B. Hill is currently a research consultant. Previously, he was Senior Research Associate at the Bureau of Social Science Research, Inc., from 1981-86 and Director of Research for the National Urban League from 1972-81.

Dr. Hill received his B.A. in Sociology from the City College of New York and his Ph.D. in Sociology from Columbia University. He has taught on the adjunct faculty of the University of Pennsylvania, universities of Maryland, Howard, Morgan State, Princeton, NYU, and Fordham. He has served on several high-level panels: the U.S. Bureau of the Census Advisory Committee on Black

Population in the 1980 Census; the 1981 White House Conference on Aging; the 1980 White House Conference on Families; and the National Academy of Science's Committee on Child Development Research and Public Policy. He is currently an Adjunct Fellow at the National Center for Neighborhood Enterprise and a member of the Association of Black Sociologists, the National Economic Association, and the American Statistical Association.

Dr. Hill's publications include: "The Black Middle-Class Defined" (1987); "Intergroup Relations" (1987); "The Future of Black Families" (1986); "The Polls and Ethnic Minorities" (1984); *Economic Policies and Black Progress* (1981); *Discrimination and Minority Youth Employment* (1980); *Informal Adoption Among Black Families* (1977); *The Strengths of Black Families* (1971), and various articles for the National Urban League's annual *State of Black America*.

DR. C. ERIC LINCOLN
Professor of Religion and Culture
Duke University

Dr. C. Eric Lincoln is internationally recognized as an authority on the sociology of black religion, and on the sociology of race and ethnic relations in the United States. He has lectured at the leading colleges and universities of the United States including: Harvard, Stanford, Yale, The University of California, Berkeley, Dartmouth, Brown, Fisk, Morehouse, Carleton, Vanderbilt, and at many distinguished colleges and universities in foreign countries.

Professor Lincoln has written or edited 19 books, his first being the internationally celebrated study entitled *The Black Muslims in America* (1961), and his most recent being *Race, Religion and the Continuing American Dilemma* (1984). Several of his books are in current use as texts in colleges throughout the United States. His other scholarly works appear in the *Encyclopeadia Brittanica*, the *Encyclopedia Americana*, the *World Book Encyclopedia*, and other authoritative works in religion and sociology. More than 100 articles have been published in scholarly journals, among them the *Union Seminary Review, Christian Century, Evangelische Theologie, Dedalus, Journal of Social Issues, Journal of Negro Education, Phylon, The Journal of Religion*, and *Evangelische Kommentare*. He is published in at least 20 books in symposia with other scholars.

A prolific writer, C. Eric Lincoln's works have been published frequently in the popular press. Dr. Lincoln has published poetry and, in 1988, a novel, *The Avenue, Clayton City*.

Professor Lincoln holds a Bachelor of Divinity from the University of Chicago and a Ph.D. from Boston University. He also holds a number of honorary degrees. He has taught at Clark, Fisk, and Union Theological Seminary (New York). He has been a visiting professor or an adjunct professor at many leading universities. He is currently Professor of Religion and Culture at Duke University.

Dr. Lincoln is a Fellow of the American Academy of Arts and Sciences, and he is Founding President Emeritus of The Black Academy of Arts and Letters. He is listed in *Who's Who in America,* and in *Who's Who in the World.* In 1984, he was cited for his scholarly work in religion by Pope John Paul II.

DR. WADE W. NOBLES
Executive Director
The Institute for the Advanced Study of
Black Family Life and Culture, Inc.
Professor of Black Studies
San Francisco State University

Dr. Wade W. Nobles is distinguished as an experimental social psychologist, who received his Ph.D. from Stanford University. He has a special interest in the social, ethnic, and cultural relativity of social science, research, and evaluation models. Dr. Nobles is a prominent theoretical scientist in the fields of cross-cultural and ethno-psychology and is one of the leading researchers of black family life and culture.

In addition to his research interest in the area of ethnic family dynamics, his research interest also covers the psychological aspect of culture, black child development, parenting, and systems of human transformation and development.

He is the author of many publications including: *Understanding the Black Family: A Guide For Scholarship and Research; Africanity and the Black Family; The Development of a Theoretical Model; The Km Ebit Husia; Authoritative Utterances of Exceptional Insight for the Black Family; African Psychology: Toward Its Reclamation, Reascension and Revitalization,* and *African-American Families: Issues, Insights and Directions.*

Dr. Nobles is a full, tenured professor in the Department of Black Studies, the School of Ethnic Studies at San Francisco State University and is the founder and current Executive Director of the Institute for the Advanced Study of Black Family, Life and Culture, Inc. He has served as a delegate to the White House Conference on Families and was a member of the President's Commission on Mental Health. He was a participant/convenor of an international group of black scholars meeting in Trinidad, the Virgin Islands, East Africa, and the United States.

Dr. Nobles is an active member of the National Association of Black Psychologists, The National Council for Black Child Development, The National Association for Social and Behavioral Sciences, and The Association for the Study of Classical African Civilizations.

DR. DAVID H. SWINTON
Dean
School of Business
Jackson State University

Dr. David H. Swinton is recognized as one of the country's leading economists. As Dean of the School of Business at Jackson State University, he has written for national publications, including the National Urban League's *The State of Black America* and the *Urban League Review.*

Dr. Swinton has held positions as Director, Southern Center for Studies in Public Policy at Clark College; Assistant Director for Research, Black Economic Research Center; and as Senior Research Associate and Director of Minorities and Social Policy Programs at the Urban Institute.

Dr. Swinton received his undergraduate degree from New York University and his M.A. and Ph.D. degrees from Harvard University. He has served as a Teaching Fellow at Harvard and a lecturer at City College of New York.

DR. REGINALD WILSON
Senior Scholar
American Council on Education

Dr. Reginald Wilson was named Senior Scholar of the American Council on Education in October 1988. He joined the Council as Director of the Office of Minority Concerns on October 1, 1981. Prior to that appointment, he was for nearly 10 years president of Wayne County Community College in Detroit. Dr. Wilson has also been Dean, Director of Test Development and Research, Director of Black Studies, and Director of Upward Bound. Prior to that, he was a psychologist in the Detroit Public Schools. Dr. Wilson has taught graduate courses in psychology and black studies at Wayne State University, the University of Detroit, Oakland University, and the University of Michigan.

He is the co-author of *Human Development in the Urban Community,* the editor of *Race and Equity in Higher Education,* and the author of *Civil Liberties and the U.S.* He is on the editorial board of *The American Journal of Education* and *The Urban Review.*

Dr. Wilson received his Ph.D. in clinical and educational psychology from Wayne State University. He is licensed as a psychologist in Michigan and in Washington, D.C., and does volunteer work with the homeless. He was honored as a Distinguished Alumnus of Wayne State University in 1980 and is a recipient of the Anthony Wayne Award and the Distinguished Service Medal of the City of Detroit.

Black America, 1988:
An Overview

John E. Jacob
President & Chief Executive Officer
National Urban League, Inc.

The state of Black America in 1988 was in marked contrast to the state of the nation. America enjoyed the continuation of its longest peacetime expansion in history — albeit a "peacetime" expansion driven by record military expenditures — while Black America remained mired in recession.

While corporate America embarked on a merger and leveraged buyout binge, the numbers of homeless increased. While presidential candidates debated their commitment to the pledge of allegiance, inner city schools deteriorated. While government officials pressed Japan to buy more goods made in the United States, Japanese companies were locating manufacturing plants in United States sites removed from black population centers.

Among the positive developments in 1988 were the passage of the Civil Rights Restoration Act over a presidential veto and the long-delayed passage of the necessary enforcement amendments to the Fair Housing Act of 1968.

On the political front, African Americans continued to make headway. Jesse Jackson's candidacy galvanized black voters and garnered many white votes. The total of black elected officials climbed over the 6,000 mark. Congressman William Gray gained the highest position held by a black person in the congressional leadership.

On the international front, too, there were important developments that have an impact on black Americans. The agreements on peace in southern Africa and Namibian independence brought a long-sought-for objective into sight, with the further possibility that more change will come to the region, specifically the achievement of political rights for South Africa's black majority.

And Secretary General Gorbachev's peace offensive that included an offer to unilaterally cut Soviet troop and tank strength gave rise to hopes that winding down the Cold War would release resources and energies to crank up the dormant war on poverty in the United States.

With the relaxation of international tensions, it is necessary for the United States to begin planning the transition to a peacetime economy that includes all of our citizens. For in 1988, as in previous years, large numbers of blacks have been excluded from participation in our economic life.

Black citizens have been too often labelled dependents of welfare programs instead of being seen as potential contributors to our economic might. In 1988, there was some movement toward an understanding of the need to equip the disadvantaged with skills and training to take their rightful place in our economy.

1

Congress passed a deeply flawed welfare reform bill that was deficient in a number of important areas, but which did focus on helping people to move from welfare rolls to payrolls. Unfortunately, the new law does not increase the shamefully low benefit levels, nor does it mandate workable training and job creation programs and day care facilities that enable mothers to work.

The continuing black focus on educating minority youth who will be the core of our future workforce began to show results in community-based programs, such as the National Urban League's Education Initiative, which is beginning to make a difference in black youth's test scores and college prep performance. The Carnegie Commission's report that charged school reform with bypassing inner city schools and the growing concern among corporate executives about the quality of their workforce may lead to more progress in urban school systems.

1988 also marked the end, not only of the Reagan presidency, but also of the Reagan Era. George Bush clearly intends to preside over an administration less ideological and more open than his predecessor's. He has spoken of leading a "gentler, kinder nation," met with black leadership in the weeks after his election, appointed minorities to key positions, and spoke eloquently of sharing minority goals.

These developments were in marked contrast to eight years of an administration that refused black access to the White House, campaigned relentlessly to roll back civil rights gains, and was ruthless in cutting federal programs that help black and poor people.

The legacy of the Reagan Era will leave its mark on our society for years to come. President Reagan is one of the few presidents to have largely achieved the goals he set for himself when he came to office — lower tax rates, a big defense buildup, federal withdrawal from social programs, and less government.

We will continue to pay the price exacted by meeting the Reagan policy goals. The combination of lower taxes and sky-high defense spending led to extraordinary deficits that will handcuff policymakers in the years to come.

Some people see the deficits as the result of a failed strategy of lower tax rates and an expensive military expansion. The result has been to get the federal debt levels so high that Congress might be unable to pass new social programs or expand old ones.

Another legacy of the Reagan Era is deeper race and class divisions. The past eight years have seen the rich get richer and the poor get poorer. In effect, there has been a huge transfer of resources from the poor to the affluent. Inequality has always been a serious national problem, but in the past eight years, we have become a far more unequal society.

Racial divisions have also increased sharply. The Reagan administration's war on affirmative action, its refusal to allow access to decision-making by minorities, its fight against civil rights legislation, and its often demeaning acts and statements about the poor, have created bitterness among blacks and encouraged racists in the white community.

So it is no accident that recent years have seen a rise in violent racial incidents or that anti-black attitudes appear to be stronger. The president who said he would use the "bully pulpit" of the White House to attack racism, instead allowed his Justice Department to give aid and comfort to enemies of civil rights progress.

The Reagan Era gave new respectability to greed and indifference to the sufferings of others. The tilt in public rhetoric away from what we need to do together as a society to a celebration of wealth without social responsibility helped make this the "age of greed."

The tragic aspect of all this is that it was unnecessary. The many billions wasted on defense programs that do not work could have been invested in training, education, and job programs that help people to get work. And even a conservative program that downgraded government's role could have been implemented without encouraging anti-social attitudes. After all, true conservatism means conserving the best of the past and cultivating responsibility toward those who have less.

History will make a final judgment on the Reagan Era, but from this vantage point it was a regressive period in our national life: a time when some Americans got richer, but our society as a whole got poorer, and blacks were driven further from the goal of equality.

That goal will be forever in the distance so long as black poverty remains so disproportionate. A third of all black people are poor — more if you use a measurement of poverty that is closer to the income needs required to meet minimally decent living standards than the current poverty index, which is based on a formula designed to determine the minimum necessary for short-term survival.

Black — and white — poverty increased in the 1980s. Some eight million more people were poor in 1987 (the last year for which there are definitive figures) than a decade earlier. Two million of the new poor are black. Nearly half of all black children live in poverty. Blacks are three times as likely as whites to be poor.

But simply to state such shocking statistics is to understate the nature of black poverty. Ideologues and the callous say that it is the result of single female-headed families, or of the refusal to work, or of generous social benefits that discourage workforce participation.

The facts argue otherwise. Compared with a decade ago, when black poverty rates were lower, black unemployment rates are the same and the percentage of the black poor living in female-headed families is lower.

The rise in black poverty can be traced to two major factors — the shift in the economy that reduced opportunities for less-skilled workers and cuts in federal programs that provide opportunities to escape from poverty.

Over the past decade, poverty rates for intact black families have risen as fast as the rates for female-headed families. The region with the highest black poverty rate is the Midwest — the region hardest hit by deindustrialization and the decline in manufacturing jobs. The Center on Budget and Policy Priorities estimates that only one in every 12 black families with children that would have been poor without government benefits was lifted out of poverty by those benefits. A decade ago, the figure was one of every six. The Center says that Census Bureau data indicate that the reduced effectiveness of federal benefit programs account for almost 40 percent of the rise in black poverty over the past decade.

Another indicator of the economic deterioration among blacks is the decline in real black income. Among the poor, more are poorer — their incomes fell from over $5,000 in 1978 to under $4,000 in 1987, adjusted for inflation. Black men working full-time experienced an inflation-adjusted decline in earnings of 10 percent. Among younger black men — the under-30 group starting families — real income is half what it was in the early 1970s. A prime cause is the extraordinary high black unemployment rate — about two-and-a-half times that for whites, and trending higher.

The gap between blacks and whites extends beyond poverty and unemployment rates to include all the key indices of life, from infant mortality rates that are at Third World levels in some ghetto neighborhoods, to education, where a recent study has found blacks disproportionately shunted into slow learner classes and excluded from programs for the gifted, to housing, where a recent study found high levels of segregation in the suburbs, as well as in urban housing.

At year-end, the tragic dimensions of that gap was heightened by the report of the National Center for Health Statistics that revealed life expectancy for blacks declined for the second year in a row — the first back-to-back annual decline in this century — while white life expectancy continued to increase.

And it is ironic that in 1989, the 200th anniversary of the adoption of the U.S. Constitution that defined blacks as "three-fifths" of other persons, black income is well below 60 of percent of white income, and other indicators find blacks at an even greater disadvantage.

The black-white gap might be barely tolerable if it were narrowing, but in the 1980s it has widened. That is why the Commission on Minority Participation in Education and American Life, which included former Presidents Ford and Carter, issued a report in 1988 that charged America was "moving backward" in its efforts to secure equity for minority citizens. The Commission's report echoed the findings of the Kerner Commission two decades earlier that America was sliding into "two societies — separate and unequal."

Because such warnings gather dust on the shelves while the black-white gap continues to widen, the National Urban League is mounting a nationwide drive behind the goal — "Parity 2000." Our objective is to secure parity between black and white citizens by the end of the century.

We have called on Mr. Bush to make this objective a key priority for his presidency. The new administration is uniquely placed to articulate the goal of eliminating the racial inequality that evades American life. It should declare that its overriding objective will be to put policies in place that lead to parity between black and white Americans in educational achievement, employment, income, housing, life expectancy, infant mortality, and other key indicators of individual and family well-being.

Undoing four hundred years of oppression and neglect in a dozen years will not be easy, but it is an achievable goal. If the black-white gap is closed by about seven percent a year between now and 2000, parity could be achieved. When we consider the vast changes that took place in the 1960s, and specifically in the progress toward dismantling southern segregation in that period, we see that enormous changes can be wrought in short periods of time.

A national Parity 2000 goal would include the private sector and the black community, as well as government. Intensive corporate and neighborhood-based initiatives to improve education, training, hiring, health, and housing will be essential.

Government clearly has to be the prime mover of such a national effort, for only it has the power and the resources to implement nationwide programs that have an impact, and only it has the moral and constitutional leadership role that can marshall private and nonprofit groups behind national objectives.

Articulation of a Parity 2000 goal by the Bush administration would give it something it lacks — a unifying objective that transcends mere muddling through. It would give it a political objective as well — to wean blacks away from the opposition party and to solidify the political center.

The Parity 2000 objective would also clarify Mr. Bush's leadership profile, for despite his public statements about the importance of ideology, he is seen as a non-ideological manager. A Parity 2000 drive would allow him to seize an ideologically pure issue and champion a vision of a more equal society, while demonstrating his managerial competence by implementing specific programs designed to meet the goal.

We should not underestimate the importance of the vision of racial equality, either. This vision was the driving force behind the civil rights progress of the 1960s, unifying blacks and whites, liberals and conservatives, rich and poor, behind the simple fairness of treating people equally and securing every person's constitutional rights. Such a vision of a fairer, more just society is desperately needed in these days when there is a burgeoning revolt against the greed that dominates national life, and when the nation needs to find new channels for its resources and energies, as the Cold War winds down.

Parity 2000 is also essential for America's economic survival in a competitive global economy. With its workforce growing blacker and browner daily, the United States will not be able to compete in the future unless it assures each and every young person the education, training, health care, and decent living conditions that will enable them to take their place as productive citizens in an open, integrated, pluralistic society.

Parity 2000 can be implemented by carefully designed federal policies that would include:

- a national effort to create jobs or training opportunities for every disadvantaged person,

- a national education policy that puts every poor child into a quality early childhood education program and brings excellent educational opportunities to all disadvantaged youngsters,

- transformation of the welfare system to provide decent living standards for all of the poor along with the education, training, and jobs to be productive,

- a massive, targeted program to end the crisis in affordable housing,

- equitable access to quality health care for the many millions who have no health insurance,

- an end to the plague of drugs that is destroying our communities and turning our school yards into combat zones, and

- aggressive national policies to protect civil rights and wipe out the last vestiges of racism and discrimination.

Such programs are not liberal or conservative — they are just common sense, rational policies to reverse the backward drift to two societies — one rich and white, one poor and black.

The huge federal deficit will be cited as a reason why such an ambitious program cannot be implemented, but it is hard to believe that a trillion dollar budget cannot accommodate investments that close the racial gap, open new opportunities for people to become productive contributors to our economy, and lay the groundwork for making our economy more competitive in the global marketplace. Conservative corporate leaders have already called for multi-billion dollar investments in child care, in education, and in housing and skills training programs, notwithstanding the deficit.

We believe the fiscal viability of the Parity 2000 program is sound, given the advisability of shifting expenditures from programs that have lesser priority and the possibility of shifting revenues from the affluent who have benefited from past policies that increased poverty, hunger, and homelessness. It would be a sad commentary on the moral strength of this nation if it decided that it is more convenient to allow the racial gap to widen and to become a more unequal society than to close the gap and bring the excluded into the mainstream, thus strengthening national unity, cohesiveness, and economic power.

The National Urban League's call for Parity 2000 is a call for helping America to live up to its ideals, to mobilize the untapped resources of its black population, and to secure a better society for all Americans.

This is a goal that deserves bipartisan support, like other great national projects of the past, such as winning the war, implementing the Marshall Plan, containing Soviet expansionism, and overturning segregation. We intend to press our Parity 2000 goal upon the new administration and the Congress and to enlist public support for it. To this end, we have asked contributors to this volume of our annual State of Black America report to focus on parity within their given areas — how wide the gap is, what is needed to close it, and what public policy initiatives will be necessary to close the gap.

We have been fortunate in securing papers from outstanding scholars. Their independent evaluations are intended to inform and to stimulate, but their views do not necessarily reflect the official position or policies of the National Urban League. Our own summation and recommendations appear at the end of this report.

This *State of Black America*, like past ones, serves to increase the nation's awareness of the reality of life within Black America and to influence the decision-making process in 1989. We express our gratitude to the authors.

The Economic Status of Black Americans

David Swinton, Ph.D.

INTRODUCTION

This report on the current economic status of black Americans comes at the end of the Reagan administration and the beginning of the Bush administration. The new administration will follow an administration which presided over eight years of stagnation and retrogression in the economic status of black Americans. As we have reported in all of the last few volumes of *The State Of Black America*, no progress was made in reducing the longstanding economic disparities faced by blacks during the Reagan administration. In fact, racial inequality in American economic life actually increased by many of the standard indicators.

In the pages of this essay we will present the updated data and discuss recent trends in the economic status of black Americans. Our emphasis this year will be on describing the magnitude and dimensions of the persisting economic inequality in economic life. As the next few pages will make clear, not only has unequal economic status persisted for blacks but also the size of the disparities are very large. We have focused on describing the dimensions and magnitude of racial disparities in economic life because we think the new Bush administration will need a clear understanding of the large magnitude of the problem of economic disparities as a precondition to finding effective remedies to the problem.

Several points should be made about the focus of this essay. First, we have deliberately avoided a lengthy discussion of the causes of the persisting disparities. We have discussed the reasons for the persisting disparities in previous essays, and we will briefly offer our explanation in the concluding section of this essay. Second, we have also chosen to focus on the broad dimensions of inequality. We will not attempt to fine tune our discussion or to analyze in detail all of the differences which exist within the black community. While such internal differences may be of interest, this essay is about the overall size and structure of the economic pyramid within the black community rather than the distribution of blacks within this economic pyramid. Third, while year to year economic fluctuations are of interest and although we will note the latest trends, the essay is about the long-term persistence of racial inequality which is observed year in and year out at all states of the business cycle. Finally, while we will present some notions concerning the implications of recent experience for public policy, we will also avoid engaging in a lengthy policy discussion. We do believe that it is transparently obvious that policy actions of the most recent past have been painfully inadequate.

9

Reasonable observers may disagree over the causes of racial inequality. the precise magnitude and dimensions of racial inequality, the importance of the latest fluctuations in racial inequality, and the most appropriate public policies to cure the racial inequality that exist in American economic life. However, the data which will be presented in this essay will identify economic gaps that are so large and so persistent that few could deny that pervasive racial inequality is a problem that requires immediate and significant national attention. Certainly this is the case if we expect to make any significant progress in reducing existing racial gaps in economic life by the turn of the century. We hope that this essay will help the new administration understand the importance and necessity of assigning a high priority to this problem.

The essay will proceed in a straightforward fashion. We will start with a brief review of recent trends and current racial gaps in income and poverty rates. This will be followed by brief review of the contribution of each source of income to the existing racial disparities. We will next look at the disparities in black participation in the American economy, which produces the persisting disparities in income and poverty rates.

This brief exploration will touch on disparities in business ownership, wealth holdings, and labor market status. Throughout the descriptive sections, we will present differences in measures of central tendency like medians and means, and occasionally discuss a distribution. Such indicators will provide measures of the level of disparity for typical black American individuals. In addition, in most instances, we will translate the individual differences into aggregate gap measures showing the total parity gap for the black population as a whole. These aggregate measures are intended to provide indications of the overall magnitude of the problem of racial disparities in economic life. Finally, we will have a brief concluding section that discusses the implications of the analysis for achieving racial parity in economic life under the new administration.

DIMENSIONS OF RACIAL INEQUALITY IN ECONOMIC LIFE

Per Capita Income

The most comprehensive measure of economic status is income. Recent trends in income are tracked in Table 1, which displays data on per capita income and aggregate income for selected years since 1970. Per capita income and aggregate income tend to increase from year to year for all racial groups. Our data show that this has been the case for blacks as well except for the aberration of the recession at the start of the Reagan administration. By 1987, black income per person was $7,499 and the aggregate income received by black Americans about 220 billion dollars. Both of these indicators are at all time high levels. However, the table also shows that white per capita income has risen and is likewise at historical high levels. Increasing per capita and aggregate income trends are generally the rule in good and bad times (except very deep recessions) and reflect normal improvements in economic productivity. In recent years this trend has been helped by declining proportions of children and increasing proportions working among working age populations.

Thus, this trend does not reflect an improvement in the relative economic status of blacks. In fact, the data in the last three columns indicate that there has been no significant decline in racial income inequality as measured by the ratio of black to white per capita income since 1970. Indeed, income inequality has increased since the end of the 1970s by this measure. For example, blacks received $594 per person for every $1,000 per person that whites received in 1978. This amount was an increase of $37 per thousand from the amount observed in 1970. This represents slow progress in closing the relative gap between 1970 and 1978. In fact, if the rate of progress observed between 1970 and 1978 had been maintained it would still have taken 73 years or until the year 2043 to obtain parity in per capita income.

However, as noted, the slow progress of the 1970s was not maintained. In fact, despite a recovery from the recession low in 1982, the current rate of per capita income in the black community in comparison with receipt in the white community, i.e., $575 per $1,000, is lower than it was in 1978. Thus, at the rate of progress which existed between 1978 and 1987, parity would never be obtained. However, even if we are very generous and measure progress from the recession low of 1982, it would still take another 131 years or until the year 2118 to obtain parity in per capita income. The generosity of the assumption is brought out by the fact that after obtaining the Reagan Era peak of $586 per $1,000 in 1985, relative black per capita income has fallen for the past two years. Without a reversal in trends per capita income, parity is nowhere in sight.

Absolute numbers will make the large size of the gap and the increasing seriousness of the problem clear. The income per black person in 1987 at $7,499 indicates that the income parity gap was equal to $5,532 for every black person

---

Table 1
Per Capita Income, Aggregate Income
And Income Gaps Selected Years
(1987$)

| | Aggregate Black Income | Per Capita Income | | | Parity Gap | |
		Black	White	B + W	Per Capita	Aggregate
1987	220 Billion	7,499	13,031	.575	5,532	162 Billion
1986	216 Billion	7,470	12,803	.583	5,333	154 Billion
1982	172 Billion	6,311	11,218	.563	4,907	134 Billion
1978	176 Billion	7,028	11,841	.594	4,813	121 Billion
1970	127 Billion	5,470	9,817	.557	4,347	101 Billion

Source: U.S. Department of Commerce, Bureau of the Census, *Money, Income and Poverty Status in 1987*, Table 13. Calculations of Aggregates and Gaps done by author.

— man, woman, and child. This shortage has increased steadily since 1970 when it was about $4,347 per person. This, incidentally, brings out the fact that constant relative incomes during periods of rising incomes imply steadily increasing absolute income gaps.

The most dramatic expression of this income gap is revealed by a quick estimate of the aggregate parity gap. As the numbers in the last column of Table 1 show the aggregate income gap is very large. In 1987, black income fell $162 billion short of the amount required for parity with white Americans.

The aggregate gap has also grown steadily since 1970 when it was already about 101 billion dollars. Between 1970 and 1987, the aggregate income gap increased by over 60 percent or about 61 billion dollars. Thus, the income of blacks is falling further and further behind in absolute terms.

Family Income

Table 2 provides similar data for family income. Although family income is a less comprehensive measure of income status for the population as a whole, it is frequently considered a better measure of the economic well being of the population since people live and raise their children in family units. Review of the data in this table reveals even greater deterioration in relative black family income than in relative black per capita income.

First, black family income during the 1980s has been significantly below the levels attained during the 1970s. Thus the absolute standard of income for black families has fallen. Indeed, even in 1987 median income for black families was still almost $900 less than it had been in 1978 and even $300 below its 1970 level. As the Table shows median family income actually declined slightly for blacks in 1987 from its 1986 level while median family income increased slightly for whites.

Second, although family income has grown slower in the 1980s than in the 1970s for all American families, black family income grew significantly slower than white family income. Thus, median white family income exceeded its 1970 highs in 1987 in contrast to the substantial shortfall for blacks.

These diverging growth trends for family income has resulted in substantially higher levels of racial inequality in family income. This data is shown in the last three columns of Table 2. For example, between 1970 and 1980 the ratio of black to white median family income fell from 61.3 to 56.1 percent. Thus, while the typical black family had about $613 for every $1,000 the typical white family had in 1970, this had fallen to $561 per $1,000 by 1978. The absolute gap had risen as well. In 1970, the family income of the median black family was $11,582 less than the family income of the median family. By 1978, this gap had increased by $2,594 to $14,176. The trends in this table suggest that family income parity will never be obtained unless something happens to change current trends.

These individual differences again have very large aggregate impacts. For example, using mean family income data not shown in the above table, we can estimate that black families received approximately $167 billion dollars in family

Table 2
Median Family Income
Selected Years
(1987$)

	Median Family Income Black	White	B + W	B + W	Aggregate Gap
1987	18,098	32,274	56.1	14,176	107 Billion
1986	18,247	31,935	57.1	13,688	*
1985	17,734	30,799	57.5	13,065	*
1982	16,011	28,969	55.3	12,958	*
1978	18,952	31,998	59.2	13,046	*
1970	18,378	29,960	61.3	11,582	58 Billion

Source: U.S. Department of Commerce, Bureau of the Census, *Money, Income and Poverty Status in 1987*, Table 13. Calculations of Aggregates and Gaps done by author.

income in 1987. If there had been income parity, black families would have received $274 billion. Thus, in 1987, the family income parity gap was $107 billion. This gap was almost double the $58 billion parity gap that existed in 1970. This 49 billion dollar increase in the family income parity gap is even more remarkable when one compares the fact that the income of individual black families actually declined in absolute terms between 1970 and 1987. Of course, much of the increase in the aggregate family income gap reflects growth in the number of families. However, the increase in inequality between 1970 and 1987 cost the average black family about $1,500 and cost the community as a whole about $10.5 billion.

Distribution of Families by Income Class

The central tendency in black income reflects two divergent trends which have impacted the distribution of family income within the black population since 1970. These trends concern the growth in the proportion of low-, middle-, and high-income families among the black and white populations since 1970. As the data in Table 3 show, if the broad middle is taken to be those with income between $10,000 and $35,000, then the proportion of both populations in this middle income group has shrunk since 1970. For blacks the proportion in this middle-income group has fallen from 56.6 percent to 47.7 percent between 1970 and 1987 while for whites the decline has been from 51.8 percent to 45.1. However, while for the period as a whole, all of the drop in the proportion of whites in the middle-income category and more was accounted for by an increase in the proportion of white families with high-income, the drop in the proportion of blacks in the middle-income category was almost evenly divided between increases in the low income category and increases in the high income category. Thus, while the proportion of blacks with low incomes increased by 16.7 percent between

1970 and 1987, the proportion of whites with low-income dropped by 6.2 percent. Although the proportion of blacks in the high-income category increased significantly between 1970 and 1978 (by 4.6 percentage points or 25.9 percent), the gain in numbers of families as a result of this improvement, 345 thousand, was almost completely offset by the increase in low-income families, 322 thousand.

The trend since 1970 has left substantial inequality in place. By 1987, blacks are over four times as likely to have very low income (under $2,500) and whites are more than 2.5 times as likely to have incomes greater than $50,000. Indeed, in 1987, about 1.5 million more black families had incomes less than $10,000 than would have had such low incomes if parity existed while about 1.7 million fewer black families had incomes over $35,000.

However, the most disturbing trend revealed by the income distribution data is the fact that for the black population most of the increase in proportions with low family incomes has occurred since 1978. Indeed, between 1970 and 1978, the percentage with very low incomes (under $2,500) actually declined by 6.6 percent. However, between 1978 and 1987, this proportion increased by 50 percent. Similarly, almost all of the increase in the proportion with high income occurred between 1970 and 1978. For example, there was a four percentage point or 22.5 percent increase in the proportion of black families with income over $35,000 between 1970 and 1978 while the increase between 1978 and 1987 was only six-tenths of a percentage point or 2.7 percent. Thus, between 1978 and 1987, the income distribution for black families has deteriorated markedly. Moreover, while there has also been a slight increase in the proportion of white families with low incomes (eight-tenth of a percentage point) this was more than offset by a 1.8 percentage point increase in the proportion of families with high incomes. Thus, income polarization or the rise of the low income population has been a much more marked phenomenon for the black population. Post-1978 trends suggest that

Table 3
Percentage of Black Families
Receiving Incomes In Selected Ranges

	1987 Black	1987 White	1986 Black	1986 White	1978 Black	1978 White	1970 Black	1970 White
Under 5,000	13.5	3.2	13.4	3.3	8.4	2.4	9.0	2.9
Less Than 10,000	30.0	9.3	29.3	9.8	26.6	8.5	25.7	9.6
10,000-34,999	47.7	45.1	48.2	45.7	51.7	47.7	56.6	51.8
More Than 35,000	22.3	45.7	22.5	44.5	21.7	43.8	17.7	38.6
More Than 50,000	9.5	24.4	9.5	23.7	8.5	21.1	5.7	16.4

Source: U.S. Department of Commerce, Bureau of the Census, *Money, Income and Poverty Status in 1987*, Table 13. Calculations of Aggregates and Gaps done by author.

parity in income distribution will not be approached without some major changes in the American economy.

For the sake of completeness, we should also note that income inequality exists throughout the income distribution. Poor blacks are generally poorer than poor whites and wealthier blacks are less well off than wealthier whites. These facts are illustrated by the data in Table 4.

As the table shows the lowest 20 percent of the black distribution has an upper income limit that is only 47 percent of the upper limit for the lowest income whites. This percentile goes up as with movement up the income distribution. However, the upper limit of the fourth quintile is still only 69 percent of the upper limit for whites. Even the lower limit of the top five percent of the black income distribution is only 72 percent of the corresponding limit for the white population. This pattern has been roughly the same since 1970.

Number of Earners and Family Headship

Part of the reason that black families have lower incomes in any given year is because they have less favorable characteristics. Data taken from the 1987 Current Population Report (see references in Table 1) substantiate these differences. Of course, part of the long-term reason for less favorable characteristics is the persistence of lower incomes. Two factors which disadvantage black family incomes are lower numbers of earners per family and fewer intact families. For example, 53.7 percent of black families have one or fewer earners as compared to 41.3 percent of white families. Similarly, only 51.3 percent of black families are headed by married couples compared to 83.2 percent of white families. Although a larger proportion of black than white married couple families has a working wife (65.9 vs 55.3 percent), only 33.8 percent of all black families are working couple families compared to 46 percent of all white families.

Table 4
Incomes of Selected Positions of
The Income Distribution
In 1987

	Black	White	Black/White
Lowest Fifth	6,800	14,450	47.1
Second	13,801	25,100	55.0
Third	22,590	36,600	62.8
Fourth	36,652	52,910	69.3
Top 5%	62,000	86,300	71.8

Source: U.S. Department of Commerce, Bureau of the Census, *Money, Income and Poverty Status in 1987*, Table 13. Calculations of Aggregates and Gaps done by author.

However, even though blacks have disadvantaged characteristics, the major part of the black disadvantage occurs because blacks of all characteristics fare significantly worse than comparable whites. Black families with every number of earners have much lower incomes than white families. For example, black families with no earners have incomes only 37 percent as high as no earner white families while one earner black families have only 54 percent as much income as one earner white families. Even four earner black families have median incomes that are only 83 percent as much as the incomes of four earner white families.

Similarly, black families with every type of headship earn less than corresponding white families. Income equality is greatest for married couple families with both spouses in the labor force. However, even these black families have only about 81 percent as much income as white families. On the other hand, the family incomes of all other headship types are less than two-thirds the median family incomes of corresponding white families. Indeed, a rough calculation suggests that differences in family headship could account for no more than 11 percent of the racial disparity in family income.

Income Trends by Census Region

Finally, we will complete our review of income disparities by looking at recent trends in family income by region. This data is displayed in Table 5. First, we should note that the pattern of income growth for blacks and whites has varied across regions and time periods. Betwen 1970 and 1978, the South was the only region which recorded growth in constant dollar family income for blacks. Income held fairly steady in the Midwest and declined for black families in the Northeast and West. During this period, the declines were greatest in the West. Inequality increased in all regions except the South during this first period with sharpest increase in inequality occurring in the West.

Between 1978 and 1982, which corresponded to a peak and trough respectively of the business cycle, black income declined in all regions, and relative inequality increased. However, the sharpest declines occurred in the Midwest. In fact, the declines in black income in the Midwest were so sharp that this region replaced the South as the region in which black incomes were lowest and racial inequality was highest.

During the post-1982 recovery, black income has improved in all regions. However, in 1987, median income for black families in all census regions except the South was still below the 1970 level. There had been at best modest attenuation in income inequality in all regions between 1982 and 1987. In fact, income inequality was still considerably higher in all regions in 1987 compared to both 1978 and 1970. Black/white income inequality as measured both by the absolute differences in black/white income and the ratio of black to white income is at record levels in all regions.

The increase in racial inequality in family income has been especially pronounced outside of the South. For example, in the Midwest the relative black to white median family income has declined from $734 per $1,000 in 1970 to $521

Table 5
Family Income By Regions

	NORTHEAST			MIDWEST			SOUTH			WEST		
	Blk	Wht	B/W	Blk	Wht	B/W	Blk	Wht	B/W	Blk	Wht	B/W
1987	20.678	35.262	58.6	16.755	32.149	52.1	17.302	30.729	56.3	20.627	32.521	63.4
1986	21.656	34.552	62.7	17.987	31.612	56.9	16.822	30.193	55.7	22.948	32.510	70.1
1982	17.180	30.101	57.1	14.428	29.038	49.7	15.210	26.922	56.5	19.249	29.441	65.3
1978	20.113	32.331	62.2	23.595	32.812	71.9	16.976	29.547	57.5	18.634	32.493	57.3
1970	21.171	31.448	67.3	23.671	32.252	73.4	15.278	26.849	56.9	23.536	31.240	75.3

Source: David Swinton. "The Economic Status of Blacks." in Janet Dewart ed. *The State of Black America*, New York: National Urban League. 1988. Page 135. Table 5. and U.S. Department of Commerce. Bureau of the Census. *Money Income Poverty Status in 1987*. Page 17. Table 4.

per $1,000 in 1987. The median black family had $8,581 less income than the median white family in 1970, and this gap had grown to $15,394 in 1987, despite the fact that there was almost no change in the median income of white families between these two years. The increase in inequality alone between 1970 and 1987 cost the median black family over $3,000 per year in the Northeast, over $3,800 per year in the West, and over $6,800 in the Midwest. Thus, no progress has been made towards attaining family income parity in any region of the country, and significant erosion has occurred in the non-South, especially in the Midwest.

Poverty

Given the discussion of income trends for the last few paragraphs, it will come as no surprise that black poverty remains high throughout the nation both absolutely and relative to white poverty. The national data to support this statement is displayed in Table 6. As can be seen from the data, in 1987 fully one-third of black persons lived in households with incomes below the poverty level. The proportions were even higher for black children who experienced a poverty rate of 45.1 percent. Moreover, over half of all families headed by females had poverty level incomes in 1987.

Poverty levels are generally higher than they were during the late seventies for all groups. Since 1970, more than 2.1 million black persons have been added to the poverty rolls, raising the total number of poor blacks to 9.7 million in 1987.

Although poverty rates have gone up for white Americans since 1970, the racial gaps which exist in 1987 are still very pronounced. Moreover, while black poverty went up in 1987, white poverty rates went down slightly. Thus, between 1986 and 1987, about 696 thousand more black persons were added to the ranks of the poor while the poor white ranks were reduced by about 774 thousand persons. Overall, blacks are more than three times as likely to be poor than whites. Black children are also more than three times likely as white children to be poor, while black families headed by females are about twice as likely as corresponding white families to be poor.

In the aggregate, about 6.6 million more blacks overall and 2.9 million more black children were poor in 1987 than would be poor if blacks had the same poverty rates as white persons. These huge parity gaps have not attenuated to any significant extent during the last two decades. This is especially true for the past ten years.

Trends in poverty within the separate census regions mirror trends in income. See Table 7. Poverty rates are higher in 1987 for blacks in all regions outside of the South than they were in 1970. Between 1970 and 1978, poverty rates declined steadily in the South, held steady in the Midwest, and went up in the Northeast and the West. Then poverty rates climbed in all regions as a result of the recession of the early 1980s and continued to rise until about 1984. Although poverty rates have been recovering somewhat since 1984, black poverty is still higher than it was in 1970 in all non-southern regions. Moreover, in the Midwest, poverty rates have never recovered to anywhere near their late 1970s levels. Poverty rates actually

18

Table 6
Poverty Rates for Selected Years
Total Persons In Poverty

	Black	White	B + W
1987	33.1	10.5	3.15
1986	31.1	11.0	2.83
1982	35.6	12.0	2.97
1978	30.6	8.7	3.52
1970	33.5	19.9	3.38

Related Children Under 18

	Black	White	B + W
1987	45.1	15.0	3.01
1986	42.7	15.3	2.79
1982	47.3	16.5	2.87
1978	41.2	11.0	3.75
1970	41.5	10.5	3.95

Female Headed Families

	Black	White	B + W
1987	53.8	26.4	2.04
1986	52.9	27.9	1.90
1982	57.4	28.7	2.00
1978	53.1	24.9	2.13
1970	58.8	31.4	1.87

Source: U.S. Department of Commerce, Bureau of the Census, *Money, Income and Poverty Status in 1987*, Table 13. Calculations of Aggregates and Gaps done by author.

increased for blacks in all regions between 1986 and 1987. Black poverty has trended up most and been most sticky in the Midwest. In fact, for most of the 1980s the Midwest has replaced the South as the region with the most pervasive black poverty.

As the data in Table 7 clearly reveals, racial disparities in poverty rates are also still at a very high level. In fact, since there was a slight decline in white poverty rates between 1986 and 1987, the parity gap in poverty rates went up in all regions in 1987. In 1987, black poverty is at least three times the rate of white poverty in every census region except the West, where the black poverty rate still exceeds the white poverty rate by better than 2 to 1. Moreover, in all non-southern regions not only has absolute black poverty gone up but also the degree of racial inequality has also increased sharply since 1970, especially in the Midwest.

In absolute terms, excess black poverty is high in all census regions. In 1987, for example, the poverty rate parity gap was 962 thousand persons in the Northeast,

19

Table 7
Poverty Rates for Regions: Selected Years

	NORTHEAST			MIDWEST			SOUTH			WEST		
	Blk	Wht	B/W	Blk	Wht	B/W	Blk	Wht	B/W	Blk	Wht	B/W
1987	28.8	8.9	3.2	36.6	9.9	3.7	34.5	11.5	3.0	24.3	11.5	2.1
1986	24.0	8.9	2.7	34.5	10.6	3.3	33.6	11.8	2.8	21.7	12.3	1.8
1984	32.2	10.7	3.0	37.9	11.5	3.3	33.6	12.0	2.8	26.6	11.8	2.3
1978	29.1	8.2	3.5	24.8	7.4	3.4	34.1	10.2	3.3	26.1	8.9	2.9
1970	20.0	7.7	2.6	25.7	8.9	2.9	42.6	12.4	3.4	20.4	10.6	1.9

Source: U.S. Department of Commerce. Bureau of the Census. Money Income and Poverty Status . . . : 1986. 1987 and Bureau of the Census. Current Population Reports Series P-60. Characteristics of the Population Below Poverty Level. 1984. 1978. 1970.

about 1.5 million persons in the Midwest, about 3.8 million persons in the South, and about 318 thousand persons in the West. Clearly blacks are far from attaining parity in poverty rates throughout the nation.

SOURCES OF INCOME AND INEQUALITY

The persisting racial disparities in income and poverty rates reflect a persistence of unequal black participation in the American economy. An overview of this participation inequality can be obtained from a quick review of the origins of black income inequality by income source. This data is displayed in Table 8 for 1970 and 1986.

As can be seen from the data, the major source of income for both black and whites in 1986 was employment. Blacks received over 82 percent of their income from employment while whites received about 80 percent of their income from this source. This is true in both 1970 and 1986, although there was a significant decline in the proportion of income deriving from employment between 1970 and 1986 as 87 percent of income originated from this source for both races in 1970.

In 1986, blacks obtained 96.6 percent of their employment income from wage and salary employment and only 3.6 percent from self employment. Whites obtained a larger share of their employment income from self employment (7.7 percent) and a correspondingly smaller percentage from wage and salary employment (92.3 percent).

Blacks receive roughly 18 percent of their income from non-labor sources. About 1.9 percent of their income from property sources while whites receive 7.6 percent of their income from this source. The share of income arising from social security or railroad retirement is roughly equal for both groups (6.4 percent for blacks and 6.1 percent for whites). The share of black income originating from public welfare payments is small at 3.6 percent but is still substantially larger than the share of income five-tenths percent that whites receive from this source. Whites receive a larger portion of their income from private pensions and annuities at 3.7 percent than do blacks who receive only 2.6 percent of their income from these sources. Finally, blacks receive more income from all other sources which include unemployment compensation, child support, alimony, and other miscellaneous sources.

The black income disadvantage derives from two factors. First, with the exception of welfare income, blacks are less likely to receive any given category of income than are whites. For example, only 84 percent of blacks versus 93 percent of whites have income from at least one source. Only 25 percent of blacks compared to 61 percent of whites have property income and 2.3 percent of blacks versus 7.5 percent of whites receive self-employment income. Similar disparities exist for each non-welfare income source. The smaller proportions of blacks receiving each source of income contribute significantly to existing disparities in income and poverty rates. About 12.5 percent of blacks and only 3.2 of whites receive welfare income (including supplemental security income).

Table 8
Per Capita Income and Aggregate Per Capita Income
Gaps By Source of Income (1987$)

1986

	Black Per Capita	White Per Capita	B/W	Per Capita Gap	Aggregate Gap	% of Gap
Wage & Salary	5823.38	9099.54	64.00	3276.16	94.8 Billion	63.69
NonFarm Self-Employed	128.17	698.70	18.34	570.53	16.5 Billion	11.09
Farm Self-Employed	.23	53.36	.00	53.13	1.5 Billion	1.03
Property	137.53	945.10	14.55	807.57	23.4 Billion	15.70
Soc. Sec. & RR	459.18	756.29	60.71	297.11	8.6 Billion	5.78
Public Asst.	262.57	72.09	364.23	−190.48	−5.5 Billion	−3.70
Ret & Annual	187.89	469.22	40.04	281.33	8.1 Billion	5.47
Other	208.70	257.46	81.06	48.76	1.4 Billion	.95
Total	7207.65	12351.76	58.35	5144.11	148.8 Billion	100%

1970

	Black Per Capita	White Per Capita	B/W	Per Capita Gap	Aggregate Gap	% of Gap
Wage & Salary	4692.07	7768.17	60.4	3076.10	71.4 Billion	70.82
NonFarm Self-Employed	143.17	719.13	19.91	575.96	13.4 Billion	13.26
Farm Self-Employed	9.62	128.52	7.48	118.90	2.8 Billion	2.74
Property	35.89	456.70	7.86	420.81	9.8 Billion	9.69
Soc. Sec. & RR	227.31	406.92	55.86	179.61	4.2 Billion	4.13
Public Asst.	283.50	64.43	440.01	−219.07	−5.1 Billion	−5.04
Ret & Annual	62.92	164.87	38.16	101.95	2.4 Billion	2.35
Other	126.04	215.61	58.46	89.57	2.1 Billion	2.06
Total	5580.52	9924.35	56.23	4343.83	100.8 Billion	

Source: Calculated by author from data in U.S. Department of Commerce, Bureau of the Census, Money Income of Households, Families, and Persons . . . 1986, 1970.

The second factor generating the parity gap is that black income recipients tend to receive lower mean income amounts when they receive income. The mean incomes received by black income recipients are again much lower than the mean amounts received by whites for every source except welfare. The disparities are greatest in property income, self-employment income, and wage and salary income. The disparities are least in social security and retirement income and the

Table 9
Wealth Ownership 1984
($ 1987)

	BLK Mean	WHT Mean	BLK %	WHT %	B/W	BLK AGG	WHT AGG	AGG GAP
Net Worth	22140.94	94435.65	100	100	23.45	210538.20	7115065	637450.40
Interest Earning at Financial								
Institutions	3429.27	18448.05	43.80	75.40	10.80	14282.71	1048008.00	117985.90
Regular Checking	655.23	1035.90	32.00	56.90	35.56	1993.77	44408.83	3611.04
Stock & Mutual Funds	3077.04	30293.53	5.40	22.00	2.49	1580.02	502129.20	61793.44
Equity in Business	37188.17	70548.90	4.00	14.00	15.06	14144.89	744151.10	79774.02
Equity in Motor Vehicle	3769.46	6242.70	65.00	88.50	44.34	23298.48	416253.80	29236.69
Equity in Home	32721.91	56814.32	43.80	67.30	37.47	136284.90	2880818.00	227301.50
Equity in Rental Property	41722.24	80761.23	6.60	10.10	33.75	26184.63	614564.10	51379.19
Other Real Estate	15776.83	38386.89	3.30	10.90	12.43	4950.72	315330.10	34846.92
U.S. Savings Bond	601.63	2870.31	7.40	16.10	9.63	423.34	34817.44	3970.95
IRA or Keoghs	3763.99	9896.21	5.10	21.40	9.06	1825.38	159560.50	18312.67

Source: U.S. Department of Commerce, Bureau of the Census, Household Wealth and Asset Ownership: 1984 Tables 1 & 3.

differences favor blacks for public assistance and welfare income. For those fewer blacks who receive each type of income, mean property receipts are only about two-fifths of the mean receipt for whites, mean self-employment income is about 57 percent of white mean self-employment income, and mean wage and salary income is about 74 percent of the white mean. The mean receipts of black social security and retirement income recipients are 82 and 81 percent of the corresponding white means. Finally, the black mean for public assistance and welfare income is about 102 percent of the white mean.

The net impact of these differences in recipiency rates and mean income levels generate the lower black per capita income. As shown in Table 8, per capita receipts from each source of income other than public assistance and welfare income are significantly smaller than the per capita receipts of whites. For example, while whites receive $9,099.54 from wage and salary employment, blacks receive only 64 percent of this amount or $5,823.38. Other gaps can be read from the table.

Since black per capita income in 1986 was about $7,208.65 and white per capita income was about $12,351.76, the income parity gap in 1986 was about $5,144.11 per black person. In the aggregate this amounted to about 148 billion dollars.

Each source of income other than public assistance contributes to this gap. As can be seen from the Table, wage and salary inequality accounts for almost 64 percent of the overall gap, inequality in property income accounts for about 16 percent of the gap, and inequality in self-employment income accounts for about 12 percent of the disparity. Thus, over 90 percent of the black/white income gap originates from disparities in current property and labor earnings. Another 13 percent of the gap is accounted for by the disparities in the other category and retirement income. Public assistance and welfare income actually reduces income inequality by about four percent.

The absolute impact of these gaps on each black person and on the population as a whole is shown in Table 8 as well. The numbers can be read from the appropriate columns. For example, wage and salary disparities cost blacks over $3,276 per person and 94 billion dollars in the aggregate in 1986. The aggregate cost of the disparity in self-employment income was $18 billion and the disparity in property receipts costs the black community $23 billion. Welfare reduced the income gap by 5.5 billion dollars, which was certainly small compensation given the large scale losses from all other sources.

Achieving economic parity for blacks will require significant improvements in the amount of income that blacks receive from each of the major earned income sources. The current low levels of income generation reflect the disadvantaged character of black participation in the various sectors of the economy. To place these disadvantages in perspective we will turn next to a review of the character of black participation as property owners and suppliers of labor.

Table 10
Total Receipts (in Billions of 1987 $) and Number of Firms (1,000's) in 1982 by Industry

	BLK RCPT	WHT RCPT	B/W	RCPT GAP	BLK FIRM	WHT FIRM	B/W	FIRM GAP
Total	13.83328	8411.19	.012	1155.92	301.43	14315	.151	1689.38
Construction	1.17112	398.65	.021	54.27	23.06	1551	.107	192.64
Manufacturing	1.16288	2804.56	.003	388.87	4.17	531	.056	69.68
Transportation and Public Utilities	.93571	747.75	.009	103.06	24.40	585	.300	56.96
Wholesale Trade	1.01104	1308.24	.006	180.93	3.65	1135	.022	59.76
Retail Trade	4.84806	1319.54	.026	178.66	84.05	2949	.025	326.07
Finance, Insurance and Real Estate	.88040	1209.60	.005	167.34	14.83	2150	.050	284.18
Selected Services	3.82407	622.87	.044	82.80	147.26	5374	.197	600.11

Source: U.S. Department of Commerce, Bureau of the Census, Surveys of Minority-Owned Businesses: Black, 1972, 1977, 1982.

BLACK PARTICIPATION AS OWNERS

Wealth Ownership

The low receipts from property and self-employment income reflect the relatively limited participation of blacks as owners of businesses and financial assets. The data for asset ownership is displayed in Table 9. As can be readily seen from this data in 1984, black disadvantages in wealth ownership derived from two factors. First, blacks were less likely than whites to own any given type of wealth. Second, the mean holdings of black wealth holders were always smaller for each type of wealth. These two factors combined to produce very large parity gaps in wealth ownership.

One can read the disparities in the various types of assets directly from the Table. The column labeled B/W provides a convenient summary measure of the extent of inequality. The numbers in this column represent the percentage of parity that blacks have obtained in each area. For example, black holdings in interest bearing accounts are only about 11 percent of the amount required for parity. We can note that the degree of equality is greatest for consumer durable assets such as vehicle and home ownership, regular checking accounts, and equity in rental property. Relative inequality is greatest for financial assets such as stocks and bonds, U.S. Government savings bonds, IRAs and KEOGHs, and interest-bearing accounts in financial institutions. For example, only five percent of black households in comparison to 22 percent of white households report owning stocks, bonds, or mutual funds. Moreover, the average holdings for black households of $3,077 is only about one-tenth the average holding of white households ($30,293). The net result is that in the aggregate, black holdings of stocks and bonds are only about 2.5 percent of the amount required to reach parity. The stock and bond parity gap in the aggregate is about 62 billion dollars. Equity in businesses and non-rental property have an intermediate degree of inequality. However, blacks have not obtained 50 percent of parity in any type of asset ownership.

Overall, the mean or per household net worth for black households was less than one-fourth of the mean holdings of white households. In the aggregate, blacks held about 211 billion dollars in all types of assets. These aggregate holdings fell about *$687 billion short of parity.* We might note also that the Census data understate wealth holdings by a great deal and so as large as this figure is, it nonetheless understate the true black disadvantage in wealth holdings.

Participation in Business Ownership

As we have pointed out in previous editions of *The State Of Black America,* blacks own a very small share of American businesses. The data in Table 10 summarize the disadvantages in business ownership.

As can be seen from the Table, overall and for each individual industry, the black presence was far below parity. This is true whether the parity gap is measured either by share of industry receipts originating in black firms or by relative numbers of firm owned by blacks. However, it is the case that the disparity is largest when it is measured by receipts. This reflects the fact that black firms tend to be significantly smaller than white firms. Nonetheless, there is no industry in which the share of firms owned by blacks exceeds 30 percent of the parity share. Black ownership in term of number of firms is closest to parity in transportation and public utilities, retail trade, and selected services. It is farthest from parity in wholesale trade, financial sectors, manufacturing, and construction.

Overall, blacks owned about 301 thousand businesses in 1982. This was about 15 percent of the number of businesses that would have been required for parity in number of businesses owned. In aggregate terms black business ownership fell short of parity by about 1.7 million firms.

The picture, however, is even grimmer when one looks at ownership from the receipts originating perspective. There is no industrial sector for which the black receipts are as much as five percent of the amount required for parity. The best black business does is in the selected services sector where the total receipts equal about 4.4 percent of the amount required for parity. In manufacturing, wholesale trade, financial sectors, and transportation and public utilities the receipts originating in the black-owned sector do not even equal one percent of the amount required for parity.

Overall, the black-owned business sector only originated about 13.8 billion dollars in receipts in 1982 in an 8.4 trillion dollar economy. Aggregate black receipts were only about 1.2 percent of the amount required to have parity in business ownership. In aggregate 1987 dollar terms, the parity receipts gap that existed in 1982 was about 1.2 trillion dollars. Obviously, blacks are not even in the universe of obtaining parity in business ownership.

LABOR MARKET PARTICIPATION

Obviously from the data reviewed so far, blacks are heavily dependent on the labor market to earn their living. For the most part, blacks continue to be a nation of wage earners. However, even here blacks have not obtained parity. A brief review of some of the recent labor market trends will make this clear.

Employment Population Ratios

Employment population ratios for selected years are shown in Table 11 for the country as a whole for the total population, men, women, and teenagers. As can be seen from this data all black demographic groups have population proportions that are below the parity level. Greatest equality is experienced by black females who for the first three quarters of 1988 were employed at over 99 percent of the white female rate. However, it should be noted that for most of this century black females have been employed at substantially higher rates than white females. Thus, the current near equality reflects a decline in the employment status of black females. Indeed, in the early 1970s black females still had a substantial employment advantage.

Black males have staged a comeback in employment since the depths of the last recession but still are employed only 90 percent as often as white males.

Table 11
Civilian Employment — Population Ratio
By Race, Sex, and Age
Selected Years

Total Population

	Black	White	Blk/Wht
*1988	56.1	63.0	.890
1987	55.6	62.3	.892
1982	49.4	58.8	.840
1978	53.6	60.0	.893
1970	53.7	57.4	.935

Men (20 and over)

	Black	White	Blk/Wht
1988	67.0	75.1	.892
1987	66.4	74.7	.889
1982	61.4	73.0	.841
1978	69.1	77.2	.895
1972	73.0	79.0	.924

Women (20 years old and over)

	Black	White	Blk/Wht
1988	53.6	53.9	.994
1987	53.0	53.1	.998
1982	47.5	48.4	.981
1978	49.3	46.1	1.069
1972	46.5	40.6	1.145

Both Sexes (16 to 19 years old)

	Black	White	Blk/Wht
1988	26.9	50.8	.530
1987	27.1	49.4	.549
1982	19.0	45.8	.414
1978	25.2	52.4	.480
1972	25.2	46.4	.543

Source: Bureau of Labor Statistics, *Handbook of Labor Statistics*, June 1985, pp. 46 and 47. *Employment and Earnings*, January 1987, October 1988.

Teenaged blacks are only about half as likely to be employed as white teenagers. This disparity holds for teenagers of both sexes. These disparities have persisted for the past two decades with little sign of any attenuation.

In the aggregate, the employment parity gap is large. On the average, through the first three quarters of 1988, blacks had an employment parity gap of about 1.4 million jobs. In other words, on the average during 1988, 1.4 million fewer

Table 12
Employment Population
By Region (1987)

	Total Blk	Total Wht	B+W	Black Male	White Male	B+W	Black Fem	White Fem	B+W	Black 16-19	White 16-19	B+W
NE	54.8	61.6	88.96	61.6	72.3	85.2	49.6	52.1	95.2	25.9	50.4	51.4
MW	50.8	63.3	80.25	56.7	73.3	77.4	45.9	54.2	84.5	24.2	55.0	44.0
SO	56.9	61.5	92.52	63.4	72.2	87.8	51.6	51.7	99.8	27.8	45.5	61.1
W	59.1	63.0	93.81	65.1	73.1	89.1	53.5	53.5	100.0	31.8	47.6	66.8

Source: U.S. Department of Labor, Bureau of Labor Statistics, *Geographic Profile of Employment and Unemployment*, 1987.

blacks were employed than would have been employed if employment parity existed. The shortfall was divided as follows: 664 thousand jobs missing for adult males, 521 thousand jobs missing for teenagers, 31 thousand jobs missing for adult females, and the remainder due to less favorable population composition (i.e., missing black males).

Of course, employment disparities exist throughout the country in every census region. Regional data for 1987 is shown in Table 12. The greatest regional disparities exist in the Midwest. In this region blacks are only 80 percent as likely as whites to have a job. Greatest employment equality by this measure is obtained in the West and the South where blacks are 94 and 93 percent as likely as whites to be employed.

Black males and teenagers experience the greatest employment difficulties by this measure in all regions relative to corresponding white groups. Black males are less than 90 percent as likely to be employed as white males in all census regions. In the Midwest where blacks continue to experience severe labor market difficulties, black male employment averaged only 77 percent of the parity level during 1988. Black teenagers in this region were only 44 percent as likely as white teenagers to be employed.

Overall, blacks have a job shortfall of over 481 thousand jobs in the Midwest, 242,000 in the Northeast, 513 thousand in the South, and 68 thousand in the West. The majority of the shortfall in each region is represented by unemployment among adult and teenage black males.

Black Unemployment

One of the major reasons for the relatively low rates of black employment is excessively high black unemployment rates. Of course, differentials in participation rates also contribute something to the employment differential, especially for males and teenagers. In fact, black females continue to have higher participation rates than white females. In any case, the data in table 13 summarize unemployment data for the past two decades.

Unemployment trends have been discussed in all of the earlier editions of the State of Black America. Black unemployment for most of the past two decades, especially since the mid 1970s, has been very high. Although, during 1988, unemployment continued its decline from the recession highs, black unemployment for the first three quarters of the year averaged 11.8 percent. Unemployment was high for all demographic groups. Both black females and black males continued to have unemployment rates over 10 percent. And fully one-third of black teenaged labor force participants were unemployed during 1988.

The gap between black and white unemployment rates has been growing throughout the 1980s. All black groups currently are experiencing unemployment rates that are 2.5 times the corresponding white unemployment rates. This is up considerably from the 2 to 1 level that existed prior to the late 1970s. This upward drift in the employment disparity has affected all black demographic groups. Black females have been hit particularly hard.

Table 13
Unemployment Rates
By Sex, Race, and Age
Selected Years

Total Population

	Black	White	Blk/Wht
1988	11.8	4.7	2.511
1987	13.0	5.3	2.453
1982	18.9	8.6	2.197
1978	12.8	5.2	2.461
1972	10.4	5.1	2.039

Men (20 years old and over)

	Black	White	Blk/Wht
1988	10.2	4.1	2.488
1987	11.1	4.8	2.313
1982	17.8	7.8	2.282
1978	9.3	3.7	2.513
1972	7.0	3.6	1.944

Women (20 years old and over)

	Black	White	Blk/Wht
1988	10.5	4.1	2.561
1987	11.6	4.6	2.522
1982	15.4	7.3	2.109
1978	11.2	5.2	2.153
1972	9.0	4.9	1.836

Both Sexes (16 to 19 years old)

	Black	White	Blk/Wht
1988	33.4	13.3	2.511
1987	33.4	13.3	2.400
1982	34.7	14.4	2.352
1978	48.0	20.4	2.784
1972	35.4	14.2	2.492

Source: Bureau of Labor Statistics, *Handbook of Labor Statistics,* June 1985, pp. 69, 71, 72, and 73. Employment and Earnings, *January 1986, p. 201.*

Even without looking at the impact on discouragement and labor force dropout, the higher unemployment rates experienced by blacks cost blacks hundreds of thousands of jobs every year.

During 1988, on average, the unemployment parity gap was over 1 million jobs. Black men experienced a 379 thousand job shortage due to lack of parity in unemployment while black women suffered even more, experiencing a 425 thousand job shortfall. Black teenagers lost 182 thousand jobs due to lack of parity in unemployment.

Table 14 displays data which shows that unemployment disparities exist in every census region. However, as was true with many of the other indicators, blacks have the highest unemployment rates in the Midwest. This is true for both black males and females. In the first three quarters of 1988, blacks were still experiencing 18 percent unemployment rates in th Midwest. Both adult black males and females experienced unemployment rates around 18 percent while teenagers had an unemployment rate over 44 percent. Moreover, inequality was also dramatic in the Midwest. Overall, the black unemployment rate was over three times the white unemployment rate.

Blacks had their best absolute experiences in the Northeast in 1988 where the overall black unemployment rate was around the nine percent level, the lowest for any region in this decade. However, even in the Northeast black males continued to experience unemployment rates over 10 percent. Moreover, the ratio of black to white unemployment remained above 2 to 1 for all demographic groups.

Black unemployment rate remained at almost 13 percent in the South in 1988. Relative to whites, blacks experienced about 2.3 times higher unemployment rates. The West had the second lowest absolute unemployment rates, although unemployment was still high for blacks in the West with all demographic groups having unemployment rates that were 11 percent or higher. The West, however, continued to have the distinction of being the region with the least racial inequality. The West was the only region in which black unemployment was less than twice white unemployment albeit just barely under at 1.9 times.

In the aggregate, higher unemployment cost blacks 523 thousand jobs in the South, 293 thousand jobs in the Midwest, 108 thousand jobs in the Northeast, and 63 thousand jobs in the West. Black women had larger job deficits than black men in the South and in the Midwest, while black men had sligthly larger deficits in the Northeast and in the West.

Occupational Status

Lower employment or higher unemployment rates are only two reasons why blacks have lower labor market earnings than whites. The other reason is that blacks tend to have more bad jobs and fewer goods jobs in terms of pay, working conditions, and status. Black jobs differ from white jobs on a number of important dimensions. There are still some persisting differences in the industry of employment. However, these industry differences apparently do not impose any economic hardships on blacks. In fact, on average, blacks may have a slightly favorable industry composition. Blacks also tend to be distributed differently across worker classes. Thus, blacks are much more likely than whites to be employed in the government sector. In 1987, for example, 24.1 percent of blacks versus only 15.7 percent of whites worked in the public sector. Blacks were correspondingly less likely to be self-employed (3.4 vs 8.7 percent) or working for wages and salaries

Table 14

	Blk Total	Wht Total	Blk + Wht	Blk Men	Wht Men	Blk + Wht	Blk Women	Wht Women	Blk + Wht	Blk Teens	Wht Teens	Blk + Wht
NORTHEAST	9.1	4.0	2.275	10.3	4.2	2.452	2.9	3.8	2.079	22.2	10.4	2.135
MIDWEST	17.9	5.6	3.196	17.9	6.09	2.983	18.0	5.2	3.462	44.3	13.4	3.301
SOUTH	12.7	5.5	2.309	11.9	5.4	2.204	13.5	5.6	2.411	35.5	16.3	2.178
WEST	11.4	6.0	1.900	11.7	5.9	1.983	11.0	6.1	1.80	27.2	17.1	1.591

Source: U.S. Department of Labor, Bureau of Labor Statistics, *Geographic Profile of Employment and Unemployment*, 1987.

in the private sector (75.9 vs 84.3 percent). However, this public sector concentration also has a positive impact on black economic status.

Other factors, such as higher proportion working on part-time jobs, do contribute negatively to black economic status. The major factor is the persistence of an unfavorable occupational distribution. Table 15 presents data for 1987 for very broad occupational categories. It should be noted that blacks have further disadvantages within each broad occupational category. This is especially true for the higher level occupations. Within these broad categories blacks tend to be concentrated in the lower paid lower status sub-occupations.

In any case, it is apparent from the data that blacks still have very large occupational disadvantages. This is especially so for males. The five top occupational groups for males are executive and managerial, professionals, sales, technicians, and precision and craft occupations. Black males are less likely than white males to hold any of these occupations. They are less than half as likely to be sales or managerial workers, about half as likely to be professionals, about two-thirds as likely to be a technician, and about three-quarters as likely to be in a precision and craft occupations. On the other hand, blacks are almost twice as likely to be employed as a laborer or in a related occupation and more than twice as likely to follow a Service occupation. Black makes are also more likely to hold an administrative support job than are white males. A similar picture exists for females as can be readily determined by perusing Table 15. Black women

Table 15
Occupational Distribution of Employed Workers 1987

	Male			Female		
	Black	White	B/W	Black	White	B/W
Exec., Admin., & Managerial	6.7	14.0	.48	6.4	10.5	.61
Professional	6.4	11.9	.54	10.8	14.8	.73
Technicians & Related Support	1.8	2.8	.64	3.2	3.2	1.00
Sales Occupations	5.1	11.9	.43	9.1	13.4	.68
Administrative Support	9.2	5.5	1.67	26.4	29.5	.90
Private Households	.1	.1	1.00	3.6	1.6	2.25
Protective Service	4.5	2.5	1.80	1.1	.5	2.20
Other Service	13.7	6.0	2.28	23.3	14.8	1.50
Precision Pro., Craft & Repair	15.5	20.6	.75	2.0	2.3	.87
Mach. Operators, Assem., & Insp.	10.8	7.2	1.50	10.3	5.9	1.75
Trans. and Material Movers	11.3	6.6	1.71	1.1	.8	1.38
Handlers, Cleaners, Helpers, Labor.	11.2	5.9	1.90	2.3	1.5	1.53
Farming, Forestry, and Fishing	3.6	4.9	.73	.4	1.2	.33

Source: U.S. Department of Labor, Bureau of Labor Statistics, *Employment and Earnings*, January 1988.

are also less likely to follow the prestigious managerial, professional, or sales occupations and more likely to be service workers, operatives, or laborers.

These disparities lead to huge parity gaps in good jobs. In 1987, blacks had a parity gap of about 645 thousand Executive and Managerial jobs — 413 thousand for black males and 232 thousand for black females. Black males were short 311 thousand and black females were short 226 thousand professional jobs. Blacks had a parity gap of 627 thousand Sales jobs, split 385 thousand for black males and 243 thousand for black females. Black males also experienced a shortfall of 289 thousand craft and precision production jobs and 57 thousand Technician jobs. Black females had a shortfall of 175 thousand administrative support jobs.

In total, the good job parity gap was over 1.4 million good jobs for black males and 873 thousand good jobs for black women. This does not even take into account the higher unemployment and lower employment rates experienced by blacks. Employed black workers experienced *a good job parity gap of over 2.2 million good jobs* in 1988.

Earnings Rates

Occupational disadvantage has many impacts. However, the most important impact is to lower earnings. Table 16 provides data on median usual weekly earnings for American workers. This data indicate that real wages continued to make their slow recovery in 1987. However, black wages continue to lag significantly behind the late 1970s level. This is particularly true for black male wages. Black female wages on the other hand are at record levels. While black males continue to earn higher usual wages than white and black females, the gaps are closing.

Racial inequality has been inching up slightly. Black males have lost considerable ground since 1980 relative to white males, and black females have lost modest ground. As of 1987, the usual weekly earnings of full-time black male workers were 72.4 percent of corresponding white wage while the usual weekly earnings for full-time black females were about 89.6 percent of corresponding white female earnings.

The median full-time black male wage and salary worker earned $124 per week less than his white male counterpart while the usual weekly earnings of full-time black females are about $32 per week less than her white female counterpart. These wage differences have large aggregate impacts. For males this wage inequality cost blacks at least $30.1 billion annually, and the black female disadvantage adds about another $7.3 billion.

CONCLUSION

The discussion in this chapter has laid out the main dimensions of racial inequality in economic life in America.

Three conclusions are apparent from the discussion to this point. First, racial inequality in economic life is still the norm throughout America. Second, the magnitude of the parity gaps is very large in all dimensions. Third, the disparities

Table 16
Median Weekly Earnings of Full-time Wage and Salary Workers by Race and Sex, 1979-1985

	Black	White	Blk/Wht
1987	301	383	.786
1986	302	383	.789
1985	292	374	.781
1984	290	371	.782
1983	291	363	.801
1982	288	358	.804
1981	291	361	.806
1980	283	361	.785
1979	311	385	.807
Males			
1987	326	450	.724
1986	329	449	.733
1985	322	441	.729
1984	333	441	.754
1983	338	448	.754
1982	325	435	.746
1981	326	435	.749
1980	335	436	.767
1979	351	467	.752
Females			
1987	275	307	.896
1986	272	305	.892
1985	267	298	.897
1984	265	289	.917
1983	261	287	.912
1982	249	283	.880
1981	252	271	.927
1980	250	277	.905
1979	258	281	.918

Source: Bureau of Labor Statistics, *Handbook of Labor Statistics*, June 1985, p. 94. *Employment and Earnings*, January 1986, 87, 88.

have been worsening in most dimensions for at least the past 10 years. If present trends continue, we can have no expectation or hope of attaining economic parity in economic life in the foreseeable future.

The new administration will face the harsh reality that racial inequality persist and is not attenuating. Regardless of one's ideology or beliefs about the efficacy of government action, one thing is certain. Whatever was going on in the American society both internal and external to the black community during the last 10 years was not sufficient to promote racial parity in economic life. It is, thus, apparent that new policies must be put in place by the new administration if progress towards racial parity in economic life is to resume and to be maintained.

Although the new administration will need to work out its own specific solutions, the analyses and facts presented here should provide some general guidance. First, it is important to pay close attention to the magnitude of the problem. We have repeatedly presented estimates of aggregate parity gaps. These estimates should sensitize policymakers to the need for large scale interventions if significant results are to be obtained. The wealth gap was well over 600 billion dollars. The income discrepancy is in the range of 150 billion dollars. We estimated an overall business ownership gap that left black businesses over one trillion dollars and 1.8 million firms short of business ownership parity. The good job deficit was over two million executive, professional, sales, and other high pay, high status job. Excess poverty exceeded 6 million persons. Almost two million fewer black families had income over $50,000 than required for parity. The large size of these parity gaps should alert the administration that significant efforts will be required to produce racial parity in economic life.

The gaps should also tell us one other thing. Namely, the capacity of the black community to develop using strictly or mainly internal resources is clearly limited. It is unreasonable to expect a community that exhibits the limited wealth and business ownership, low incomes, and high poverty rates characteristic of the black community to provide the resources internally to overtake the more advantaged segment of the population. This is especially so since the black population also lacks parity control over all of the other political, educational, and social institutions as well. To ask blacks to overcome the centuries of racism and discrimination that have left the population without the wealth and control required to develop is to promote the impossible. No economist has yet to develop a workable model for economic development without resources.

Indeed, the main reason that prior efforts to eliminate racial disparities have probably failed is that they have never been implemented at anywhere near the magnitude required to repair the damage to ownership, family structure, human capital, and control created by the legacy of racism and discrimination that all blacks inherit. While there may be disagreement about the best way to achieve parity, any meaningful program must infuse ten of billions of dollars into the black community annually for many years. Unless the Bush administration recognizes this reality, we are destined to continue the pattern of stagnation and retrogression in the relative economic status of the black population that has existed for the past 10 years.

Some general principles may guide the administration's planning for eliminating racial inequality in economic life. It is still the case that the lowly economic status of blacks is caused primarily by three factors. Past and current discrimination, limited ownership of capital (business, human, financial, and social), and the dysfunctional individual and community behavior. Scholars and researchers will always disagree about the role and relative importance of these various factors. However, it is apparent that at any point in time they all contribute to the maintenance and perpetuation of racial disparities. Moreover, it seems perfectly clear that all of the factors are mutually interdependent and reinforcing. Thus, it is apparent that any successful assault on economic disparities must simultaneously impact all of these factors.

An effective policy must prevent current discrimination in all aspects of economic life. There are many approaches to achieving this. However, all approaches require a consensus on the meaning of discrimination and methods of detecting it. One of the worse legacies of the Reagan administration was its destruction on the emerging consensus concerning the appropriateness of the use of numerical data to detect and correct discrimination. While such methods are not perfect and certainly needed refinement, the failure of the administration to accept the notion that parity implies equality of end results has greatly hampered efforts to prevent discrimination. One would hope the detection and prevention of discrimination would become a high priority for the Bush administration.

Past discrimination has resulted in blacks having inappropriate placements in the labor market and limited opportunities to gain the type of experience that leads to parity in employment. Programs to prevent current discrimination may have only limited impact on those who have already started on a particular career path. There is, thus, a need for efforts to upgrade existing workers and to restore them to their appropriate places in the work force. There has been no significant effort in this direction in the past, but it is a necessary ingredient to any strategy to make significant progress against racial disparities in a reasonable period of time.

Of course, one of the major legacies of the racial history of this country is the limited ownership that blacks currently have of all types of capital. Indeed, one of the main reasons why discrimination has such a powerful impact on blacks is the limited ownership of capital within their own population. Any strategy to eliminate racial inequality must break this black dependency. This implies the need for substantial efforts to build capital ownership within the black community. The number and size of black-owned businesses need to increase substantially. Gaps in the level and quality of black and white education also must be diminished. Black-owned or controlled social infrastructure would also have to be substantially strengthened if racial parity is to be attained. Indeed, it seems very unlikely that any effort to bring about racial parity could be successful without a substantial capital development component.

Finally, the social, familial, and individual dysfunctionalism within the black community must also be reduced if parity is to be attained. However, it is very likely that this problem would largely take care of itself if a major effort to end racial discrimination and capital disparities were to be initiated. However, there may still be a need to have special efforts in certain cases. In any case, policymakers do need to recognize that pathological community patterns could disrupt efforts to eliminate racial inequality in economic life.

The most important ingredient of all for bringing about racial parity is a commitment at the highest levels of the administration to make this a high priority. It is certainly time that the nation took this problem seriously. The administration must be willing to recognize that it will neither be easy nor cheap to rectify the centuries of deprivation and discrimination experienced by the black population. There are no free lunches. If there was any doubt about this, the poor record of progress under the last administration should have made this clear.

It is the responsibility of the Bush administration to educate the American public on the dimensions, magnitude, and seriousness of the problem of persisting racial disparities in economic life. Its challenge in this area will be to rally the American public to finally make the commitment required to achieve racial parity in economic life and to eliminate this problem from the national agenda within a reasonable period of time.

Given the challenges facing the society both within the international community and domestically at this critical historical juncture, a unified and productive citizenry which includes all segments of the population is necessary for future prosperity. The elimination of racial disparities will free the country for unfettered pursuit of a better future for all.

Critical Issues For Black Families By The Year 2000

Robert B. Hill, Ph.D.

INTRODUCTION

After making unprecedented strides during the 1960s, black families experienced sharp social and economic setbacks during the 1970s and 1980s. Not only was the poverty rate for black families higher in 1987 (30 percent) than the rate in 1969 20 percent; there were also 700,000 more poor black families. Similarly, not only was the unemployment rate for blacks twice as high in 1988 (12 percent) than it was in 1969 (6 percent), but three times more blacks were unemployed in 1988 (1.7 million) than in 1969 (570,000).

Such severe economic instability led to family instability. While black unemployment soared from six percent to 20 percent between 1969 and 1983 due to four back-to-back recessions, the proportion of female-headed black families jumped from 28 percent to 42 percent. Each percentage point rise in black unemployment was correlated with a comparable increase in one-parent black families.

Black families continue to be disproportionately disadvantaged in other aspects as well. Although out-of-wedlock birth rates declined steadily among black teens during the 1970s and 1980s, while rising among white teens, black adolescents are four times more likely than white adolescents to have babies out-of-wedlock. And, over half of all black births today are out-of-wedlock, compared to only 13 percent of all white births.

Unprecedented levels of crime and gang violence have also destabilized many black families. With drug trafficking rampant in most inner-city areas, drug-related homicides among blacks have reached record-levels. The disproportionate surge in deaths among blacks has resulted in the first declines in black life expectancy since 1962. While life expectancy from birth rose among whites from 75.3 to 75.4 between 1984 and 1986 (the latest year available), life expectancy among blacks declined from 69.7 in 1984 to 69.5 and 69.4 in 1985 and 1986, respectively.

Black families have also been disproportionately devastated by the declining stock of affordable housing due to abandonment, urban renewal, commercial development, gentrification and condominium conversions. About half a million low-income units have been disappearing each year. Thus, the number of homeless individuals and families has soared to about two to three million. In addition, there are hundreds of thousands "hidden homeless" who "double-up" with relatives and friends for varying periods of time. Blacks are overrepresented among the thousands of families and children living in welfare hotels and shelters for the homeless.

Contrary to popular belief, these severe social and economic dislocations have not been confined to blacks in poor or one-parent families. As was the case among whites, thousands of middle-class, working class and two-parent black families were also adversely affected during the 1970s and 1980s.

For example, unemployed black husbands doubled from 84,000 to 188,000 between 1969 and 1985, while their jobless rate soared from three percent to seven percent. During the 1970s, female-headed black famlies increased ten times faster among wives who were college-educated than among wives who were high school dropouts. Not only has there been a shrinking in the size of the black middle-class since 1978, but also poverty rates among black two-parent families have risen more rapidly than among black single-parent families.[1]

While poverty among female-headed black families edged up from 51 percent to 52 percent between 1978 and 1987, these rates jumped from 12 percent to 14 percent among male-headed black families. Although the proportion of middle-income ($25,000 & over) black families grew from 33 percent to 38 percent between 1970 and 1978, it declined to 36 percent by 1987.[2]

The disproportionate declines in living standards experienced by low-income and middle-income black families led to a widening in the economic gap with white families. While the income ratio between black and white families in general declined from 59 percent to 56 percent between 1978 and 1987, the ratio between white and black couples fell more sharply from 81 percent to 77 percent. Furthermore, since the strongest economic gains over the past two decades were made by upper-class whites and blacks, the gap between the rich and poor in this nation is now wider than it has been in generations.[3]

What can be done to narrow the socio-economic gap between black and white families? In order to make significant strides toward parity between blacks and whites by the year 2000, it is important to address the following questions:

- What will be the demographic characteristics (i.e., size, age composition, family structure and labor force patterns) of the black population by the year 2000?;

- What are the critical issues that will be confronting black families during the 1990s?; and

- What strategies must be adopted by the public and private sectors for black families to achieve equity with white families by the 21st century?

FUTURE DEMOGRAPHIC STATUS OF BLACKS

Population Size

While the Census Bureau's middle-growth series projects the total U.S. population to increase from 245.3 to 268.0 million between 1988 and 2000, the black population is anticipated to rise from 30.5 to 35.8 million.[4] Since the black population is expected to grow twice (+17 percent) as fast as the total U.S. population (+9 percent) over the next 12 years, the proportion of blacks would rise from 12.4 percent to 13.4 percent between 1988 and 2000.

It is frequently asserted in the media that Hispanics will outnumber blacks by the year 2000. Yet, the Census Bureau projects blacks to outnumber Hispanics not only by 2000, but also into the middle of the 21st century as well. Although Hispanics are estimated to increase twice as fast (+ 34 percent) as blacks between 1988 and 2000, the Hispanic population is expected to rise (from 18.8 million) to 25.2 million—10.6 million fewer persons than blacks by 2000. Similarly, while the Hispanic population is projected to reach 50.8 million by 2050, the black population is projected to number 52.3 million by mid-century.[5] Due to the sharp increases of blacks and Hispanics, non-whites are expected to soar (from one-fifth in 1988) to one-fourth by 2000 and to one-third of the U.S. population by 2050. (Table 1)

Age Composition

With the maturing of the "baby boom" cohort (born between 1947 and 1961), the median ages of all groups are expected to increase markedly in the coming decades. For example, while the median age of the total U.S. population is expected to rise from 32.3 to 36.3 between 1988 and 2000, the median age of blacks is projected to rise from 27.1 to 30.2. (Table 2)

Although the pre-school population (under six years old) in the total U.S. is expected to decline by six percent between 1988 and 2000, the number of black pre-schoolers will fall by two percent. On the other hand, the elementary (6-13 year-olds) and (jr/sr) high school (14-17-year-olds) age populations will increase sharply among all racial groups. While the elementary and high school age populations in the total U.S. are projected to grow by 13 percent between 1988 and 2000, the 6-17-year-olds among blacks will rise by 24 percent. It should be

---

Table 1
Population Projections By Race and Ethnic Group, 1985-2050

| Year | Numbers (in millions) | | | Percent Distribution | | |
	Total	Black	Hispanic	Total	Black	Hispanic
2050	309.5	52.3	50.8	100	16.9	16.4
2030	304.8	47.6	41.9	100	15.6	13.7
2010	283.2	40.0	30.8	100	14.1	10.9
2000	268.0	35.8	25.2	100	13.3	9.4
1990	249.7	31.4	19.9	100	12.6	8.0
1988	245.3	30.5	18.8	100	12.4	7.7
1985	238.6	29.1	17.0	100	12.2	7.1

Sources: U.S. Bureau of the Census, "Projections of the Population of the United States, by Age, Sex, and Race: 1983 to 2080," *Current Population Reports*, Series P-25, No. 952, May 1984; U.S. Bureau of the Census, "Projections of the Hispanic Population," *Current Population Reports*, Series P-25, No. 995, November 1986.

Table 2
Population Projections of Median Age By Race and Sex, 1985-2050

(Median Age)

RACE	1985	1988	1990	2000	2030	2050
All Groups	**31.4**	**32.3**	**33.0**	**36.3**	**40.8**	**41.6**
Male	30.2	31.1	31.7	34.9	39.1	39.5
Female	32.7	33.6	34.2	37.7	42.6	43.7
White	**32.3**	**33.3**	**33.9**	**37.4**	**42.1**	**42.6**
Male	31.1	32.0	32.7	36.1	40.3	40.5
Female	33.7	34.5	35.2	38.8	43.8	44.8
Black	**26.2**	**27.1**	**27.7**	**30.2**	**35.5**	**38.1**
Male	24.9	25.7	26.3	28.5	33.7	36.3
Female	27.6	28.5	29.2	32.0	37.3	39.9

Source: U.S. Bureau of the Census, "Projections of the Population of the United States, by Age, Sex, and Race: 1983 to 2080," *Current Population Reports*, Series P-25, No. 952, May 1984.

noted that the first graders of 1988 will constitute the high school graduating class in the year 2000.

In contrast to the elementary and high school age groups, the college-age population (18-24-year-olds) is expected to decline sharply among all racial groups by 2000. While college-age blacks are projected to decline by four percent between 1988 and 2000, all college-age persons in the U.S. are expected to fall twice as fast—by eight percent. (Table 3)

Among the "younger" (age 25-44) working-age population, the 25-34-year-olds are expected to decline among all racial groups over the next 12 years, while the 35-44-year-olds are expected to rise sharply. Blacks age 25-34 will fall by six percent between 1988 and 2000, while blacks age 35-44 will soar by 49 percent. Among the "older" (age 45-64) working-age population, the 55-64 year olds will increase more slowly than the 45-54 year olds. While blacks age 45-54 will rise by 66 percent, the blacks age 55-64 will increase by only 18 percent.

Even among the elderly (65 years and over), blacks are expected to grow faster than the U.S. population over the next 12 years. While the total U.S. aged are projected to increase by 14 percent (from 30.5 to 34.9 million) between 1988 and 2000, the black aged are expected to rise by 20 percent (from 2.5 to 3.50 million). Because of the higher fertility rates among blacks relative to whites, the proportion of blacks will rise in every age category during the 1999s. Thus, blacks will become more widely represented at all stages of the life cycle by the year 2000.

Table 3

A. Projections of Black Population By Age, 1988-2050

Numbers (in thousands)

AGE	1988	2000	2050
All Ages	**30,474**	**35,754**	**52,297**
Under 6	3,792	3,702	3,966
6-13	4,171	5,153	5,441
14-17	2,054	2,544	2,753
18-24	3,921	3,773	4,815
25-34	5,662	5,316	6,983
35-44	3,908	5,811	6,901
45-54	2,491	4,124	6,275
55-64	1,995	2,355	5,936
65 & over	2,480	2,976	9,227
Median Age	**27.1**	**30.2**	**38.1**

B. Percent Black of Total Population, 1988-2050

(% Black)

AGE	1988	2000	2050
All Ages	**12.4**	**13.3**	**16.9**
Under 6	16.7	17.4	18.7
6-13	15.3	16.8	18.8
14-17	15.0	16.5	18.9
18-24	14.6	15.3	18.8
25-34	13.0	14.6	18.2
35-44	11.1	13.3	17.8
45-54	10.4	11.1	17.0
55-64	9.3	9.9	15.9
65 & over	8.1	8.5	13.7

Source: U.S. Bureau of the Census, ''Projections of the Population of the U.S., by Age, Sex, and Race: 1983 to 2080,'' *Current Population Reports*, Series P-25, No. 952, May 1984.

Family Structure

While the total families in the U.S. are projected to increase by 11 percent (from 65.3 to 72.3 million) between 1988 and 2000, the total black families are expected to rise by 17 percent (from 7.2 to 8.4 million) Female-headed families are expected to increase twice as fast as married couples among all racial groups during the 1990s. While couples are expected to grow by eight percent (from 52.1 to 56.3 million) by 2000, female-headed families in the U.S. are projected to rise by 18 percent. Consequently, the proportion of all U.S. families headed by women is expected to rise from 16 percent to 18 percent between 1988 and 2000.

Somewhat similar patterns are anticipated among black families. While black couples are expected to rise by 11 percent (from 3.6 to 4.0 million) between 1988 and 2000, black female-headed families are expected to increase by 25 percent (from 3.2 to 4.0 million). Thus, the proportion of black families headed by women would rise from 44 percent to 48 percent by the year 2000. (See Table 4)

In sum, between 1988 and 2000: (a) the median age of the black population will rise from 27.1 to 30.2 years; (b) the total black population will increase from 30.5 to 35.7 million; (c) the number of female-headed black families (+25 percent) will increase twice as fast as the number of black married couples (+11 percent); and (d) the proportion of black families headed by women will rise from 44 to 48 percent.

Labor Force Patterns

What will be the labor force characteristics of blacks at the turn of the 21st century? The U.S. Bureau of Labor Statistics (BLS) provides alternative projections of the civilian labor force (which includes both the employed and unemployed) by race from 1986 to 2000. For our purposes, we will use the BLS intermediate (or "moderate") growth projections which assume two "mild" recessions and a decline in the U.S. unemployment rate from 7.0 percent in 1986 to 6.0 percent in 2000.[6]

While BLS projects the total white labor force (16 years and over) to increase by 15 percent (from 101.8 to 116.7 million) between 1986 and 2000, the black labor force is expected to soar by 29 percent (from 12.7 to 16.3 million). Similarly, black men in the labor force are expected to increase by 24 percent by 2000, compared to only a nine percent rise among white men. Black women in the labor force are anticipated to increase by 33 percent by 2000, compared to a rise of only 22 percent among white women.

The largest gains in the U.S. labor force during the 1990s will occur among adults age 25-54. Black adult men are projected to increase in the labor force by 34 percent—twice the 16 percent rise among white adult men. Similarly, black adult women are expected to increase in the labor force by 42 percent, compared to a 33 percent rise among white adult women. Thus, black male and female family heads, 25 years and over, are expected to experience more favorable job opportunities during the 1990s.

However, because of the "baby bust" of the 1970s, youths age 16-24 in the labor force are projected to decline among whites during the 1990s, but to rise among blacks. While white males age 16-24 in the labor force should fall by nine percent between 1986 and 2000, black male youths in the labor force are expected

Table 4
Projections of Number of U.S. Families By Race, 1986-2000
A. Number of Families (in millions)

Year	Total U.S. Families			Black Families		
	All Families	Married Couples	Female-Headed	All Families	Married Couples	Female-Headed
2050	72.3	56.3	12.7	8.4	4.0	4.0
1998	71.3	55.7	12.4	8.2	3.9	3.9
1996	70.3	55.2	12.1	8.1	3.9	3.8
1994	69.2	54.5	11.8	7.9	3.8	3.6
1992	68.1	53.8	11.5	7.7	3.8	3.5
1990	66.8	53.0	11.2	7.5	3.7	3.4
1988	65.3	52.1	10.8	7.2	3.6	3.2
1986	63.8	51.1	10.4	7.0	3.6	3.1

B. Percent Distribution of Family Structure By Race, 1986-2000

Year	Total U.S. Families			Black Families		
	All Families	Married Couples	Female-Headed	All Families	Married Couples	Female-Headed
2050	100.0	77.9	17.6	100.0	47.6	47.6
1998	100.0	78.1	17.4	100.0	47.6	47.6
1996	100.0	78.5	17.2	100.0	48.1	46.9
1994	100.0	78.8	17.1	100.0	48.1	45.6
1992	100.0	79.0	16.9	100.0	49.4	45.5
1990	100.0	79.3	16.8	100.0	49.3	45.3
1988	100.0	79.8	16.5	100.0	50.0	44.4
1986	100.0	80.1	16.3	100.0	51.4	44.2

Source: Derived from data in U.S. Bureau of the Census, "Projections of the Number of Households and Families: 1986 to 2000," *Current Population Reports*, Series P-25, No. 986, May 1986.

to rise by six percent. Similarly, while white females age 16-24 are expected to decline in the labor force by three percent by 2000, black female youths are expected to increase by 11 percent. Thus, with declining competition from white youths, black male and female youths are expected to have wider job options during the 1990s. (Table 5)

Although the black labor force is expected to grow twice as fast as the white labor force during the 1990s, whites, particularly males, are still expected to maintain higher labor force participation (LFP) rates than blacks throughout the decade. While the proportion of the white working-age population working or

Table 5
Projections of U.S. Labor Force By Race, Sex, and Age, 1986-2000

RACE	Civilian Labor Force[1]		Labor Force Participation Rates	
	1986	2000	1986	2000
Blacks	**12,684**	**16,334**	**63.5**	**66.0**
Males	**6,373**	**7,926**	**71.2**	**70.7**
16-24	1,416	1,497	63.0	64.9
25-54	4,289	5,753	88.4	88.1
55 & over	668	676	35.8	28.5
Females	**6,311**	**8,408**	**57.2**	**62.1**
16-24	1,349	1,490	53.6	59.1
25-54	4,356	6,195	72.7	79.0
55 & over	606	723	24.2	22.8
Whites	**101,801**	**116,701**	**65.5**	**68.2**
Males	**57,216**	**62,252**	**76.9**	**75.3**
16-24	10,528	9,552	75.3	77.2
25-54	38,766	45,077	94.6	93.5
55 & over	7,922	7,623	40.8	34.5
Females	**44,585**	**54,449**	**55.0**	**61.5**
16-24	9,511	9,191	66.7	72.7
25-54	29,682	39,510	70.7	81.3
55 & over	5,392	5,748	21.7	21.0

[1]Numbers in thousands.

Source: U.S. Bureau of Labor Statistics, "Projections 2000," *BLS Bulletin*, No. 2302, March 1988

looking for work is expected to rise from 65.5 to 68.2 percent between 1986 and 2000, the LFP rate for black workers is expected to increase from 63.5 to 66.0.

Partly due to early retirement, black and white adult men age 25-54 are expected to have declining labor force participation. LFP rates for white adult men are expected to fall from 94.6 to 93.5 by 2000, while rates among black adult men will drop from 88.4 to 88.1. However, the LFP rates are projected to rise among white males age 16-24 (from 75.3 to 77.2) as well as among black males age 16-24 (from 63.0 to 64.9) during the 1990s. Nevertheless, by 2000, the LFP rates for white male youths are projected to be 20 percent higher than the rates for black male youths.

Unlike the patterns among men, labor force participation rates are projected to increase for black and white women—adults and youths—during the 1990s. While the proportion of white women age 25-54 working or looking for work is expected to rise from 70.7 to 81.3 percent between 1986 and 2000, the LFP rates of black adult women will increase from 72.7 to 79.0. The LFP rates for white adult women are expected to surpass those of black adult women by the year 2000. Similarly, the LFP rates of white females age 16-24 are expected to increase from 66.7 to 72.7 between 1986 and 2000, while the rates of black females age 16-24 will rise from 53.6 to 59.1. Thus, the LFP rates for white female youths are likely to be 23 percent higher than the rates for black female youths by 2000.

What unemployment levels are projected for blacks? BLS forecasts six percent for all U.S. workers by 2000—equivalent to the U.S. jobless rate for 1988. Since black jobless rates are usually double the nation's, we project 12 percent unemployment rates for blacks and five percent rates for whites by 2000. In order for blacks to attain jobless rates equal to those of whites by the year 2000, black unemployment rates would have to decline 60 percent. And, to equal the LFP rates of white youths, black male and female youths would have to increase their LFP rates by 20 and 23 percent, respectively, by 2000.

CRITICAL ISSUES CONFRONTING BLACK FAMILIES

To achieve parity with white families by the year 2000, black families must successfully confront several important issues:

- Attaining economic self-sufficiency;
- Strengthening and stabilizing families; and
- Developing viable and healthy communities.

We will examine each of these issues in greater detail and offer recommendations for the public and private sectors to equalize the life-chances of black and white families by the 21st century.

Attaining Economic Self-Sufficiency

Demographic projections suggest more favorable job opportunities for male and female heads of black families as well as for black youths by the year 2000. However, before effective policies can be developed to enhance economic self-sufficiency among black families during the 1990s, it is essential to assess the intended and unintended consequences of key social forces and policies on black families during the 1970s and 1980s.

Recessions and Inflation: The state of the economy during the 1990s will determine the quantity and quality of job opportunities available to all workers, regardless of race, by the 21st century. Despite the current record-level budget deficit, most economists do not forecast a recession for 1989, but many anticipate a mild recession during 1990. The U.S. Labor Department projects two "mild" recessions by the year 2000.[7]

Historically, all recessions—however "mild"—have had disparate effects on black workers and their families. Indeed, each of the four recessions (1970-71,

1974-75, 1980, and 1981-82) affected blacks more adversely than whites, due to the "last hired, first fired" principle of seniority. At the same time that black families were being hit by back-to-back recessions, they were battered by double-digit inflation.[8]

Industrial Shifts: Black families were also adversely affected by structural industrial changes, especially the exodus of jobs from central cities to the suburbs and the shift from higher-paying manufacturing jobs to lower-paying service jobs. These industrial shifts eroded the earnings of middle-class and working-class blacks and widened their economic gap with white workers. For example, the real median weekly earnings ($315) of full-time black workers did not increase in purchasing power between 1980 and 1987. Moreover, black full-time workers continue to earn about 20 percent less per week than white full-time workers.[9]

Jobs Mismatch? Many analysts predict that poorly educated blacks will experience a severe jobs mismatch by the 21st century, since the number of high-skilled jobs are to increase markedly, while the number of unskilled jobs are supposed to decline rapidly. Yet, while many of the fastest-growing jobs are high-paying, high-tech, and service occupations, the Labor Department predicts the largest number of new jobs to be low-paying service and sales jobs in which blacks are already overrepresented.[10]

For example, while the number of computer analysts and programmers are expected to increase by 586,000 between 1986 and 2000, five times as many (3.2 million) new jobs are projected for janitors, maids, food service workers, nurses' aides and cashiers. Not only are most of the new jobs likely to be low-paying, they are also likely to be part-time. Seven out of 10 new jobs created during the 1970s and 1980s have been part-time. Consequently, in addition to a mismatch with high-paying jobs, blacks may be plagued by "too perfect a fit" with low-paying jobs.

Obviously, if concerted efforts are not taken to reduce the alarming rates of high school dropouts, functional illiteracy, and declines in college and graduate school enrollments among minorities, this nation will be sharply polarized by the year 2000 between high-paying jobs held largely by whites and low-paying jobs held largely by blacks and Hispanics.

Immigration: Although blacks are expected to have declining competition from whites during the 1990s, there will be increased competition from Hispanic and Asian immigrants—who are projected to increase twice as fast as blacks. For example, Hispanics obtained the same number of new jobs created between 1975 and 1980 as blacks, although they were about half the size of the black population, while Asians secured half as many new jobs as blacks, although they were only one-fifth the size of the black population. Clearly, the extent of legal and illegal immigration over the next decade will be an important determinant of the economic status of black families by the year 2000.[11]

Federal Budget Cuts: Other government policies will also play a major role in the social and economic progress of poor black families during the 1990s. Working poor black families were impacted severely by the sharp cuts in federal programs for the poor and jobless during the Reagan administration. The AFDC budget cuts enacted in 1981 removed 400,000 working poor families from the rolls and reduced AFDC benefits for another 300,000 families. Food stamp recipients were affected adversely by the 15 percent cuts in federal spending between FY 1981 to FY 1987. Blacks were disparately hit by these cuts, since they comprised 40 percent of the recipients of these programs.

Several research studies revealed that the budget cuts of the 1980s contributed to the sharp increase in poverty (from 1.44 million to 1.82 million) among black families with children between 1979 and 1987. Only nine percent of these black families were lifted from poverty by cash entitlement programs (i.e., public assistance, unemployment insurance, and Social Security) in 1987, compared to 16 percent in 1979. If these programs had the same anti-poverty effects as they did in 1979, 143,000 fewer black families with children would have been poor in 1987. Thus, the economic progress of low-income black families will depend on the extent to which programs for the poor and jobless bear the brunt of deficit-reduction policies during the 1990s.[12]

Tax Reform: The well-being of working poor black families was enhanced markedly by several important tax initiatives. With the erosion of the personal exemption and standard deduction by spiraling inflation during the 1970s, poor families not only paid higher income tax rates, but larger payroll taxes as well. Consequently, the Earned Income Tax Credit (EITC) was enacted in 1975: (a) to restore poor families to their former status of not paying any income taxes, and (b) to refund a portion of the payroll tax to the working poor.

Because of the increased regressivity due to the tax cuts of the 1980s, however, poor families were paying higher actual tax rates (10 percent) than many affluent individuals (5 percent) and corporations by 1985. Thus, the Tax Reform Act of 1986 not only exempted working poor families from paying income taxes, but also raised the thresholds of the personal exemption, standard deduction and the EITC. Moreover, these thresholds were indexed, for the first time, to keep them abreast of rising inflation. About three million working poor families (one-fourth of whom are black) may be removed from the income tax rolls by the 1986 legislation. Similar tax reforms are needed during the 1990s to enhance economic self-sufficiency among poor and working-class families.[13]

Welfare Reform: Although conventional wisdom contends that the growth in one-parent black families during the 1970s and 1980s was mainly due to an "overgenerous" welfare system, numerous studies reveal that spiraling inflation eroded the value of welfare benefits sharply, since most states failed to raise AFDC needs and payment standards from their mid-1970 levels. A consensus emerged among conservatives and liberals that the current welfare system needed to be overhauled radically since it was only maintaining families in poverty and not helping them to climb out.

Although the final legislation is far from the extensive "welfare reform" originally conceived, The Family Support Act of 1988 contains several key provisions to help welfare recipients achieve economic self-sufficiency: (1) the ineffective

WIN (Work Incentive) program was replaced by JOBS (Job Opportunities and Basic Skills Training)—a comprehensive education, training and employment program; (2) states must guarantee child care for welfare mothers required to participate in JOBS; (3) child care and Medicaid coverage must be extended for 12 months for the families of recipients who leave welfare rolls due to employment; and (4) there is a mandated extension of the AFDC-Unemployed Parent (AFDC-UP) program to all 50 states.

On the other hand, the 1988 Family Support Act has a number of deficiencies: (1) it does not mandate increases in the AFDC benefit levels; (2) it does not set nationwide minimum AFDC needs and payment standards; (3) it allows newly-participating states the option of limiting participation in their AFDC-UP program to six months; and (4) fails to assign high priority to enhancing the employability of low-income and young noncustodial fathers. Although many of these defects will be addressed by various demonstration projects, they must be rectified during the 1990s if poor families are to move toward economic independence by the year 2000.

Non-Cash Benefits: The role of in-kind benefits in reducing poverty will continue to be a major policy issue affecting black families during the 1990s. In response to criticism that poverty in the U.S. was overstated by conventional "cash-only" statistics, the Census Bureau began issuing experimental annual data on noncash benefits from 1979. Yet, these data reveal not only that sizable numbers of low-income blacks and whites receive no in-kind benefits for the poor, but also that poverty continues to remain at high levels even after noncash benefits are included.[14]

At least two out of five poor black families receive no cash or in-kind "means-tested" benefits. While half (48 percent) of all poor black families receive no public assistance in 1986, two-fifths received no Medicaid (41 percent) or food stamps (43 percent), and two-thirds (67 percent) were not recipients of either subsidized rent nor public housing. Moreover, poverty among blacks only fell from 33 percent to 27 percent in 1987 when the value of food, housing and medical benefits were factored in. Thus, even when in-kind benefits were "cashed out," poverty among blacks surged from 22 percent to 27 percent between 1979 and 1987—which is faster than the rise in the official poverty rates for blacks from 31 percent to 33 percent.

Yet, these in-kind programs provided vital support to the three out of five poor black families that received them. While over two million blacks received Medicaid, food stamps, or school lunches, about one million were recipients of subsidized rent or public housing. Clearly, in-kind benefits must be targeted more effectively to the poor during the 1990s.

STRENGTHENING AND STABILIZING FAMILIES

Many low-income and middle-income black families were destabilized acutely during the 1970s and 1980s by factors at the societal, community, and family levels. Several important issues must be addressed by the public and private sectors to strengthen and stabilize black families by the 21st century.

Single-Parent Families: While the proportion of black families headed by women rose from 22 percent to 28 percent between 1960 and 1970, it soared to 44 percent by 1985. However, during 1986 and 1987, female-headed black families fell to 42 percent—the first major declines in single-parent black families in three decades. Nevertheless, by 1987, half (52 percent) of black children lived in female-headed families, compared to 37 percent in 1970. Moreover, while 45 percent of all black children live in poor families, 68 percent of black children in single-parent families are poor.

Contrary to popular belief, school dropouts account for only a tiny fraction of the growth in female-headed black families since 1970. In fact, single-parent families increased 50 times faster among college-educated (+ 496 percent) black women between 1970 and 1985 than among black women who did not complete high school (+ 10 percent). Thus, school dropouts accounted for only six percent of the female-headed black families formed over that 15-year span, while college-educated women comprised 35 percent.

However, never-married women comprised the bulk of the new single-parent black families formed since 1970. While separated and divorced women accounted for 86 percent of the white female-headed families formed between 1970 and 1985, never-married women accounted for 67 percent of the black female-headed families formed during that 15-year period. Contrary to conventional wisdom, most of these never-married female family heads are adults, not teenagers. Since nine out of 10 black unwed adolescent mothers do not set up independent households, teenagers account for less than five percent of black female-headed family households.

Adolescent Pregnancy: Although out-of-wedlock births have steadily declined among black teenagers, while rising among white teens, adolescent pregnancy will continue to be a major area of concern for blacks thoughout the 1990s. Out-of-wedlock birth rates fell among black teens (from 90.8 to 79.4 per 1,000 unmarried women age 15-19) between 1970 and 1985, but rose among white teens (from 10.9 to 10.5 per 1,000 unmarried women age 15-19). Nevertheless, black teenagers are still four times more likely than white teenagers to have children out-of-wedlock.[15]

Moreover, it is estimated that teenagers will account for about one million pregnancies—400,000 abortions and 500,000 births—each year. Since blacks will account for about half of the adolescent out-of-wedlock births, the social and economic viability of black families will be acutely affected. Because of inadequate health care and nutrition, babies born to black teenage mothers are at-risk of dying in infancy or having a low birth weight. Furthermore, high dropout rates increase the risk of black teenage mothers becoming unemployed and going on welfare. Comprehensive strategies will be needed to combat adolescent pregnancy in black families during the 1990s.

Child Support: More sensitive child support policies will be needed to enhance the functioning of single-parent black families by the year 2000. Black mothers arc less likely than white mothers to be awarded child support, but more likely to receive smaller payments when awarded. Two out of three white single mothers were awarded child support in 1985, compared to only one out of three black single mothers. Since child support accounts for only about one-fifth of the total income of single custodial mothers, many of them remain in poverty—after receiving child support payments![16]

Although high rates of unemployment among black noncustodial fathers contribute to the low child support payments received by black single mothers, the failure to establish paternity for out-of-wedlock children is the major reason for the low rates of court-ordered child support awards. To facilitate the collection of child support for low-income single mothers, the Family Support Act of 1988 strengthens state efforts to establish paternity and instituted automatic withholding of the wages of noncustodial fathers—even when they were not in arrears. Since low-income fathers often pay higher proportions of their income for child support than middle-income fathers, this Act urges more equitable court guidelines.

Child Care: With labor force participation among black women expected to jump from 57 percent to 62 percent, the need for child care by working parents will be more pervasive by the 21st century. For example, the proportion of black wives in the labor force with children under age 18 rose from 56 percent to 70 percent between 1970 and 1984, while the proportion of black single mothers in the labor force went from 53 percent to 62 percent. Mothers of pre-school children are also expected to enter the labor force in record numbers during the 1990s. While the proportion of black wives in the labor force with children under age six rose from 50 percent to 72 percent between 1970 and 1984, the proportion of black single mothers with pre-schoolers increased from 44 percent to 51 percent.

Due to the unavailability of day care for thousands of working parents, it has been estimated that between 6 and 7 million school-age children are "latchkey," i.e., are minors who return to an unsupervised home. However, a special survey conducted by the Census Bureau in 1984 found only seven percent (or 2.1 million) of all 5-13 year olds with working parents to be "unsupervised." Moreover, white families (eight percent) were twice as likely as black families (four percent) to have "latchkey" children.

Informal Adoption: A major reason for the low incidence of "latchkey" children among blacks is the availability of child care providers in black extended families. Although it is often asserted that extended families are largely nonexistent among blacks today, numerous research studies reveal the kinship networks continue to provide vital support to two-parent, one-parent, middle-income and low-income families. Nine out of 10 babies born out-of-wedlock to black teenage mothers live in three-generational families with their mothers and grandparents (or other adult relatives). Almost half (45 percent) of all black working mothers rely on relatives for child care—inside and outside their homes.[17]

Economic hardships and the lack of affordable housing contribute to surges in "doubling-up" with kin. Due to the 1974-75 recession, for example, the proportion of black children living with their mothers in the households of relatives jumped from 30 percent to 39 percent between 1973 and 1975. Furthermore, while the number of black children living with kin increased from 1.3 million to 1.6 million between 1970 and 1987, the proportion of black children in informally adoptive families soared from 13 percent to 17 percent. Undoubtedly, back-to-back recessions, double-digit inflation and housing shortages led to sharp increases in "doubling-up"among black families during the 1970s and 1980s.[18]

Foster Care and Adoption: Although the total number of children in foster care declined after 1977, the proportion of black foster children rose sharply. As the number of foster children fell from 500,000 to 250,000 between 1977 and 1983, the proportion of foster children who were black increased from 28 percent to 34 percent. Since 1983, the number of foster children has surged due to soaring homelessness, drug abuse, and AIDS. Alarming numbers of babies born to mothers who are alcohol-addicted, drug-addicted, or AIDS-infected are placed in foster care or hospital wards.

While black foster children are less likely than white foster children to have physical or mental disabilities, they remain in foster care much longer than white children. Unfortunately, many black families that want to adopt are screened out by insensitive criteria that place higher priority on middle-class status, two-parents, heads under 40, and no children of their own. Thus, hundreds of black foster children are never adopted and must "age out" of the system. Many studies reveal that long-term foster children have a high risk of becoming delinquents, criminals, mentally ill, drug addicts, prostitutes, alcoholics, and welfare recipients. About half of the homeless youths in New York City, for example, were formerly in foster care. More sensitive foster care policies are needed for the 1990s that build on the informal adoption and foster care practices among blacks.

Family Violence: Traditionally, black families have had lower rates of child abuse and neglect than white families of similar economic status. According to the national study of child abuse and neglect conducted by HHS between 1979 and 1980, 652,000 children under age 18 were identified as abused or neglected—yielding a national incidence rate of 10.5 per 1,000 children. Contrary to conventional wisdom, blacks had lower rates than whites for all forms of child abuse (i.e., physical, sexual, and emotional) and neglect (i.e., physical and emotional), except for educational neglect. Studies have found the lowest levels of child abuse and neglect in families with strong kinship networks.[19]

However, the proliferation of the cocaine derivative, "crack," in the black community has led to sharp increases in child abuse and other forms of family violence. There are regular news accounts of children who were abused or killed by parents who were addicted to drugs or alcohol. Although alcohol abuse has been strongly correlated with wife abuse in black families for a long time, drug addiction has become more preeminent.

Drug Abuse, AIDS, and Alcohol Abuse: According to the 1982 National Survey on Drug Abuse, one-third of blacks and one-third of whites used drugs illicitly, while 13 percent of blacks and 12 percent of whites were currently using drugs illicitly. Moreover, blacks comprised one-fourth of the clients admitted to federally funded drug treatment centers in 1983. Although black youths have about equal rates of drug abuse as white youths, drug-related violence has risen sharply among black youths in inner-cities. Rising drug abuse among black women has led to a steep rise in the births of drug-addicted babies—many of them spending years in hospitals as "boarder" babies.

One of the most ominous consequences of extensive drug abuse has been the spread of AIDS (Acquired Immune Deficiency Syndrome) among blacks.

Blacks comprised one-fourth of 24,5000 AIDS cases reported in the U.S. between 1981-1986. AIDS is likely to be transmitted disproportionately among blacks through intravenous drug abusers and their sexual partners, while homosexual or bisexual men with AIDS are disproportionately white. Moreover, black children are 15 times more likely than white children to contract AIDS. Furthermore, blacks are expected to comprise about 12,000 of the 179,000 AIDS-related deaths predicted in the U.S. by 1991.[20]

Although alcohol abuse has long been associated with spousal abuse, child abuse, homicides, divorce, separation, desertion, mental illness, and physical illness, its devastating effects have been conspicuously omitted in conventional studies of black families. Moreover, many studies have found strong associations between alcohol and drug abuse. Despite the severe destabilization of black families due to alcohol abuse, the black community has not indicated a sense of urgency in combatting this disease.

Shortage of Men: A perennial obstacle to stabilizing black families has been the shortage of men relative to women. Although single-parent families grew at about the same pace among blacks and whites during the 1970s, black women had much lower remarriage rates than white women because of the greater unavailability of marriageable black men. Among persons of all ages, there are 95 white men to 100 white women, while there are only 90 black men to 100 black women.

Among blacks, the sex ratio is widest among those in their prime working years. Among persons age 25-44, there are only 85 black men for every 100 black women, while there are about equal numbers of white men and women in that age category. However, when one corrects for the disparate undercount of black men, the gap narrows markedly to about 96 black men for every 100 black women between the ages of 25-44.

Yet, a shortage of marriageable black men continues to exist, since they are forced to run a "gauntlet" of school expulsions, special education placements, dropouts, foster care placements, delinquency, arrests, incarceration, unemployment, drug addiction, alcohol abuse, homelessness, homicides, and suicides from the cradle to the grave. It is clear that the functioning of black families cannot be enhanced by the year 2000—until highest priority is assigned to insuring that black boys, male youths, adult men, and fathers are able to fulfill their responsibilities as productive members of this society.[21]

DEVELOPING VIABLE COMMUNITIES

In order to enhance the social and economic functioning of black families by the 21st century, comprehensive public and private initiatives must be undertaken during the 1990s to develop vibrant black communities.

Segregation in Poverty Areas: A major barrier to the social and economic development of black communities has been the residential segregation of the overwhelming majority of working-class and poor black families in low-income areas that have experienced large declines in jobs. While 85 percent of poor blacks lived in poverty areas of the nation's five largest cities in 1980, 60 percent of non-poor central city blacks also lived in poverty areas. Moreover, while 39 percent of poor blacks lived in poverty areas with 40 percent or more poverty rates, 17 percent of non-poor blacks also lived in these "extreme" poverty areas. In contrast, only 32 percent of poor central city whites lived in poverty areas in 1980.[22]

It should be noted, however, that strong working-class role models continue to exist in low-income black areas. Even in the "extreme" poverty areas, three out of five families are in the labor force, half are not on welfare and half are headed by two parents. Yet, the progress of black families in poverty areas is impeded, since these areas are "redlined" for substandard housing, inferior schools, inadequate community services, crime, and "open air" drug markets. Bold housing initiatives will be needed in the 1990s to insure that: (a) blacks have the same residential options as whites of similar economic status; and (b) working-class and poor black families are able to revitalize their communities socially and economically.

Community Development: Fortunately, there are countless examples across the nation of residents of low-income areas enhancing the vitality of their communities. Some of the most spectacular accomplishments have occurred in public housing. With the assistance of the National Center for Neighborhood Enterprise, several resident management corporations have demonstrated that they can maintain safe, pleasant, and comfortable living environments more efficiently and cost-effectively than local public housing authorities. For example, after three years of tenant management in Kenilworth-Parkside in Washington, D.C., there were sharp declines in vandalism, welfare dependency, school dropouts, teenage pregnancy and unemployment, and sharp increases in building repairs and rent collections.

Some of the other successful resident management initiatives are: Bromly-Health in Jamaica Plains, Massachusetts; Cochran Gardens in St. Louis, Missouri; A. Harry Moore in Jersey City, New York; LeClaire Courts in Chicago, Illinois; and B.W. Cooper in New Orleans, Louisiana. A key to their success is establishing numerous resident-operated small businesses in such areas as: maintenance, day care, laundry cleaning, tailoring, barbering, beauty salons, catering, and thrift shops. Other reasons for their effectiveness include: setting form behavioral and maintenance standards for their residents, enhancing the residents positive self-esteem, and sense of personal efficiency.[23]

To increase the stock of affordable housing to low-income families, grassroots groups have adopted many strategies. One popular approach is "sweat equity" to help low-income families overcome high down payments or the lack of credit through their own labor. Self-help housing efforts have been successfully implemented by urban and rural groups, such as: Jubilee Housing in Washington, D.C.; Delta Housing Development Corporation in Indianola, Mississippi; and Flanner House Homes in Indianapolis, Indiana. Other community-based groups that have successfully converted declining neighborhoods into thriving ones include: Operation Better Block in Pittsburgh, Pennsylvania; Bedford-Stuyvesant Restoration Corporation in Brooklyn, New York; Collinwood Community Service Center in Cleveland, Ohio; Urban League affiliates and numerous black churches throughout the nation.

Economic Development: Numerous community-based groups have undertaken innovative business development efforts in black communities. Some of these groups are: South Arsenal Neighborhood Development Corporation (SAND) in Hartford, Connecticut; Business Opportunities System in Indianapolis, Indiana; and Jeff-Vander-lou in St. Louis, Missouri. Many grassroots groups are enhancing the entrepreneurial skills of black youth. For example, the Educational Training and Enterprise Center in Camden, New Jersey, has helped hundreds of youths to create businesses in such areas as food vending, janitorial services, etc.

In addition to outstanding accomplishments in increasing the supply of low-income housing, black churches have also launched numerous economic development efforts. For example, Zion Investment Corporation, a development arm of Zion Baptist Church in Philadelphia, has built a shopping center and created several small businesses. In Washington, D.C., the United House of Prayer for All People has constructed McCullough Plaza—a huge complex of affordable housing, shopping facilities and small businesses. Moreover, Allen AME Church in Jamaica, New York, has established a housing corporation, a senior citizens complex, a 480-pupil elementary school, a health service facility, and a home care agency for the elderly and the handicapped. The Congress of National Black Churches has also undertaken innovative efforts in such areas as education, strengthening families, community development, and economic development. Such creative community revitalization efforts must be reinforced by public policies through the 1990s, if the well-being of black families is to be enhanced.

RECOMMENDATIONS FOR ENHANCING BLACK FAMILIES

In order to develop effective strategies for attaining parity between black and white families by the year 2000, we have examined: (a) future demographic characteristics projected for black individuals and families and (b) critical issues that will confront black families during the 1990s. More specifically, we examined critical issues related to: attaining economic self-sufficiency, strengthening families, and community development. We shall now offer specific recommendations to enhance the social and economic functioning of black families by the 21st century. However, to place our recommendations in proper context, it is necessary to be explicit about key guiding principles that cut across each of them.

58

Guiding Principles

Self-Help and Government Aid: Since neither the black community nor the government—alone—can resolve all of the problems affecting black families, partnerships and coalitions are required that involve all segments of the public (i.e., federal, state, county, and city) and private (i.e., business, labor, non-profit groups, and all institutions in the black community) sectors. Thus, community-based minority organizations (notably, churches, CDCs, and neighborhood groups) with demonstrated capabilities for strengthening black individuals and families should be used as major conduits, contractors, sub-contractors, advisors, etc., for such efforts.

Combatting Racism: To insure that these recommendations have enduring positive effects on black families, this nation must make a major commitment to eradicate racism in all of its forms—individual and institutional. Firm public and private actions should be taken to remove racial barriers—intended and unintended—from all of the institutions of American society.

Family Impact Analyses: Prior to 1987, all proposed policies were required to have an environmental impact statement that assessed their potential effects on the physical environment, but not on families and individuals. However, on September 3, 1987, President Reagan signed an executive order requiring all levels of government to assess the intended and unintended consequences of current and proposed policies and regulations on American families. The black community must closely monitor government agencies to insure that the potential and actual effects of public policies on black families are assessed appropriately. The Black Family Impact Analysis Program of the Baltimore Urban League might be used as a model for conducting sensitive impact analyses for black families.

Cost-Effective Strategies: Record-level budget and trade deficits, volatile stock markets, and impending recessions suggest an austere economic climate that will require family-strengthening policies that are more efficiently targeted. Policymakers should not be permitted to use a stagnant economy as justification for neglecting the needs of the economically and racially disadvantaged.

Strategies for Achieving Economic Self-Sufficiency

Stimulating Economic Growth: Although reductions in the budget deficit are essential if the American economy is to sustain steady growth during the 1990s, programs for the poor and jobless must not bear the brunt of such initiatives. If tax increases are instituted to reduce the deficit, they should not erode the 1986 Tax Reform Act provisions to aid the working poor. Moreover, policymakers should not be permitted to fight inflation by inducing recessions, as was the case for the four slumps between 1970 and 1982.

Achieving Full Employment: This nation must rededicate itself to the goals of the Employment Act of 1946 and the Humphrey-Hawkins act of 1978 to provide everyone willing and able to work with jobs at liveable wages. Accordingly, the federal minimum wage should be raised to at least $4.35 per hour to enhance the well-being of low-wage American workers. Moreover, larger tax incentives should be given to businesses that create full-time jobs at liveable wages than to those creating part-time jobs at minimum wages.

Enhancing Job Training: Strong emphasis on quantitative outcomes has encouraged ''creaming'' of job-ready persons and an underrepresentation of ''hard-core'' workers with deficient work and educational skills. Eligibility and performance criteria for job training programs should be modified to give higher priority to ''long-term'' jobless adults and youths, adolescent parents (male and female), and to female heads of low-income families.

Reforming AFDC: Building on the 1988 Family Support Act, these provisions should be included in the welfare reform of the 1990s: (a) periodic increases in AFDC benefits should be mandated to keep abreast of inflation; (b) national minimum standards for AFDC needs and payments standards should be established; (c) the income ceiling to be eligible for AFDC should be raised to the poverty level; (d) the onerous prior work history eligibility requirement for AFDC-UP and its 100-hour ceiling should be eliminated; and (e) low-income and young noncustodial fathers should be given high priority for basic skills and job training in the JOBS program.

Strategies for Strengthening Families

Aiding Single-Parent Families: Public and private efforts to help low-income single-parent families over the next decade should be directed toward the following initiatives: (a) remedial education, high school equivalency assistance, and basic skills training for school dropouts; (b) classroom training, work experience, job search, and job training; (c) affordable day care for working parents; (d) affordable medical care; (e) affordable and decent housing that permit children; (f) child support enforcement; (g) family violence assistance; (h) enhancing parenting skills; and (i) counseling and mentoring.

Aiding Young Fathers: Since most fathers of children born to adolescent mothers are sincerely interested in being responsible parents, government policies are needed to reinforce, and not discourage, such bonds. Under no circumstances should the in-kind services that noncustodial fathers provide their children be ''cashed out'' to reduce their welfare grants. Higher priority should be given to enhancing the employability of young parents. Child support policies should be made more sensitive to the circumstances of low-income and young noncustodial fathers. Male responsibility media campaigns, like those conducted by the National Urban League, should be widely supported.

Expanding Child Care: A major barrier to the labor force participation of many black women is the lack of affordable child care. Unfortunately, the current Dependent Care Tax Credit (DCTC) is not used by most working poor parents, since their incomes are too low to have tax liabilities. Thus, the DCTC should be made ''refundable,'' similar to the Earned Income Tax Credit, to insure that working poor families receive tax rebates for child care—even when they do not have to pay taxes. Moreover, this nation should give serious consideration to implementing a children's allowance.

Reforming Foster Care: The foster care system needs to be radically overhauled to: (a) provide quality family preservation services; (b) reduce unnecessary placements; (c) provide more effective permanency planning; (d) use culturally-relevant adoption criteria; (e) assign highest priority to extended family networks for foster care and adoption placements; (f) reduce sharply the time minority children spend in foster care; and (g) raise the exit age to 21 in order to provide youths who "age out" of foster care with adequate educational, employment training, and life skills to be productive citizens in society.

Strategies for Developing Viable Communities

Expanding Low-Income Housing: The increasing unavailability of affordable housing for low-income families has led to overcrowding, homelessness, foster care placements, child abuse, family violence, physical illness, and mental illness. This nation must expand the supply of low-income housing by: (a) expanding the availability of subsidized rental units; (b) restoring thousands of abandoned and boarded-up housing; (c) supporting the development of resident management of public housing; (d) expanding homeownership option for low-income families, such as urban homesteading, "self-help," and "sweat equity." Community-based groups, especially churches and community development corporations should be used as major conduits for constructing housing in low-income communities.

Enhancing Economic Development: Policies are needed that target entrepreneurial development in inner cities. The successful efforts of several states with enterprise zones in low-income communities should be emulated across the nation. The development and maintenance of black businesses should be encouraged through set-asides and other targeted approaches. The innovative entrepreneurial ventures on public housing sites by resident management corporations should be replicated at other public housing facilities. Recipients of welfare and unemployment insurance should be encouraged to establish small businesses through "enterprise allowances," which have been effective in several European countries. Black churches should be encouraged to expand into economic development efforts.

Black Children In America

Marian Wright Edelman

A Day in the Lives of Black Mothers and Infants

Each day in 1986, 1,702 infants were born to black women of all ages.

- Almost one in four was born to a teenager.
- 1,042 were born to unmarried mothers.
- 450 were born to mothers with less than a high school education.
- 62 were born to mothers who had received no prenatal care.
- 103 were born to women who received prenatal care only in the last three months of pregnancy.

Each day in 1986, about 700 black girls between the ages of 15 and 19 became pregnant, and an estimated 250 had abortions.

Each day in 1986, 388 babies were born to black teenagers.

- Nine in 10 were born to unmarried teens.
- One in four was born to a teenage mother with at least one other child.
- 16 were born to mothers younger than age 15.
- 19 were born to teenage mothers who had received no prenatal care at all.
- 38 were born to teenage mothers who received prenatal care only in the last three months of pregnancy.
- 51 weighed less than 5.5 pounds at birth.

Millions of black children today live in a desolate world where physical survival is a triumph, where fear and hopelessness reign, and where the future holds no promises and few opportunities. As America positions itself for passage into the 21st century, its current policies conspire to abandon these children and their families. Unless we change this country's course, many black children will be left behind completely, suffering from poor health care and nutrition, stifled by inadequate education and training, and trapped in lives of impoverishment and despair.

Our prospects as a nation now depend in large part on our ability to cultivate a new generation of citizens and employees and leaders and parents from a pool of children that, without intervention, will remain disproportionately poor, under-educated, and untrained. By the year 2000, the total number of minority children will increase by over 25 percent and will constitute one-third of all children; the number of white, non-Hispanic children will increase by only two-thirds of one percent.[1]

In 1978, young people age 16 through 24 were 27 percent of the working age population (age 16-64). By 1995, these young adults will be only 18 percent of Americans of working age, and one in three of our new workers will be minority.[2] As the number of workers steadily declines, business and industry will be forced to rely upon workers and potential workers in whom we traditionally have failed to invest, including large numbers of blacks. Between now and the year 2000, only one in four of new labor force entrants will be white males; in 2000, the Hudson Institute estimates that only 15 percent of all new labor force entrants will be white males born in the United States.[3]

To ignore these facts is to jeopardize America's future and undermine the competitiveness and productivity of our economy in the twenty-first century. And for black children, continued failure to recognize the need for public, private, and community intervention only increases the already high odds against their survival.

Today, compared to 1980, black children are now more likely to be born into poverty, lack early prenatal care, have a single mother, have an unemployed parent, be unemployed themselves as teenagers, and not go to college after high school graduation:[4]

- A black baby is almost three times as likely as a white baby to be born to a mother who has had no prenatal care at all.

- A black infant is more than twice as likely as a white infant to die during the first year of life.

- A black child's father is twice as likely as a white child's father to be unemployed. If both parents of a black child work, they earn 84 percent of what a white family earns.

- A black child is 40 percent more likely than a white child to be behind grade level in school and 15 percent more likely to drop out.

- A black youth is twice as likely as a white youth to be unemployed. A black college graduate faces about the same odds of unemployment as a white high school graduate who never attended college.

- A black male teenager is six times as likely as a white male teenager to be a victim of homicide.

What America needs is a comprehensive, long-term investment in policies and programs which help all poor children and their families. We need a new national commitment to ensure as well as we can that every child, black and white, has basic health and nutrition services and the opportunity to attend good schools, to develop strong basic academic skills, and to become economically independent as a young adult.

POVERTY

Black children, youth, and families remain worse off than whites in every economic indicator of American life — and the gap is widening. In 1987, nearly one-half (45.1 percent) of all black children were living in poverty; that means that there were 4.3 million black children living in poverty in 1987. Between 1959 and 1968, the poverty rate among black children fell from 65.5 percent to 43.1 percent, a drop of more than a third. But, between 1968 and 1987, the poverty rate among black children dropped by less than 1 percent. In fact, in 1984, the poverty rate had risen to 46.2 percent, a rate higher than at any point since 1967. By comparison, in 1987, only 15.0 percent of white children lived in poverty.[5]

High poverty rates among black children are closely related to the eroded employment and wage base among black families. While the nation's overall unemployment rate in October 1988 was 5.3 percent, among blacks it was 11.0 percent. In 1987, of the 4.2 million black working families with children younger than 18, one in six (17.9 percent) had at least one working-age person unemployed. Among two-parent black families with at least one person unemployed, 34.1 percent had no other person in the household employed.[6]

For a growing number of black children, living in a family where the parents are employed does not provide an escape from poverty. Many black adults trying hard to provide for their children often have work that does not pay enough to support a family. The federal minimum wage of $3.35 per hour is worth today only about 70 percent of its 1979 value. It has not been raised to compensate for inflation since 1981.

This wage stagnation has had a dramatic impact on a family's ability to provide for itself. Full-time, year-round work at the minimum wage now yields annual earnings that are less than 70 percent of what is needed to lift a family of three out of poverty ($9,690) and less than 60 percent of what is needed to lift a family of four out of poverty ($11,650). Overall, for both whites and blacks, from 1979 to 1987, the number of Americans paid on an hourly basis who were paid wages so low that full-time work could not lift a family of three out of poverty jumped from 2.8 million to over 14 million.[7]

But, despite evidence of programs with proven success and signs of rising child poverty, programs which help poor children and their families have been cut drastically in this decade.

In 1981, cuts in programs for low-income families and children totalled $10 billion per year for 1982 and a roughly equivalent amount for each subsequent year. The effects of the $10 billion annual cut from federal survival programs for poor families and children were clear.

- From 1979 to 1985, 30 percent of the increase in poverty among families with children (and half of the increase since 1981) was due to declining federal assistance.

- In 1979 nearly one of every five families with children that otherwise would have been poor was lifted out of poverty by Social Security, unemployment insurance, or public assistance. In 1985, the comparable figure was only one out of every nine families.

- Only 704,000 children were lifted out of poverty in 1983 through 1987 — five years of economic "recovery." At that rate of improvement (assuming no more recessions), it would take seventeen years — nearly another generation of children — just to get back to the high 1979 level of child poverty.[8]

The combined effect of declining federal commitment and the social and economic changes has taken a serious toll on black families and their children is abundant as the discussion which follows reveals.

Increasing Poverty Among Young Black Families

Young families (those with family heads under age 30) have been especially hard hit by economic change and earnings losses over the last decade. For example, there has been a significant decline in the proportion of young men with earnings sufficient to support a family. Only 48 percent of white men and 27 percent of black men ages 20 to 24 earned enough to support a wife and one child above the poverty level in 1984. In contrast, in 1973, 64 percent of white males and 57 percent of black males in this age group could support a family of three.[9]

Living below the poverty line is becoming far more frequent among young families. Poverty rates among young white families have more than doubled, from 12 percent in 1973 to 26 percent in 1986. Poverty rates among younger black families were higher to begin with and still increased by nearly half, from 43 percent in 1973 to 59 percent in 1986.[10]

While the economic losses experienced by young white families have been large, young black families as a group have fared far worse. They started the period in 1973 with considerably lower earnings and family incomes than whites, and they suffered larger percentage reductions than whites from 1973 to 1986.

The median annual earnings of young blacks who head families fell by one-half between 1973 to 1986, from $11,965 to $6,000. More than half of all young black family heads without a high school diploma had no earnings whatsoever in 1986. Even young black college graduates who head families had their median earnings decline by 31 percent during this period.[11]

More than 600,000 young black families — nearly one-half (46 percent) of all young black families in America — were poor in 1986. In contrast, slightly more than one-third of all young black families lived in poverty in 1973.[12]

In the past, when young parents were getting started or when good paying jobs were scarce, many extended black families lived together and were better able to make ends meet and to absorb wage losses. But, with many extended families now living far apart from one another, many family units can no longer pool their earnings or share living expenses. Many black children who used to be supported by or cared for by the efforts of two parents and grandparents now often have only one parent at home and have grandparents who are themselves living on the margin.

DWINDLING YOUNG BLACK MARRIAGES

Basic changes in the numbers and kinds of jobs available to young workers have had a tremendous impact on the ability of young blacks to form families and to support themselves. The end result is that, in the black community, young marriages have declined dramatically, leaving many black babies and children in single parent, female-headed families. The economic consequences of these changes have been disastrous for black children.

The decline in the employment rates and in good paying jobs among black males has had a devastating impact on the number of marriages among young blacks. Professor William Wilson, Chairman of the Department of Sociology at the University of Chicago, has studied the link between black male joblessness and declining black marriage rates extensively. He says that:

> . . . both the black delay in marriage and the lower rate of remarriage, each of which is associated with high percentages of out-of-wedlock births and female-headed households, can be directly tied to the labor market status of black males. Our data show that black women, especially young black women, are facing a shrinking pool of "marriageable" (that is, economically stable) men . . . the problem of black joblessness should once again be placed as a top priority item in public policy agendas designed to enhance the status of families.[13]

A look at current proportions of marriages among young blacks and young whites bears this out. Among all white 20- to 24-year-old women, almost 40 percent are married. But among black 20- to 24-year-old women, almost 80 percent are still single. Among white males aged 20 to 24, 22.6 percent have married; among black males of the same age, only 10.7 percent have married. Among white males aged 25 to 29, 66.1 percent have married; among black males of the same age, only 39.7 percent have married.[14]

The failure of first marriages to form among young blacks has fueled the growth in female-headed families, and the almost inescapable poverty which follows. Young black women are not having more babies; black teens had 179,100 babies in 1970 and 141,606 in 1986. In fact, the proportion of black women younger than 20 who have given birth has fallen fairly steadily since the early 1970s. The birth rate for unmarried black teens is also decreasing, although it remains much higher than that of white teens. (The birth rate among unmarried white teens is increasing: by 97 percent between 1970 and 1986.)[15]

The crux of the problem facing the black family today is that young black women who become pregnant are far less likely to marry than they used to be, nor are they as likely to marry as young pregnant white women are. The whole of the increase in the proportion of black children in female-headed families over the last decade is accounted for by the increase in those who live with unmarried mothers, and not by the increase in the proportion who live with divorced or separated mothers.[16]

When a single woman is pregnant and wants to bear the child, marriage is most likely under active consideration. If the father of the child, presumably a few years older than she, is potentially a good provider, marriage may well result, as has been the pattern in the past. But, if the proportion of young males who are potentially good providers falls, it could be expected that the prenatal marriage rate would decline.

That is precisely what has happened in the black community. Since 1947, the marriage rates for pregnant black 15- to 17-year-olds has dropped about 80 percent; for pregnant black 18- and 19-year-olds, the marriage rate is down about 60 percent.[17]

There is another important factor, however, that contributes to the rising proportion of black out-of-wedlock births. Married black women have among the lowest birth rates of any racial or ethnic group in the country. In 1983, pregnant married black women were more than two and one-half times as likely to have an abortion as pregnant married white women. Having a child (or an additional child) may mean a substantial loss of family income to a married black woman. Among two-parent families with incomes over $25,000, 86 percent of black women work as compared to 68 percent of white women. And the black woman's salary contributes a bigger share of total family income than does the white woman's.[18] For many black families, an additional child may tip the scales back toward economic insecurity.

The combined statistical impact of fewer black marriages and a low birth rate among black married women results in higher proportions of black babies being born out-of-wedlock, even though the number of black babies born to unmarried black women is declining. As a result, in 1986, over 61 percent of all births to black women were out-of-wedlock.[19]

Currently, only four out of ten black children live in two-parent families as compared to eight out of every 10 white children. If the share of births to unmarried women grows in the black community at the rate of the last decade, by the year 2000 only one black baby in five will be born to a married woman.

This virtually guarantees the poverty of the next generation because even today, black children in young female-headed households are the poorest in the nation.

Young black female-headed families had an astounding 81.5 percent poverty rate in 1986. While a black child born in America has a one in two chance of being born poor, a black child in a female-headed household has a two in three chance of being poor. For white children living in female-headed families, 45.8 percent lived in poverty in 1986.[20]

If a household is headed by a young black mother under 25, that baby has a nine in 10 chance of being poor.[21] The median annual earnings of all young female-headed families were extremely low ($2,171) in 1973, but nonetheless declined still further, to only $1,560, in 1986[22]

If these trends are to be stopped or reversed, two efforts must remain high priorities within the black community: working to improve job opportunities and wages for black parents, and encouraging young people to delay having children until they are financially secure.

CHILD CARE

Black women have a long history of working outside of the home to help provide income for their families. Over the last 20 years, their wages have become even more important to black economic survival. Between 1967 and 1985, wives' contributions to income for black families with children increased from 19.4 percent to 31.1 percent.[23] In fact, for many two-parent families today, black or white, the second income is all that stands between them and poverty. In 1985, a study for the Congressional Joint Economic Committee found that 53.8 percent more two-parent families would live below the poverty line if the wives in them were not employed.[24]

Most mothers of young children have joined the labor force, a massive demographic shift that has made decent child care a necessity for families from every income group. Among single mothers in 1987, 73.8 percent worked. Of employed women, more and more are working full time. In 1987, 81.7 percent of black employed mothers and 69.0 percent of white employed mothers worked full time.[25]

Rising numbers of mothers with very young children are working outside the home. Fifty-six and one-tenth of one percent of all mothers with preschool children are in the labor force. More than half of all married mothers with infants younger than age two are in the work force — a 116 percent increase since 1970.[26] By the year 2000, seven out of 10 preschool children will have mothers in the labor force.[27]

Black children, regardless of age, are more likely than white children to have working mothers. In 1987, 57.1 percent of black children under age six had working mothers.[28]

For low-income families, whether headed by a single parent or by two parents, quality child care is a critical first step in getting and keeping economic self-sufficiency. But our current patchwork child care system cannot meet the growing demand, forcing many low- and moderate-income families to leave their children in inadequate and sometimes dangerous child care situations. Too few children are in good child care conditions. Too many are left alone, with slightly older siblings, or in overcrowded, unsafe, or unstimulating substitute care.

These inadequacies in child care availability and quality have hit black families particularly hard. Higher proportions of black children need full-time care and at earlier ages than do white children. Too many black children spend long periods of time in makeshift or unlicensed care.

Child development experts agree on the key contributors to quality child care: small group size and adequate adult supervision; continuity of care; a staff that has received adequate training; cooperation between caregivers and parents; and activities geared to a child's development. Affordable child care of any kind is

69

difficult to locate; but, affordable, quality care is virtually unavailable to too many poor black children.

Yet, the federal government has not taken a significant role in helping low-income working parents meet their child care needs. The Title XX Social Services Block Grant, a broad federal program helping states meet a wide range of social service needs, is the major source of direct federal assistance to child care. Funding for this program has been slashed and is now one-half (in real terms) of what it was a decade ago, $2.1 billion down from $4.2 billion. Even before funding cuts, Title XX only served 472,000 of the 3.4 million children younger than six living in poverty. By 1988 there were 5.0 million poor children in that age group and less money to serve them.[29] Head Start reaches only 18 percent of eligible children, and usually is a part-day, part-year program.

The costs of day care continue to rise and consume a large share of family income among low-income families. The typical cost of full-time child care is $3,000 per year for one child, or one-third of the poverty level for a family of three. With two children in full-day care, a family of four with poverty-level wages would need to spend more than half its income on child care.[30]

Research shows that lack of child care is a key barrier to employment for some AFDC mothers. Eighty-five percent of them have children younger than 12, and more than 60 percent have children younger than six. Nearly two-thirds cite child care as the major difficulty in participating in employment programs.[31]

A growing majority of all American families daily confront the need for safe and affordable child care. Basic child care is the key to getting and holding jobs for many low-income families.

An increased federal role in day care is absolutely essential for these families, their children, and for our future as a nation.

HEALTH AND NUTRITION

Poverty has always fallen disproportionately on black children, and it breeds infant and maternal deaths and childhood sickness and disease. Child poverty is strongly correlated with increased health risks. Black children in the United States face far greater health risks than white children. In 1986:

- a black infant born in the United States was more than twice as likely to die as a white infant born that year;

- a black infant was more than twice as likely as a white infant to be born at low birthweight;

- a black infant was far less likely than a white infant to be born to a mother who had received early prenatal care;

- a black infant was more than twice as likely as a white infant to be born to a mother who did not begin prenatal care until the last three months of pregnancy or who had no care at all.[32]

70

One of the most disturbing side effects of growing black poverty is the increase in black infant mortality. The mortality rate among the youngest black infants (under 28 days of life) rose nationally in 1985 for the first time in over 20 years. If America's overall infant mortality rate were equal to that for black infants, it would have placed 28th in the world in keeping babies alive in the first year of life. A black baby born in America had less chance of surviving than a baby born in Cuba or Bulgaria and was about equally likely to survive as one born in Costa Rica.[33]

Maternal mortality among black women is also higher than among white women. A black woman in 1986 was almost four times as likely as a white woman to die from a pregnancy-related cause, although 75 percent of all such deaths are considered preventable.[34]

Although early and continuous prenatal care is one of the most effective ways to combat low birthweight, in 1986 nearly 40 percent of black infants were born to mothers who did not receive early care; more than one in 10 black infants were born to a mother who received either no care at all or care only in the last three months of pregnancy.[35]

Good nutrition is also a factor in preventing low birthweight and in sustaining a baby's health. But, federal nutrition efforts have been curtailed and their beneficial impact has been undermined. As a result of inadequate funding, the federal WIC program (which provides food supplements and other services to low-income infants, children, and pregnant and nursing women) reaches only 3.4 million people, or fewer than half of those eligible for it.[36]

Even black children's immunization status is sliding backwards. In 1985 one in every ten nonwhite children one to four years of age received no doses of polio vaccine — nearly double the percentage in 1980.[37]

The threat from major childhood diseases pales in comparison to the new and graver threat to black babies — AIDS. Black children constitute more than half of all reported cases of AIDS in children younger than age 13. The Centers for Disease Control estimate that within two years at least 10,000 children will be infected by the AIDS virus; the majority of them will be poor children.[38]

The greatest barrier to health improved status for black children is financial. Decent health care, including preventive care, is very expensive in this country. Few can afford health care unless they are insured, and insurance is very expensive unless it is provided through employers or public financing. Millions of families — especially lower-income working families and unemployed families — are covered by neither private nor public health insurance. The recent erosion in black access to health care is largely a result of poverty, the decline in public health programs, and a lack of health insurance.

In 1984, there were 35 million Americans without either public or private health insurance; one-third of them were children. One in every four black children is completely uninsured.[39]

Cutbacks in public health programs like Medicaid have also played a major role in the worsening health status of black babies and children. Medicaid served

200,000 fewer poor children in 1986 than in 1979 (when there were nearly one-third fewer poor children). Medicaid works and saves money in the long run. In the 15 years following Medicaid's enactment, black infant mortality fell 49 percent, nine times the rate in the 15 years before it was enacted. But, between 1976 and 1986, the percentage of poor families covered by Medicaid fell from 65 percent to 46 percent. In 1987, Medicaid served fewer than 50 percent of the eligible poor, and eligibility is very restrictive in some states.[40]

Decent health care, including preventive care, is very expensive in this country. Of all age groups, children are most affected by weaknesses in the public and private health insurance systems. The eroding status of black child and maternal health must be viewed in the broader context of the eroding status of poor black families generally. In many ways, the poor health status of black children is the cumulative end result of poverty, inadequate nutrition, and stressful and unsafe living conditions.

Steps must be taken to improve prenatal care for black mothers and to increase black children's access to health care. Only then will the dreadful black health indicators change.

EDUCATION AND EARLY CHILDHOOD DEVELOPMENT

Education remains one of the black community's most enduring values; it is sustained by the belief that freedom and education go hand in hand, that learning and training are essential to economic equality and independence. Yet, fewer and fewer young blacks are receiving the basic skills and education necessary to survive and compete in today's world. With good paying jobs which require little or no education nearing extinction, a solid education is in many ways more important now than at any time in the history of black Americans. Educating black children and youth has never been more critical, for blacks and for the nation.

Most American parents and educators recognize that nothing is more important to a child's development as a student than quality early education. Unfortunately, low-income children generally and many black children in particular are not able to attend preschool without financial help. While two-thirds of four-year-olds and half of three-year-olds in families with annual incomes of $35,000 or more attend preschool programs, less than half of preschoolers in families with incomes under $20,000 are in such programs. For children in families with incomes near the poverty level, access to preschool is even more limited. Less than 38 percent of four-year-olds and 17 percent of three-year-olds in families with annual incomes under $10,000 were enrolled in such programs in 1986.[41]

The Head Start program is the federal government's attempt to provide early childhood services to the neediest three- to five-year-old children. Ninety percent of Head Start children are from families which live on incomes less than the poverty level ($9,690 for a family of three in 1988).[42]

Despite Head Start's proven effectiveness, the program has never been funded at a level which would allow it to meet the needs of all eligible children. Head Start now reaches only 18 percent of the 2.5 million children who need its services, or about 451,000 disadvantaged youngsters. Hundreds of thousands of children are on Head Start waiting lists.[43] This successful program should be offered to many more eligible children and eventually to every eligible child.

Over 86 percent of American children from all income groups are educated in the public school system;[44] yet, the public schools are failing to educate many, especially those from economically disadvantaged backgrounds.

In 1987, the Committee for Economic Development issued a report, *Children in Need*, which discussed how crucial good schools are to low-income children and to the country as a whole:

"The nation's public schools have traditionally provided a common pathway out of poverty and a roadway to the American Dream. But, today, in too many communities, the schools are hard pressed to serve the needs of disadvantaged children. . . . An early and sustained intervention in the lives of disadvantaged children, both in school and out, is our only hope for breaking the cycle of disaffection and despair."[45]

Indeed, too many disadvantaged students do fail to acquire needed basic academic skills in elementary school, and the consequences are harsh. A recent analysis revealed that more than half of the 15- to 18-year-olds surveyed with family incomes below poverty have basic skills in the lowest of five skills groups. Poor teens are four times as likely to have poor basic skills as are teens with family incomes above poverty. Among teens living in poverty, more than six out of 10 black teens fall in the lowest quintile skills group.[46]

Poor basic skills hurt young people and society in the long run. Youths who by age 18 have the weakest reading and math skills, when compared to those with above-average basic skills, are eight times more likely to have children out of wedlock; nine times more likely to drop out of school before graduation; five times more likely to be both out of work and out of school; and four times more likely to be forced to turn to public assistance for basic income support.[47]

The combination of poverty and weak basic skills accounts for virtually all of the racial disparities in teen childbearing rates. Young women with poor basic skills, whether black, white, or Hispanic, are more than three times as likely to be parents as those with average or better basic skills. Eighteen- and 19-year-old men with poor basic skills are three times as likely to be fathers as are those with average basic skills.[48]

If we want to help prevent our children from having children, it is crucial for us to understand who is having babies and why; futures already foreclosed contain no incentive to delay too-early pregnancy and parenthood. The links between poor basic skills and early parenthood are unmistakable; increasing and improving programs which further basic skills development is crucial for black students.

The federal Chapter 1 compensatory education program supports remedial education programs serving poor children, but this cost-effective program reaches only about half of all low-income students in need of its assistance. Despite its success and cost effectiveness, in real terms, between 1979 and 1985 federal funding for Chapter 1 dropped roughly 29 percent. Chapter 1 served only 54 students for every 100 poor school-age children in 1985, down from 75 in 1980.[49]

For students who drop out of school, the costs are high and are shared by all. Between October 1985 and October 1986, 682,000 students aged 14 or older dropped out of school. Dropping out disproportionately afflicts the poor, including higher proportions of students from racial and ethnic minority groups. Among blacks, the dropout rate is 17.4 percent. However, when poverty rates are controlled for, black and white dropout rates are essentially identical: regardless of race, youths from poor families are three to four times more likely to drop out than those from more affluent households.[50]

The repercussions from dropping out are very serious. Dropouts are much less likely to be employed: in 1987, only 76 percent of men and 45 percent of women age 25 to 64 who did not have a high school diploma were working, while 90 percent of men and 67 percent of women with a high school diploma were employed.[51] More than half of all young black high school dropouts who head families with children reported no earnings whatsoever in 1986.[52]

Dropping out also takes a toll on the next generation. In 1982-83, in families where both parents were high school graduates, fewer than seven percent of the children were poor. If only one parent was a high school graduate, slightly more than 20 percent of the children were poor in those families. When neither of the parents was a high school graduate, more than 39 percent of the children were poor.[53]

A bachelor's degree, although not a guarantee of employment or success, is almost a precondition for survival in today's job market. This is especially true for young blacks. In 1987, the average unemployment rate among black high school graduates under 25 was 22.0 percent — more than one in every five. Among black college graduates under 25, it was 11.4 percent — more than one in every nine. Among young white college graduates, it was 5.1 percent or one in twenty.[54] For black youth, having a college degree still does not raise their employment rates to parity with whites, but it is still an important factor in reducing the gap.

The difference college makes on earnings is especially dramatic among young black women. Between 1973 and 1984, those with no college (both dropouts and high school graduates) saw their earnings plummet by nearly 40 percent, whereas those with a college degree saw their earnings climb by more than 60 percent.[55]

College attendance rates among black students have declined significantly in recent years. Those black students who graduate from high school are now less likely than whites to attend college. Young black and white high school graduates were equally likely to attend college in 1977 (for whites, 51 percent, for blacks, 50 percent). By 1986, whites were more than 53 percent more likely to attend college than blacks (for whites, 56 percent attended, for blacks, 37 percent).[56]

Poverty is the key to low college attendance among blacks. Less than one poor black high school graduate in five attends college. Among whites and blacks living above poverty, more than two high school graduates in five go on to college.[57]

Declining financial aid availability is obviously a significant factor in reduced black college attendance rates. In 1985, more than one-fifth of black college students came from families with annual incomes of less than $10,000, compared to less than six percent of their white peers.[58]

But those students in need of financial aid, as are most black students, are increasingly hard pressed to find it. Between 1980 and 1988, there was a 4.1 percent drop in student aid from all federally supported programs. This figure masks the much larger loss between 1980 and 1983 — almost 18 percent. Federal student aid has been increasing since 1983, but it is still less than it was in 1980. This loss has increased the importance of supplemental grants, college work-study, direct loans, and state student incentive grants in helping needy students meet the cost of college. Appropriations for some of these programs have declined since 1980; however, funding for the work-study program has declined by 25 percent in real dollars.[59]

These reductions have also led to an increased reliance on loans. This change has a disproportionate impact upon students from low-income families. For women and minorities, who traditionally earn less than their white male counterparts once they enter the full-time work force, the burden of repayment will be heavier and may serve as a deterrent to college.

The education of low-income and black youth is in serious trouble. As the Committee for Economic Development report *Children in Need* aptly observes:

"The price of corrective action may be high, but the cost of inaction is far higher." According to Fred M. Hechinger, education columnist for *The New York Times*, 'We have raised too many children without allowing them expectations of success, without giving them hopes of useful lives ahead. To continue to do so, in an era that has no economic or social use for the uneducated, is to court disaster.' "[60]

POLICY RECOMMENDATIONS

Despite repeated and constant attack over the last eight years, programs which bolster black and poor children's most basic needs have been able to survive. Although some have been damaged, none has prospered, and little new has been added. It is absolutely essential that the federal government make substantial new and additional investments in black children and families if we are to break the cycle of poverty, poor education, ill health, and unemployment which doom so many today.

Here is what must be done:

- Child Care: Enact and fund the Act for Better Child Care Services (ABC) bill currently pending in Congress. This legislation would make child care more affordable for low- and moderate-income families; increase the number of child care facilities; and improve the quality of day care services and help coordinate child care resources.

- Health: Full funding for the WIC program to ensure that it reaches all rather than just half of women and children needing nutrition supplements. Extend Medicaid coverage to all uninsured pregnant women and children with incomes less than twice the poverty line. Full funding for childhood immunization program in order to ensure that all American children are fully immunized.

- Education and Early Childhood Development: Increase Head Start funding by $400 million annually for each of the next five years, allowing the program to extend to at least half of the poor three- to five-year-olds by 1992. Add $500 million in each of the next five years to the Chapter 1 program, fully funding the program and enabling it to reach all eligible educationally disadvantaged children by 1992.

- Income: Raise the minimum wage to $4.65 by 1990. Increase other family income supplements. Expand the Earned Income Tax Credit (EITC) to give more help to low-income working black families. Build upon the successes of programs like the Jobs Corps and add $200 million which would allow its services to reach an additional 25,000 youths.

The needs of poor children, black and white, will continue to be neglected without the concerted efforts of thoughtful and caring adults. The price we pay for that neglect is already too high. These recommendations must be woven into our national priorities if we are to reverse the mounting tide against black child survival and success.

To Make Wrong Right: The Necessary and Proper Aspirations Of Fair Housing

John O. Calmore, J.D.

For Blacks, the task at hand is to devise ways to wage ideological and political struggle while minimizing the costs of engaging in an inherently legitimating discourse. A clearer understanding of the space we occupy in the American political consciousness is a necessary prerequisite to the development of pragmatic strategies for political and economical survival. In this regard, the most serious challenge for Blacks is to minimize the political and cultural cost of engaging in an inevitably co-optive process in order to secure material benefits. Because our present predicament gives us few options, we must create conditions for the maintenance of a distinct political thought that is informed by the actual conditions of Black people. Unlike the civil rights vision, this new approach should not be defined and thereby limited by the possibilities of dominant political discourse, but should maintain a distinctly progressive outlook that focuses on the needs of the African American community.[1]

INTRODUCTION

Becoming law one week after the death of Martin Luther King, Jr., Title VIII of the Civil Rights Act of 1968 declares that it is national policy ". . . to provide, within constitutional limits, for fair housing throughout the United States."[2] The fair housing commitment of antidiscrimination and desegregation complemented the Civil Rights Act of 1866, 42 U.S.C. § 1982, which provides that blacks, as citizens of the United States, possess the same right "as is enjoyed by white citizens . . . to inherit, purchase, lease, sell, hold, and convey real and personal property."[3] Additionally, Title VIII refined the commitment Congress made in the Housing Act of 1949 that 'every American family' be provided 'a decent home and a suitable living environment . . . as soon as feasible.'"[4] These three fair housing commitments, singularly and combined, however, have come to represent more hope than help as Black America's cumulative, circular, and synergistic harms associated with *housing deprivation, racial discrimination,* and *segregative disadvantage* persist in placing us uniquely outside the American Dream.[5]

Redress in housing is Black America's Sisyphean rock. As a group blacks stand as a contrast conception to equal housing opportunity and, with each passing day, the problems and harms inherent in that image appear not only persistent, but also intractable.[6] Appropriately, housing has been described as "the last major frontier in civil rights."[7] Housing is "the area in which progress is slowest and the possibility of genuine change is most remote."[8] The 1980s will be recorded as the decade of radical fair housing retreat.[9] The 1990s will likely present the last chance for making "fair housing" both.[10]

As fair housing themes evolve, we see that today's world has changed in significant ways from the way the world was in 1968 when Title VIII was passed. New directions are now necessary if progress in fulfilling the promise of 1968 is to be made. We must evaluate the consequences of change in the economic, demographic, social, political, and attitudinal contexts of today's America. As Robert Lake, for instance, asks:

"To what extent has the progress foreseen by the act's sponsors in an expanding economy and liberal sociopolitical climate been subverted, in both pace and direction, in a recessionary economy and conservative political atmosphere?"[11]

As a final introductory caveat, let me say that, although this writing addresses fair housing in the traditional sense of antidiscrimination, because of Black America's disproportionately high poverty rate, in a normative as well as practical sense, I do not believe that we can reasonably and honestly expect to secure and advance viable housing rights and opportunities as a group without paying significant attention to the need to improve the conditions of housing deprivation plaguing the African-American poor.[12] Thus, for me, fair housing advocacy necessarily incorporates that of low-income housing as well: "Can 'fair' housing come about if the economic disparity between white and black citizens is not first lessened?"[13]

The following article will discuss the national housing crisis, with particular regard to blacks; the phenomena of discrimination and segregation that are unique to Black America; aspects of integration progress and resistance; the enforcement of fair housing, considering the important 1988 statutory amendments; and finally, ways to move from existing social conditions to a closer approximation of the way things ought to be, arguing for "spatial equality of results" generally and discussing particularly the notion and potential of black neighborhoods becoming black cities.[14]

NATIONAL HOUSING CRISIS

During the past decade, it has grown increasingly difficult to obtain and retain housing that is affordable, well maintained, secure, and located in a supportive neighborhood of one's choice. Indeed, for many poor, nonwhite, and female-headed households, the problems of housing deprivation have reached extreme levels.[15]

In 1982, President Reagan's Commission on Housing assured the nation that "Americans today are the best housed people in history."[16] Recently, however, a report from the Joint Center for Housing Studies of Harvard University declared:

"Despite the noticeable reductions in homeowner costs in recent years, homeownership rates among young households continue to fall. Despite high levels of new construction and equally high levels of housing rehabilitation expenditures, the supply of low-cost rental housing continues to shrink. Only one in four renter households with incomes at or below the poverty level lives in public or other subsidized housing. Some 5.4 million poverty-level renter households are left to compete for the dwindling supply of low-cost rental housing available in the private market. The result is further tightening at the low end of the rental housing market, and a growing rental payments burden for low- and moderate-income households."[17]

As William Apgar, director of the Joint Center, recently warned a Senate panel, "America is increasingly becoming a nation of housing 'haves' and housing 'have nots.'"[18]

Presidential commissions notwithstanding, the United States approaches the 1990s mired in a deep, long-term crisis that will likely cause a qualitatively different housing future for Americans, black and white. The crisis is reflected in terms of *unaffordability, unavailability, overcrowding, poor quality, forced displacement,* and *inequality.*[19] Regarding inequality, suffice it to say that non-whites suffer disproportionately from all of the mentioned crisis manifestations. When we talk about "fair housing," we must recognize that "housing" denotes a variety of disparate things that must be consumed in a bundle, packaged together.[20] As Achtenberg and Marcuse point out: "Housing, after all, is much more than shelter: it provides social status, access to jobs, education and other services, a framework for the conduct of household work, and a way of structuring economic, social and political relationships."[21] Fair housing, thus, must seek to reduce inequality and inequity in housing as it relates to these broad features.

The national consciousness of housing conditions allows the crises to go unreorganized or underestimated because it is still influenced by the extraordinary progress of the housing sector in the decades following World War II.[22] Between 1940 and 1970, the nation's population grew by half, and the number of occupied units increased by 80 percent; crowding decreased from 20 percent to 8.2 percent of all households; substandard housing dipped from 49 percent of all occupied units in 1940 to seven percent in 1970;[23] and homeownership, particularly of single-family, suburban homes, increased dramatically from 44 percent in 1940 to 68 percent in 1980.[24]

These numbers tend to obscure the substantial population of urban and rural poor who continue living in slum conditions and the deterioration extant in many central-city communities. Also, older Northeastern and Midwestern areas are experiencing population loss, deteriorating housing stock, and continued abandonment. Over the last two decades, there has been an overall reversal of performance in the housing sector, as the nation suffered a variety of harsh economic setbacks.[25] First, the housing conditions of those suffering housing deprivation during the 1950s, 1960s, and 1970s found their problems worsening. Second, both new problems and new victims have come into public view.[26] From the mid-1960s, the household income available for housing expenses has shrunk as a result of declines in the nation's economic growth which in turn has produced the double whammy of unemployment and inflation, and as a result of labor markets shifting from manufacturing toward "managerial-professional-technical and service jobs."[27] Simultaneously, the cost of producing, acquiring, and maintaining housing has risen, primarily as a function of high land and financing costs.[28]

Affordability

Unaffordability is the principal measure of the current crisis. An increasingly large proportion of disposable family income is now consumed by housing costs.[29] Even in HUD low-income housing programs, federal legislation has increased the rent-to-income ratio from the traditional 25 percent to 30 percent.[30] For renters generally the median gross rent-to-income ratio increased from 22 to 29 percent from 1973 to 1983. Over 10 million renter households paid at the rate of 35 percent of income in 1983; 6.3 million paid 50 percent or more; and 4.7 million paid 60 percent or more. Even 3.1 million *homeowner* households paid 50 percent or more in 1983.[31]

The housing cost burden inflicts extreme hardship — other common necessities are not purchased so there is a shortage of food or an inadequate diet is consumed; the children's clothing is almost always outworn or outgrown; people crowd into smaller units than needed; transportation costs keep people shut in as if they were sick; utility bills cannot be met, so the telephone or heat or lights are shut off; eventually, in order to "meet" these other needs, rent is not paid and people are evicted and the scenario repeats itself. At the extreme, the scenario increasingly leads to homelessness.[32]

The aspirations for homeownership among newly formed households or first-time buyers are frustrated by the lack of a down payment and the high costs of purchase and financing.[33] The traditional ways of coming up with a down payment are saving, borrowing from a relative, or reducing the down payment in exchange for higher monthly payments. Generally, lenders require 10 to 20 percent of the purchase price as a down payment.[34] How does one do this when house prices are increasing faster than incomes and Americans typically save only four to 10 percent of their income? According to David Schwartz, chairman of the National Housing Institute: "The down payment dilemma is the worst it's been since the Great Depression. We are living in a situation today where the average 30-year-old man or woman who wants to buy a house is being asked to put up 50 percent of their annual income for a down payment."[35] Mortgage interest rates, while tax deductible, are now fixed in the range of 11 to 14 percent, up from 8.75 percent in 1975 and 6.83 percent just 20 years ago in 1968.[36] It is noted that "[w]hen combined with rapidly escalating house prices, monthly mortgage payments rise geometrically, far faster than incomes."[37] Even if one owns a house and has no, or low, mortgage costs, the price of utilities and property taxes are substantial burdens on many.[38]

The ramifications of the affordability problem hit blacks hard, whether they be low-income or midddle-income. Rental problems are particularly important for our people. In 1980, while white home ownership had climbed to 68 percent, black home ownership was only 44 percent.[39] Additionally, in 1986, the black poverty rate was 31.1 percent.[40] Thus, preserving the supply of low-income rental housing and increasing that supply are of paramount importance not only to the nation at large, but also and particularly to the nation's black citizens.

While definitions of "middle-class" vary,[41] it is conservatively estimated that at least 80 percent of black middle-class families as of 1984 were first-generation middle-class.[42] Consequently, the black middle class has not had time to accumulate the wealth of similarly situated whites.[43] One cause is the absence of prior homeownership and its appurtenant income and investment opportunities.[44] Moreover, as the gap between black and white homeowners would indicate, as first generation middle-class members, many blacks have reached the status traditionally enabling one to buy a home precisely at one of the worst periods in history to do so: In 1975, the average-priced, new single-family house cost $44,600, and the conventional mortgage interest rate averaged 8.75 percent. On an 80 percent mortgage and housing costs at 25 percent of income, in 1975, a family would have needed a down payment of $8,920. This would constitute 65 percent of median family income that year. On a 30-year fixed payment mortgage, there would have been a monthly mortgage payment of $280.69, which in turn required a minimum annual income of $13,473. In 1981, the average-price, new single-family house had risen to a cost of $94,100, and the mortgage interest rate had risen to an average of 14.1 percent. On an 80 percent mortgage and housing costs at 25 percent of income, in 1981, a family would have had an $897.93 monthly mortgage payment, which in turn required a $43,101 minimum annual income. The 1975 required minimum annual income of $13,473 was two percent below the median family income for that year, while the $43,101 required in 1981 was nearly double the nation's median family income that year.[45]

Availability

The lack of affordable, "decent, safe, and sanitary housing" remains a problem, especially for the poor, for large families needing more than three bedrooms, for families with children, for female-headed households, and for general categories of discrimination victims whose locational choices are restricted. According to the National Low-Income Housing Coalition, using 1980 census data, it is estimated that for very low-income renter households, i.e., those whose income is 50 percent of median or lower, there is a shortfall of 1.2 million units between the number of these households and the number of rental units needed to rent at 30 percent of their incomes.[46] The unavailability problem is caused by various factors: (1) urban disinvestment and planned shrinkage; (2) condominium and co-op conversions of rental units; (3) inflated rental prices; (4) landlord abandonment; (5) arson; (6) urban revitalization; and (7) the federal government's withdrawal from subsidized new construction.[47]

An important consideration here is the concept of "filtering."[48] This "trickle-down" process is the primary means for providing housing to low- and moderate-income households in the United States. According to Anthony Downs, this process shapes the entire structure of urban development in our country; hence, understanding it is a key prerequisite to understanding how various housing subsidies would affect urban development."[49] A basic part of the trickle-down process is the federal government's provision of an "indirect subsidy" or "tax expenditure" on behalf of homeowners, primarily in the form of a deduction for payment of mortgage interest and property tax.[50]

These tax expenditures serve to stimulate the demand for new and better housing. Historically, that housing has been away from the central-city core.[51] As families who can afford to move outward to new homes do so, they initiate the filtering process. Initially, better structured dwellings become available as they trickle-down to poorer households. Thus, in lieu of building new and better housing in neighborhoods where working class and poor households live, such housing is built away from them, and one moves up *and away*, leaving it for a poorer household. Ultimately, the worst sectors of the inner-city housing stock are abandoned and demolished.[52] The counter strategy of rehabilitation exits but is little employed.[53]

As relatively poor homeowners occupy the filtered housing, the increasing age of the dwelling brings increasing maintenance obligations that are deferred or, more often, not met. For absentee landlords, as original higher income tenants are lost, rental income is decreased. Management expenses increase, compounded by late and nonpayment of rent and increased maintenance. This leads to the housing investment's profit being reduced and landlords often hastening the process of deterioration through reduced maintenance expenditures as they decide "to maximize short-term profitability rather than long-term returns on investment."[54] This is followed by tax delinquencies, both in renter and owner-occupied dwellings.

The effects of filtering on the condition of African Americans are intensely and disproportionately felt because our segregation within metropolitan areas is manifested by the pattern of black concentration in central city areas. We seldom occupy and own new houses or live in new multiple dwellings, relying instead on trickle-down housing opportunities. Blacks do tend to benefit from new construction, however, if we are able to move into a home vacated by a white household.[55]

Downs points out that the filtering process is "remarkably efficient . . . neatly matching up the quality and cost of housing with the income levels of households."[56] He then adds, however: "But for many of the urban poor, the 'trickle-down' process is a disaster. It compels the poorest and often least [able] households to live concentrated together in the worst quality housing in society. This concentration has a 'critical mass' effect which multiplies the negative impacts of poverty."[57] Montgomery and Mandelker further point out that there is a tendency to confuse filtering as a model describing what seems to be a market dynamic with ideas about what ought to be: "This conclusion, of course, is nonsense. In a specific situation, given the constraints of time and place, it may be the best thing we can do. But that is a long way from saying it is what we should do.

Yet, this error is rampant. Public policy seems almost to be founded on it. To the degree that is so, our thinking is the poorer for it and so are the housing satisfactions of many real people."[58]

President Reagan's Commission on Housing relied on filtering to direct its low-income rent subsidy program.[59] During the 1980s authorized funds for federal housing programs have plummeted almost 80 percent — more than any other domestic social program — from the $30 billion authorized for fiscal year 1981 to the $7.17 and $7.3 billion authorized respectively for fiscal years 1988 and 1989.[60] Reduced dollars, of course, translate into reduced units: from fiscal 1981 to fiscal 1988, appropriated units fell from 280,000 to 88,000.[61] Along with the Reagan administration's retrenchment in funding, there has been a shift in emphasis to privatization and subsidies for existing housing while providing virtually no subsidies for increasing the supply of low-income housing through new construction and substantial rehabilitation.[62] In October 1981, President Reagan's Commission on Housing concluded that affordability rather than an inadequate supply of housing was the major problem facing poor families. It thus recommended "that the primarily federal project for helping low-income families achieve decent housing be a consumer-oriented housing assistance grant."[63] This notion represented the primary policy of the Reagan housing program, such as it was. HUD's present fiscal 1989 budget request calls for 108,000 new assisted housing units, primarily vouchers.[64]

HUD's budget request continues the trend set in the early 1980s.[65] In 1983, Congress repealed the authority for additional units of Section 8 new construction and substantial rehabilitation. What little new construction funding that has been allocated has largely been restricted to Section 202 housing for the elderly and handicapped,[66] although the predominant identified need is for family housing, a particularly acute need for blacks and other people of color.[67] The Reagan administration was not content to abandon new construction and substantial rehabilitation; it also acted counter to preserving the existing inventory of federally subsidized housing.[68]

Since 1981 and the coming of Ronald Reagan, the federal administration has virtually declared war not on poverty, but on poor people, and federal housing programs have been the principal target. On February 5, 1988, the President signed the Housing and Community Development Act of 1987.[69] This represents the first free-standing federal housing bill in seven years.[70] While it is a welcome end to the drought, it is too little, too late for many.

Section 121 of the 1987 Act provides new restrictions regulating the Public Housing Authority (PHA) application to HUD for the approval of public housing demolition and sale. Under this provision, demolition now cannot take place unless the project is obsolete and unusable for housing and no feasible modifications could restore it to useful life. PHAs wishing to sell or demolish any units must develop a plan to provide additional decent, safe, sanitary, and affordable units for each unit to be sold or demolished.[71]

Subsidized Section 236 Housing is a Great Society program, established in 1968.[72] It was created to further the government-private sector partnership as it intended to subsidize new constructions of privately owned housing for lower income families. Under the program, either non-profit or limited dividend sponsors built or substantially rehabilitated apartments which were financed with FHA-insured mortgages. In 1973, President Nixon's impoundment prevented the authorization of new Section 236 units.[73] Hence, while Section 236 cannot be used to add to the low-income housing supply, it is important to prevent the loss of units that occurs primarily through mortgage defaults and HUD disposition of these foreclosed properties without ensuring their continued low-income character.[74] Presently, the threat of mortgage prepayments further jeopardizes the Section 236 housing stock. The federally insured mortgages run 40 years, but there is a prepayment option available to the sponsors after 20 years. If the owners exercise that option, then they are relieved of the obligation to maintain the housing as low-income. Both the disposition and prepayment issues are addressed by the new legislation.[75]

As many subsidized projects approach their 20th year, the prepayment threat grows significantly.[76] The problem occurs as many tax incentives supporting low-income housing owners have been eliminated under recent tax reforms. According to Jane Lehman, low-income housing investors are primarily interested in tax benefits rather than economic returns, and now they can no longer use their project losses to offset other income under the new passive loss rules.[77] Former HUD Secretary Carla Hills has warned that in markets where housing is booming, if the project is not lucrative, "the owners are only too happy to have the use restrictions expire."[78] In economically deprived neighborhoods in depressed areas of the country, where the market is not hospitable, a different problem may arise. When this is joined with the loss of tax benefits, Hill has predicted that these investors may default on their loans and discontinue upkeep, thus removing even more habitable units.[79]

Prepayment is now governed by Sections 201 through 235 of the new Act. A host of significant restrictions are now imposed. The owners must submit a prepayment plan of action for HUD's approval. Section 224 provides for HUD to supply a variety of incentives in exchange for the extension of low-income use restrictions. HUD is limited to approving a prepayment plan only if (1) it will not (a) materially increase the economic hardship for current tenants or (b) involuntarily displace current tenants where comparable affordable housing is not readily available; and (2) the supply of comparable vacant housing is adequate to ensure that prepayment will not materially affect (a) the availability of affordable, decent housing in the area, (b) the ability of low- and very low-income families (those respectively not exceeding 80 and 50 percent of the area median income) to find affordable, decent housing near employment, or (c) the housing opportunities of minorities in the community. As indicated by the National Housing Law Project, "Under this standard, it is hard to imagine many prepayments being approved by HUD, so close scrutiny of HUD's approval process will be essential."[80]

The pressing Section 8 issue also currently revolves around the loss of units. The project-based programs, such as New Construction and Substantial Rehabilitation, are at risk because their 15-year subsidy, or housing assistance payments, contracts made under the programs in 1976 will run out in 1991. Even sooner, Section 8 owners who entered the programs prior to 1981 are permitted to opt out of the program every five years.[81] Under Section 262 of the 1987 Act, required opt-out notices are extended to one year rather than the previous 90 days. The notices must be sent to HUD and the affected tenants, and HUD is to evaluate whether the terminations are lawful and whether there are additional actions HUD could take to avoid the termination.

The new provisions, however, are modest at best. According to the report to Congress by the National Housing Preservation Task Force, released February 18, 1988, "The greater risk of loss is not from the area about which most of the concern has been expressed."[82] The report explains that while prepayment could result in the loss of about 316,000 units by 1995, over 700,000 units could be lost by then as a result of expiring Section 8 housing assistance payments contracts. Additionally, the report indicates that more than 960,000 units house tenants using Section 8 certificates or vouchers, and contracts on at least 636,000 of these units will have run their course by 1995.[83]

Since August of 1985, the voucher, or housing allowances, program has operated as a $1 billion demonstation. Section 143 of the new Act reinforces the importance of the voucher program by removing its demonstration status. At a news conference, February 8, 1988, HUD Secretary Samuel R. Pierce, Jr., reiterated that the program is "the cornerstone of the Reagan administration's housing policy."[84] As of February 5, 1988, 100,000 voucher units were under lease using fiscal 1987 appropriations. This improves on the 36,000 units under lease as of May 22, 1987. The voucher program's biggest obstacle has not been acceptance by PHAs or private landlords, but, rather, in voucher holders being able to find a unit within the 60-day deadline in tight real estate markets.[85]

Based on earlier experiments with housing allowances, when strict housing quality standards were introduced as a program requirement (as in the present program), there was a disproportionate reduction in participation of nonwhites, large households, and poorer shelter seekers.[86] The programs, moreover, must proceed not only in the face of tight rental markets, but also in the face of private sector housing discrimination against people of color, the handicapped, single-parent families, families with children, gay people, and the poorest of the poor. At a minimum the voucher program should be an entitlement rather than the token it is. It cannot be the only, or primary, federal housing program.[87]

Quality

By virtually every indicator, the problem of substandard housing that existed 20 years ago has been substantially eliminated. Traditionally, substandard housing has been characterized as (1) dilapidated or in substantial violation of housing codes with respect to its physical condition; (2) lacking in facilities such as plumbing, heat, etc., or (3) overcrowded, exceeding two occupants per bedroom. If these characteristics seriously interfere with health and safety or "the reasonable conduct of family life," then the housing is substandard.[88] While housing occupied by blacks has improved along with the general trend because we generally occupy existing housing stock rather than new contruction, we are more likely to occupy lower-quality housing. There remain significant racial differences in housing quality with blacks continuing to face higher odds than whites, living in aged housing that is structurally deficient and overcrowded, even though both blacks and whites may have had approximately similar improvement in their housing quality between 1960 and 1978.[89]

For Black America, the serious issues of poor quality housing are now primarily a concern with neighborhood conditions. Studies indicate that when one's household status exceeds one's neighborhood status, the neighborhood will get a low evaluation, and thus whites, homeowners, and those with higher educations tend to rate their neighborhoods more poorly than blacks, renters, and the less-well educated living in the same neighborhoods. But, subjective responses should not lead us to deemphasize the problems and actual conditions that need to be improved. As Craig St. John explains:

> "[E]quity in final outcome, satisfaction, does not necessarily mean there is equity in conditions. The discrepancy between evaluations and actual conditions points out the fallacy of using subjective evaluations, at least of neighborhood quality, as social indicators to inform this type of policy. An undesirable situation might exist if there were, hypothetically, no significant group difference in satisfaction with the residential environment but because of variations in standards of evaluating this environment some groups were, in fact, far less well-off than others."[90]

Two problems of poor quality deserve special mention: public housing maintenance programs and efforts to improve poor housing through urban revitalization. Conventional public housing is the paradigm federal housing program. Enacted pursuant to the United States Housing Act of 1937, public housing, for better or worse, is Black America's most significant federal low-income housing. A majority of the 3.4 million tenants in public housing is nonwhite, and we can ill-afford to allow its history or image to scare us into ignoring it or turning our backs on it; it must be preserved and expanded.

As public housing surpasses its 50th year, many projects across the nation suffer from mismanagement, deferred maintenance, and advanced decay. A recent *Wall Street Journal* reports that in 1984, the New Orleans PHA, which shelters one-tenth of the city population, was sued an average of three times a day over poor living conditions.[91] *The Wall Street Journal* article also indicates that according to HUD, about 70,000 units of public housing are boarded up, and 1,000 units are demolished across the nation every year because costs for repair exceed the units' worth. While the 1987 Housing Act authorizes $1.7 billion for comprehensive improvement assistance grants, it is not enough. For example, it is estimated that in San Francisco alone there is a need for $500 million to upgrade the city's 42 public housing projects.[92]

On August 22, 1974, President Ford signed the Housing and Community Development Act of 1974.[93] Among the Act's purposes, it intended to further the achievement of the nation's housing goal of a decent home and suitable living environment for every American family. Also, it sought to foster the undertaking of housing and community development activities "in a coordinated and mutually supportive manner by federal agencies and programs, as well as by communities."[94]

Historically, even during better times when a variety of housing programs were available, the beneficial relation between community development and housing has been tenuous at best.[95] From slum clearance to urban renewal to community development and urban revitalization, a major hindrance in the attempts to coordinate housing and overall neighborhood improvement has persisted: poor people have been ignored or victimized more often than helped.[96] And among the victims, blacks have been disproportionately represented. Most of us remember urban renewal being aptly characterized as "Negro removal."[97] Today is little different than yesterday:

> "The responsible officials tend to be much more concerned about the well-being of the buildings and other physical elements of the neighborhood than the well-being of the residents. Too often, federal programs improve the neighborhoods and provide new or rehabilitated housing, but not for the benefit of poor people or the long-term neighborhood residents. Instead, the poor are displaced into other, deteriorated urban areas with grossly overpriced substandard housing. All the while, HUD officials stand by, doing nothing. What is worse, the bureaucrats often vigorously argue that they cannot be concerned about the plight of the displaced poor because that concern might undermine the revitalization momentum of private investors."[98]

Forced Displacement

Richard Le Gates and Chester Hartman's 1981 study indicates that 2.5 million Americans are victims of forced displacement.[99] As homelessness grows, this number will climb.[100] Indeed, some of the homeless advocates estimate that there are three million or more of this group alone.[101] In 1984, HUD estimated the number to be 250,000[102] and recently, an Urban Institute Study has estimated the U.S. homeless population to be 600,000.[103] Based on the Urban Institute sample, the majority of the homeless are male, nonwhite, and between 31-50 years old.[104]

Forced displacement is caused by a variety of factors and impacts disproportionately on the poor, nonwhites, and elderly. Among the causes: "gentrification, under-maintenance, formal eviction, arson, rent increases, mortgage foreclosures, property-tax delinquency, speculation in land and buildings, conversion of low-rent apartments to luxury units or condominiums or nonresidential uses, demolition, planned shrinkage, or historic preservation."[105]

The primary improvement brought about by the new legislation is its establishment of "[t]he most far-reaching displacement provisions ever enacted."[106] Section 509 of the 1987 Act requires for all CDBG- and UDAG- assisted development projects, a residential, anti-displacement, and relocation plan that should improve chances that the revitalized cities will also benefit poor residents as well as the gentrifiers and the industrial/commercial developers.[107]

HOUSING DISCRIMINATION'S DIVERSE REALITIES

Discrimination is a slippery term, which can be interpreted according to anyone's subjective motives. But, it has become a technical term of art within the international community. Article 1(1) of the International Convention on the Elimination of All Forms of Racial Discrimination defines racial discrimination as:

"any distinction, exclusion, restriction or preference based on race, coulour, descent or national origin which has the purpose or effect of nullifying or impairing the recognition, enjoyment or exercise, on an equal footing, of human rights and fundamental freedoms in the political, economic, social, cultural or any other field of public life."

Housing discrimination, however, can be difficult to analyze because housing is a broad, mixed bundle of goods and services. Provided in a variety of situations and transactions.[108] Both the overall context in which housing transactions take place and the events themselves can be subject in turn to a variety of discriminatory acts and effects.[109] Traditional housing discrimination has been an isolated act of treating a black unfavorably because of his race, generally with the effect that the black cannot complete the transaction he wants or he must do so on terms less favorable than they would be if he were not black.[110] Here, then, the focus is on "race-dependent" decisions that intentionally disadvantage blacks through disparate treatment.[111] On other occasions discrimination will reflect a "color-blind" decision or practice that has a disproportionate adverse impact on the members of a racial minority group.[112] This latter form of discrimination is the more controversial.[113]

Traditional forms of discrimination are becoming harder to detect, as these aspects of discrimination have now become quite subtle, covert, and sophisticated.[114] Indeed, victims often do not even know they were discriminated against.[115] As example, an on-site manager allows blacks to go through the same application process required of white applicants. When submitted to the main office for review and evaluation, however, the black applications are marked on the backs with pencil while the white applications are marked with pen. With the applications thus coded for the landlord, only those applications marked in pen are fairly considered for tenancy.[116]

Another case of "the new technology" in discrimination involves the use of the telephone answering machine. When an applicant is detected as being a black or other "undesirable," the housing provider simply does not return the call. If the address or telephone exchange left on the machine by a black homeseeker is identified as being in a nonwhite area of the community, the inquiry regarding housing availability is ignored.[117]

As these traditional acts of differential treatment aggregate and pervade society, along with other limitations on the housing stock, unbalanced by additional sources of supply, the result is white market restriction and the establishment and support of the dual housing market.[118] Discrimination, institutionalized in this way, creates the systemic condition of discrimination.[119] It places the black consumer in a captive market devoid of significant free choice.[120]

Thus, the potential is created for a third dimension of discrimination to result. Given the systemic condition of discrimination, other individuals act to take advantage of the racially dual market: "Upon the specially disadvantaged position of blacks trapped by the systemic condition of discrimination, social and economic mechanisms operate, though often in a manner not traditionally discriminatory, to misallocate resources — blacks end up with less in the way of goods and services per dollar spent than do their white counterparts."[121] As we move away from the isolated act of disparate treatment, courts recognize that "race discrimination is by definition a class discrimination . . . [A]lthough the actual effects of a discriminatory policy may . . . vary throughout the class, the existence of the discriminatory policy threatens the entire class."[122]

As I have indicated, discrimination comes into housing decisions in ways that are more subtle than a clear desire to harm the victims. Three of the ways emphasized in legal scholarship are: "racially selective sympathy and indifference;" generalizations and stereotypes; and perpetuation of past discrimination. In each case, victims are subjected to differential treatment because of their race, or other impermissible factors, without any necessary intent on the part of the perpetrator to discriminate.[123]

The notion of racially selective sympathy and indifference refers to "the unconscious failure to extend to a minority the same recognition of humanity, and hence the same sympathy and care, given as a matter of course to one's own group."[124] This selectivity results — "often unconsciously — from our tendency to sympathize most readily with those who seem most like ourselves. Whenever its cause, decisions that reflect this phenomenon, like those reflecting overt racial hostility, are unfair; for by hypothesis, they are decisions disadvantaging minority persons that would not be made under the identical circumstances if they disadvantaged members of the dominant group."[125] The concept of selective sympathy and indifference corresponds to the general problems posed by stereotypes, "conscious and unconscious temptations that inhere in we-they generalizations."[126] The bias resulting from stereotype "is not confined to isolated individuals of ill will, but reflects the social conditions of the times."[127]

Presently, the most significant aspect of housing discrimination relates to the effects of, and the perpetuation of, past and remote discrimination. According to Paul Brest:

"The effects of discrimination may attenuate over time or be submerged in superseding events. But the injuries inflicted by discrimination can place its victims at a disadvantage in a variety of future endeavors, and discrimination can also perpetuate itself by altering the social environment to harm new generations of victims. Discrimination often works its injuries through practices, not themselves race-dependent, implemented by institutions that have not themselves discriminated. Past and remote discrimination often manifest themselves in racially disproportionate impact, and the antidiscrimination principle may therefore support its amelioration or elimination."[128]

Also, when a substantial time period passes between an initial act of intentional discrimination and the subsequent conduct which causes that act to harm a victim, the total sequence of events can be characterized as the "perpetuation of past discrimination."[129] This concept refers to acts by different parties, to different transactions, or to "institutionalized" discrimination — "a situation that occurs when a discriminatory act creates physical or social circumstances that endure and cause injuries in the future."[130]

Unfortunately, this aspect of discrimination is often viewed as a minor corrective matter, and when there is a recognition of the problem, the commitment concedes an inadequate theoretical framework."[131] Instead, this type of institutionalized discrimination — not intentionally discriminatory acts — is the primary problem that plagues our society: "The essence of effective racial discrimination was and remains the creation of rules and circumstances that minimize the necessity for new acts of intentional discrimination. Once such a system has been established, all that is accomplished by forbidding further intentional discrimination is interference with the ability of biased officials to fine-tune the system and adapt it to unforeseen developments."[132] In the United States today, discrimination can no longer be viewed as primarily an issue of isolated, individual acts, intentionally designed to disadvantage particular groups.[133] Rather than subjugation stemming from conscious personalized discrimination, it now flows from what Lawrence Tribe describes as a "subtle mosaic of oppression."[134]

THE UNIQUE NATURE AND EXTENT OF BLACK RESIDENTIAL SEGREGATION

We could reasonably have expected during the 1970s that the segregation of blacks from whites would have been substantially reduced.[135] The Fair Housing Act was in effect for the entire decade,[136] there was a modest improvement in the economic status of some African-Americans,[137] the racial attitudes of whites grew more liberal,[138] and there was a continuing push for black civil rights.[139] While segregation declined in central city and metropolitan areas, both the rate of decline and the extent of decline have been unremarkable.[140]

Table I presents 17 city indexes of segregation for 1970 and 1980. The indexes of dissimilarity range from 0 (no dissimilarity or segregation) to 100 (complete dissimilarity or segregation). As of 1980, these cities contained the nation's largest black populations. In 12 of these cities there was a decrease in black-white residential segregation between 1970 and 1980. In Los Angeles there was a change from 90-81; in Washington there was no change, 79 at both dates; and in Phil-

Table I
Measures of Racial Residential Segregation in 1970 for Those Metropolitan Areas Containing 250,000 or More Blacks in 1980*

	Black population in 1980 (thousands)	Metropolitan areas			Central city		
		1970	1980	Change	1970	1980	Change
Atlanta	499	82	77	–5	92	86	–6
Baltimore	557	81	74	–7	89	86	–3
Chicago	1,428	91	86	–5	93	92	–1
Cleveland	346	90	88	–2	90	91	+1
Dallas-Fort Worth*	419	n.a.	76	n.a.	96	83	–13
Detroit	891	89	87	–2	82	73	–9
Houston	529	78	72	–6	93	81	–12
Los Angeles	944	89	76	–13	90	81	–9
Memphis	364	n.a.	n.a.		92	85	–7
Miami	280	86	77	–9	n.a.	n.a.	
New Orleans	387	74	70	–4	84	76	–8
New York	1,941	74	73	–1	77	75	–2
Newark	418	79	79	0	76	76	0
Philadelphia	884	78	77	–1	84	88	+4
St. Louis	408	87	82	–5	90	90	0
San Francisco-Oakland**	391	77	68	–9	70	59	–11
Washington	854	82	69	–13	79	79	0
Average	679	82	77	–5	86	81	–5

*These indexes were computed from block data and compare the distribution of blacks to all nonblacks in 1980 or blacks to whites in 1970. The measure is the index of dissimilarity, which equals 100 if all blacks live in racially homogenous blocks.

**Segregation indexes refer to the central city with the larger black population: Dallas and Oakland.

Sources: Karl Taeuber, "Racial Residential Segregation, 28 Cities, 1970–1980," University of Wisconsin-Madison, Center for Demography and Ecology, CDE Working Paper 83–12, table 1; Karl Taeuber, Arthur Sakamoto, Jr., Franklin W. Monfort, and Perry A. Massey, "The Trend in Metropolitan Racial Residential Segregation," paper presented at the 1984 meetings of the Population Association of America, Minneapolis, May 5, 1984.

adelphia there was an increase from 84 to 88. The overall change averaged five points as the typical score fell from 86 to 81. Between 1970 and 1980, reductions of 10 points occurred in only three cities: Dallas, Houston, and Oakland, with the 13-point change in Dallas being the most substantial. Along with Philadelphia, only Cleveland had an increase. Also, as indicated by Table I, segregation in metropolitan areas with 250,000 or more black residents declined in the 1970s, with the average range going down from 82 to 77. In metropolitan areas, however, the indexes are high.

Our segregation within metropolitan areas is manifested "both by the large *extent* of residential varied separation within and between neighborhoods and by the *pattern* of black concentration in central city areas."[141] Blacks in 1980 comprised about 24 percent of the population in central cities, up from only 12 percent in 1950 and 20.6 percent in 1970. For the national population, however, the percentage of residents in central cities decreased from 35.5 in 1950 to 30 in 1980. While blacks increased in the suburbs between 1970 and 1980 at a rate almost three times that of whites, the proportion of blacks to whites residing in the suburbs increased only from 4.8 to 6.1 percent. Still in 1980, there was a large degree of social isolation. The respective black and white populations living in the suburbs were 20 and 42 percent.[142]

The political separation of the city and suburbs has placed within central cities twice as many poor residents as suburbia, four blacks for every one living in the suburbs, little potential for growth, and a shrinking share of the metropolitan population and economic base.[143] By restricting most cities from the benefits of urban growth, and concentrating the most serious urban problems within city limits, the development of relatively independent and autonomous suburbs has been a key factor in the worsening plight of older cities. Independence from the city exempts residents of suburbs from most of the public responsibility of providing for poor families who live in the city. Local autonomy also improves the ability of suburbanites to exclude lower-income and nonwhite groups, thus intensifying the concentration of the poor and blacks within city boundaries. These developments, in turn, enhance for whites the attraction of independent suburbs because they can insulate their residents and businesses from the people and problems of the cities.[144] Blacks primarily tend to move to "spillover" suburban communities that are contiguous to the central city area housing other blacks.[145] On occasion, the more favorable residential environment on the inner suburban margins of the advancing black community is occupied by a population of better-educated, middle-class, young black families. The other primary form of black suburbanization is the "leap-frog" type, most often an enclave situated beyond the spill-over area. Here, however, the black pockets are often relatively undesirable areas characterized mostly by "deteriorated, cheaply constructed early postwar tract housing which whites have abandoned . . . ."[146]

The present-day trend toward black suburbanization is a phenomenon of too little, too late in many ways. Compared with today, suburbs in the 1940s and 1950s were less different from each other, and racial exclusion was so complete it was appropriate to lump suburbs together and contend that blacks in simply crossing the line from city to suburb had achieved a real racial breakthrough.[147] As Orfield points out, however, that measure which might have been justified a generation ago to evaluate progress in a very different social and economic milieu can be extremely misleading. Over the past 20 years there have been developments that render analysis of today's events much more complex.

"Many blacks now enter suburbs with fewer resources, with fewer positive ties to cities, less rising economies, more fiscal problems, less financially viable public school systems, and greater isolation from the socio-economic mainstream of upwardly mobile Americans as compared to the suburbs that whites entered earlier. Blacks have gained less financially, as very few have been able to buy homes in the suburbs when the investments were the least and the gains the greatest. Most black suburbanites do not own property, and now they must overcome significantly higher obstacles to ownership. Rental consideration regarding the market, construction, and subsidies are far more cricial to black than to white suburbanites. As Orfield states:

"Black suburbanites, whose hold on suburban life is more precarious and whose gains have been smaller, also face the real possibility that a number of their communities will go through the entire ghettoization cycle, ending with segregated slums, falling population, and effective nullification of everything the early immigrants believed they had won. It has already happened in some areas."[148]

Although there is considerable evidence that blacks moving to the suburbs entered neighborhoods whose former occupants were white,[149] suburbanization has not led to significant residential integration.[150] As we have discussed, black suburbanition generally occurs in neighborhoods which either already had blacks or were close to concentrations of black populations, repeating a process similar to that which occurred in may central cities subsequent to World War II.[151] After an investigation of racial change in 1,600 separate suburbs in 44 metropolitan areas, it was found that black-white residential segregation in suburban rings was as substantial in 1980 as it had been in 1970.[152]

Black segregation is unequally intense in that blacks are more isolated from whites than are the other major racial and ethnic minorities and for decades it has persisted at high levels while the segregation of ethnic minorities from native whites has declined over time. Moreover, even the newest minority groups to come to American cities in large numbers are less segregated from whites than are blacks.[153]

In Table III, for instance, in comparing ethnic groups separated from the English in America, we see that blacks are far more segregated than are the other European groups. Comparing the most segregated of the Europeans, the Russians (many of whom are Jewish), with that of blacks shows that in our nation's capital, the respective indexes of segregation are 51 for Russians and 68 for blacks. The respective averages for the 16 metropolitan areas are 59 and 75. Regarding the newer arrivals such as Hispanics and Asians, Table II shows that in all 16 areas African Americans were considerably more residentially segregated from whites in 1980 than were the Hispanics and Asians: The average respective residential segregation score for blacks, Hispanics, and Asians is 79, 48, and 43. In New York City the numbers are 81, 65, and 35; in Los Angeles, 81, 57, and 47; in Miami, 78, 53, and 34; and in Washington, 70, 32, and 31. As Farley and Allen

Table II
Measures of the Residential Segregation of Blacks, Hispanics, and Asians from Non-Hispanic Whites, Metropolitan Areas in 1980*

| | Segregation of three groups from non-Hispanic whites | | |
	Blacks	Hispanics	Asians
Atlanta	77	31	39
Baltimore	74	38	44
Chicago	88	64	46
Cleveland	88	55	42
Dallas	79	49	43
Detroit	88	45	48
Houston	75	49	45
Los Angeles	81	57	47
Miami	78	53	34
New Orleans	71	25	54
New York	81	65	49
Newark	82	65	35
Philadelphia	79	63	47
St. Louis	82	32	44
San Francisco	74	41	47
Washington	70	32	31
Average	79	48	43

*These are indexes of dissimilarity which were calculated from census tract data. Data are shown for all metropolitan areas with 250,000 or more black residents in 1980, except Memphis.

Source: U.S. Bureau of the Census, *Census of Population and Housing: 1980,* Summary Tape File 3.

state, the indexes in Table II "suggest that a continuation of the trends of the 1970s will leave blacks highly segregated in the foreseeable future. That is, if the average black-white segregation score declines by five points each decade, it will take about six decades for black-white residential segregation to fall to the current level of Asian-white or Hispanic-white segregation."[154]

Finally, in looking at Tables II and III, the persistence of black-white segregation as a result of the "birds of a feather" hypothesis is rebutted.[115] The notion that because ethnic groups tend to voluntarily segregate themselves and that the black isolation from whites is rather typical, not unusual, is just not true.[156] It is not true in terms of comparing black isolation to that of traditional European immigrants or to that of newer arriving Hispanics and Asians.

Another unique aspect of black residential segregation is the fact that improved black socioeconomic mobility is no guarantee of spatial mobility. Freedom to move into a white residential area of one's choice subject to ability to pay is a freedom not indicated for African Americans. This contravenes an assumption commonly held by black and whites that segregation is substantially determined by the races' respective economic differences.[157] How many times do those reading the pages of *Ebony* or *Jet* magazines see stories describing the "fantastic" homes of black professional entertainers and athletes who are living in some of the best white neighborhoods. The implicit message is that if you make enough, you can live anywhere whites live.

On the other hand, in seeing the blacks who are still trapped in segregation one is apt to recognize the tremendous differences in black and white financial status. In 1986, 31.1 percent of the national black population was below the poverty line compared to only 11 percent of the white population. Black median income was only 57.1 percent of whites, $17,604 to $30,809. Only 8.8 percent of the blacks had more than $50,000 in income compared to 22 percent of the whites. For blacks 14 percent had incomes less than $5,000 and 30.2 percent had less than $10,000, while the respective figures for whites were only 3.5 and 10.2 percent.[158] The median white household net worth in 1984, $39,000, exceeded black household net worth by 11 times.[159]

While one might expect blacks and whites to live in more integrated settings according to their similar incomes, indications are that blacks at every economic level are significantly segregated from whites of similar economic status. Table IV reveals that blacks are significantly segregated from whites regardless of how much income we have obtained or how many years we have gone to school. The segregation index for families in the $50,000 and over range is 79 and that for families with incomes under $5,000 is 76. The 1980 census data reveal, moreover, that educational attainment means little in terms of escaping segregation: The segregation indexes comparing black and white college graduates were 80 in Detroit, 76 in Chicago, and 72 in New York.[160] The corresponding residential segregation indexes for blacks and whites who failed to finish of high school were 77 in Detroit, 80 in Chicago, and 68 in New York. As Farley and Allen indicate: "In contrast to the situation among blacks, as income or education increased, Asian-white residential segregation declined. This implies that social and economic factors account for some of the residential segregation of Asians since segregation levels varied by status. Asians with high incomes or extensive educations apparently could move into neighborhoods of similar whites much more easily than could blacks."[161]

ATTITUDINAL CHANGES REGARDING INTEGRATION: PROGRESS AND RESISTENCE

A key question in this area focuses on the extent to which residential separation reflects public attitudes and preferences of both blacks and whites. Anti-black prejudice is generally measured by four factors: (1) whether blacks would be welcome to dinner; (2) whether whites have a right to prevent blacks from moving into their neighborhoods; (3) whether blacks should "push" themselves into areas

Table III
Measures of the Residential Segregation of Blacks and Selected Ethnic Groups from the English Ethnic Group, Metropolitan Areas in 1980*

	Blacks	Germans	Irish	French	Scots	Swedes	Dutch	Italians	Poles	Hungarians	Greeks	Russians
Atlanta	75	19	12	22	26	38	26	34	37	n.a.	n.a.	63
Baltimore	73	24	21	30	32	n.a.	37	34	45	48	56	73
Chicago	80	28	35	33	32	30	52	49	52	44	55	64
Cleveland	83	24	27	35	33	n.a.	n.a.	41	47	33	55	60
Dallas	77	16	14	23	27	33	28	33	37	n.a.	n.a.	n.a.
Detroit	85	21	20	27	28	36	37	45	42	44	52	66
Houston	73	17	17	22	31	35	33	29	35	n.a.	n.a.	n.a.
Los Angeles	78	14	17	24	28	25	34	25	37	41	46	55
Miami	712	18	17	27	29	32	37	29	50	48	44	61
New Orleans	63	27	23	31	n.a.	n.a.	n.a.	37	n.a.	n.a.	n.a.	n.a.
New York	67	39	43	40	n.a.	n.a.	n.a.	55	52	52	64	49
Newark	77	25	26	36	30	33	39	41	44	42	48	48
Philadelphia	77	27	32	35	32	n.a.	41	41	40	44	62	64
St. Louis	78	26	20	24	35	35	31	39	35	44	n.a.	75
San Francisco	71	15	21	26	25	25	32	30	28	41	45	43
Washington	68	15	17	25	27	36	33	25	29	41	46	51
Average	75	22	23	29	30	33	35	37	41	44	52	59

*These are indexes of dissimilarity calculated from census tract data. Data are shown for all metropolitan areas with 250,000 or more black residents in 1980 except Memphis. Each group is compared to the residential distribution of those who gave English as their only ancestry. Blacks are defined by the race question. Ethnic groups consist of individuals who reported one specific ancestry such as German or Irish.

n.a. = Indexes not calculated if the group size was less than 10 times the number of census tracts.

Source: U.S. Bureau of the Census, *Census of Population and Housing: 1980*, Summary Tape File 3.

Table IV
Measures of Residential Segregation, Controlling for Income for Education, Metropolitan Areas in 1980

	Black-white segregation In 16 areas*	Segregation in three metropolitan areas** Black-white	Asian-white
Family income in 1979			
Under $5,000	76	77	66
$5,000 to 7,499	76	77	71
$7,500 to 9,999	76	78	69
$10,000 to 14,999	75	76	59
$15,000 to 19,999	75	78	58
$20,000 to 24,999	76	77	57
$25,000 to 34,999	76	78	53
$35,000 to 49,999	76	78	53
$50,000 or more	79	79	56
Educational attainment of persons 25 or over			
Less than 9 years	76	77	57
High school, 1 to 3 years	77	79	56
High school, 4 years	76	77	50
College, 1 to 3 years	74	74	48
College, 4 years or more	71	69	47

*These residential segregation scores are average values for the 16 metropolitan areas listed in the previous table. They were computed from census tract data. The index shown for $20,000 to $24,999, 76, compared the residential distribution of black families in this income category to that of whites in the identical category.

**These segregation scores are average values for those three metropolitan areas which contained both one-quarter million blacks and one-quarter million Asians: Los Angeles, New York, and San Francisco.

Source: See table 3.

when they are unwanted; and (4) whether laws should prohibit black-white marriage.[162]

Firebaugh and Davis found that as measured by these indications anti-black prejudice has declined during the period from 1972 to 1984.[163] In light of the growing conservatism on social issues, the possibility of white backlash based on "perceived" black gains, the increased black-white competition, and the continuing de facto segregation, such a finding is surprising. Their explanation for the decline is that attitudinal change has been supplemented by "cohort replacement," each accounting for roughly 50 percent of the decline in traditional anti-black prejudice.[164] According to Firebach and Davis, "[i]ndeed, with cohort replacement, societies on the whole can become more tolerant, even though no single individual does. If successive cohorts of whites continue to be less prejudiced than their predecessors — and if racial attitudes formed early tend to persist throughout one's life — then the downward trend in prejudice is likely to continue."[165]

Data on national trends related to white attitudes show a sharp increase in support for the principle of residential integration specifically and a drop in the support for any kind of racial discrimination. For example, by 1985, 74 percent of the white population expressed disagreement with the statement that "white people have a right to keep blacks out of their neighborhoods, and blacks should respect that right." This figure is up from 39 percent in 1963.[166] Simultaneously, however, the same surveys indicate that whites do not support implementation of black rights through open-housing laws as much as they support integration in principle. In 1986, white support for implementation reached only 48 percent.[167] Moreover, as earlier indicated, actual desegregation of neighborhoods has decreased only slightly over long periods of time.

Discrepancies between white attitudes regarding general fair housing principles and white attitudes regarding implementation have provoked disagreement among social scientists interpreting the attitude data. Some have seen the discrepancy as indicating a masked intolerance as whites pay "lip service" to democractic platitudes, while hiding strong objections to actual integration that come out whenever serious implementation measures are proposed.[168] The theory of "symbolic racism" claims that racism today primarily avoids expressions of explicit beliefs in black inferiority or outward support for segregation. Instead, new stereotypes have come into play that depict blacks as uppity or pushy, pressing illegitimate demands, and benefiting from preferential treatment and welfare programs. These symbolic racial views become the new foundation for opposing the implementation of social changes that benefit blacks.[169] The theory of "symbolic tolerance" focuses on the weak or non-existent link between education and support for social reform. Here, the better educated recognized the value in advocating egalitarian norms, but do not apply them if doing so will undermine their own position of privilege.[170]

Attitudes may reflect prejudice, erroneous judgment, or rational and moral convictions.[171] In recent studies of the Detroit area, white residents were found to hold three general beliefs about neighborhood racial change:

"First, they felt that stable inter-racial neighborhoods were rare: Once a few blacks entered an area,they thought that more would come and that eventually, the neighborhood would become largely black. Second, many whites presumed that property values were lowered by the presence of black residents so it was seen as risky to hold property in an area undergoing racial change. Third, whites agreed that crime rates are usually higher in black neighborhoods than in white ones. In particular, if whites are a minority in a black area, they may be exposing themselves to a high risk of victimization."[172]

In 1973, Downs identified eight principal sources of opposition to open suburbs: (1) resistance to rising property taxes, (2) resistance to higher federal taxes for housing subsidies, (3) fear of falling property value, (4) fear of rising crime and vandalism rates, (5) decline in the quality of schools, (6) desire to maintain "social distance," (7) central-city fears of loss of leaders, and (8) the black nationalist position. One recent study found that the perceived presence of government coercion is an important factor in opposition to fair housing.[173]

Finally, white opposition to open-housing laws has been found to rest on white beliefs that enforcement of such laws will adversely change status relationships.[174] Tied to this, some researchers have found that some personal objections to blacks seem to rest on perceived class differences rather than on race differences per se. This appears to be especially true for middle-class whites.[175]

In light of the array of attitudinal factors giving rise to an opposition in fact of residential integration, both prospects for initial integration, as well as those for stable integration, are implicated. As indicated by Table V, in 1978, 85 percent of the national black sample preferred a neighborhood that was half black and half white, whereas only 36 percent of the whites perferred such a neighborhood. Only three percent of the blacks preferred a neighborhood mostly white, while 29 percent of the whites preferred this neighborhood. And over one-third of the whites — 34 percent — preferred an all-white neighborhood. Five percent of the blacks preferred an all-black neighborhood. Farley's 1978 study of Detroit indicates that this preference gap is a serious impediment to residential integration:

> "Whites strongly endorse the ideal of equal opportunities for blacks but would be uncomfortable if more than token numbers of blacks entered their neighborhoods. Blacks desire to live in mixed areas, but are reluctant to be the pioneers. It appears that whites are saying that integration is acceptable so long as black representation is minimal. Blacks, on the other hand, see integration as desirable but think the ideal neighborhood is one with a sizable black population — a number that will only make whites uncomfortable, but will terminate white demand for housing in the neighborhood."[176]

In another study by Farley, the following hypothetical situation was presented to all respondents: "I'd like you to imagine that you're going to move. You have a choice of buying two houses that are identical, except that one is located in northwest Detroit and the other is located in a desirable suburb. The house in the suburb costs $8,000 more than the house in Detroit. Which of the two houses would you choose to move into?"[177] Given these options, 90 percent of the whites chose the suburban house while 75 percent of the blacks chose the city house. This study was done in 1976, and the housing market has changed, but it is probably still the case "[a]lthough endorsing the ideal of integration, many whites would actually spend large sums of money to avoid living in an area which they believe 'belongs to blacks.'"[178] As recently as 1985, consistent with the Farley study, Muth stated that "the basic reason for black residential segregation . . . is that whites are willing to pay more for housing in segregated white residential areas than blacks are."[179] The preference explanation of segregation has, thus, generated two controversies: (1) should access of blacks to buildings or neigh-

Table V
Summary of Recent Neighborhood Preference Studies*

	All black	Mostly black	Half & half	Mostly white	All white
Black preferences					
National 1978	5.0%	7.0%	85.0%	3.0%	***
Detroit** 1977	12.0	14.0	62.0	10.0	
Kansas City 1982	4.0	3.0	87.0	6.0	***
Cincinnati 1983	7.0	8.0	69.0	7.0	***
White preferences					
National 1978	***	1.0	36.0	29.0	34.0
Kansas City 1982	***	0.0	25.0	39.0	36.0
Cincinnati (Hamilton County) 1983	***	6.0	34.0	34.0	26.0

*"No difference" responses allocated proportionately to other choices.

**Central cities only; suburbs excluded.

***Not asked.

Sources: National and Detroit studies, *Armour* v. *Nix*, Defendants' Exhibit No. 22, prepared by David J. Armor for *Jenkins* v. *State of Missouri;* and Cincinnati from survey by W.A.V. Clark for *Bronson* v. *Board of Education of the City School District of the City of Cincinnati.*

borhoods be restricted to maintain "stable integration"; (2) should tolerance be subsidized?

The disparities between blacks and whites in their assessment of the proper integration mix has caused an increased concern on maintaining stable integration. The process of residential integration has two stages. The first stage focuses on the elimination of segregation, usually by making it easier for blacks to enter previously all-white areas, while the second stage seeks to maintain a stable racial balance to prevent white flight and resegregation. The first stage typically is furthered through prohibitions against racial discrimination, along with affirmative marketing to encourage nonwhite buyers to move into white areas by informing them about housing opportunities. Because black entry often leads to white flight, however, such programs may fail to produce stable integration.[180]

Thus, integration maintenance programs are instruments for controlling white fight. Techniques include primarily "benign" steering and quotas and affirmative marketing. The goal is to maintain stable integration, in light of the dynamics of residential segregation: Founded on the fear of "the process by which a previously all white community becomes an all black community" these programs restrict the proportion of black residents so that whites will be encouraged to enter or remain in the community.[181] In other words, the quota is intended to prevent resegregation by limiting the percentage of blacks to just short of the point that would "tip" the housing or community from white or black. Studies show this point to range from 6 to 60 percent, with most studies fixing the point at between 20-30 [182] percent. The potential restrictions on black access to housing and the implicit acceptance of white prejudice involved in these programs have provoked heated dispute among traditional advocates of racial integration.[183]

While some view integration as an end in itself, most blacks view it as a pragmatic means to suitable housing and a decent residential environment. Integrationists link various values to integration, such as quality public schools, low crimes rates, effective provision of good municipal services, and increased access to better jobs. Integration maintenance places a very high value on second-stage integration as a social goal "even if an effect of that policy is to reduce the number of blacks moving into certain areas of the city.[185] Hence, a conflict in Title VIII goals is manifested because integration maintenance promotes antisegregation or integration policy while defeating the antidiscrimination or freedom-of-choice policy.[186]

As Leigh and McGhee point out, the conflict can be resolved through pragmatic analysis:

"Historically, the National Urban League has opposed any activity that would limit for any reason the access of minority group members to any housing that they could afford. At the same time, the organization has concerned itself with limiting the diffusion of black political power, acquiring jobs, limiting urban displacement, and a myriad of other, separate issues related to housing. Although the National Urban League opposes any policy of so-called 'spatial deconcentration,' for example, it does not object to the movement of blacks to suburbs by personal choice. Even if this movement eventually results in neighborhoods that are no longer racially integrated, the League would opposed any action that would maintain housing integration by denying free access to housing to minority group members . . . . Residential racial integration per se is not now and may never have been the desideratum among blacks. The more fundamental concern among black Americans has been freedom from impediments to the fulfillment of their human potential. If blacks get the housing units that they want, and the characteristics include a racially integrated neighborhood, they are willing to accept integration as a useful although not essential outcome."[187]

Many argue that, although stronger Title VIII enforcement might lead to a reduction in the incidence of the housing discrimination proscribed, it would have little impact upon the extent of black segregation. If whites remain reluctant to enter areas where blacks are attracted or even to remain in areas where blacks are represented, provides motivation for real estate dealers to steer blacks and whites to distinct locations. Many of these violate the Fair Housing Law but, if commonly practiced, they help to account for the persistence of racial residential segregation."[188]

In Muth's view the only ways to reduce black segregation are (1) to subsidize black families to live in white areas or (2) to subsidize white families to live in black areas. Muth sees the present voucher program as a means of providing a tolerance subsidy by simply increasing its value for blacks or whites who move to predominantly other neighborhoods.[189] Downs would provide special "moving adjustment" grants to low- and moderate-income household moving from central cities into suburban neighborhoods.[190] Sander would provide "mobility grants" in the form of direct payments or mortgage interest subsidies.[191] Silverman, in considering low-income dispersal, sees it desirable to subsidize communities that would receive low-income or subsidized housing. His strategy would supplement other dispersal strategies such as persuasion, accommodation, and coercion. According to Silverman, the reform mission he adopts is to change "active opposition" at least into "dispassionate tolerance."[192] Silverman, in 1977, saw the subsidizing to tolerance as a last resort; while controversial, it is certainly preferable to quotas.

FAIR HOUSING ENFORCEMENT

There are three separate and independent means of enforcing Title VIII: (1) a private civil action brought directly without a prior administrative complaint or resolution; (2) a civil action brought by the Justice Department in "pattern or practice" and "general public importance" cases; and (3) an administrative complaint filed with HUD.[193]

A direct privately enforced suit brought in federal court is preferably in many ways to other enforcement means. There are cases, however, where a direct suit is not the most feasible alternative as, for instance, when a complainant lacks the necessary funds to initiate and sustain litigation. As Professor Schwemm notes, "Whatever the reason, thousands of complainants initiate [administrative] proceedings with HUD every year, far more than the number who file court [private enforcement] suits."[194]

Under the administration enforcement provisions of the Fair Housing Act, HUD refers complaints to the appropriate state or local agency wherever a state or local fair housing law provides rights and remedies for alleged discrimination which are "substantially equivalent" to the rights and remedies provided by Title VIII. As of June 25, 1988, HUD recognized such laws in 36 states and 76 localities.[195] The number of complaints referred to state or local agencies increased from seven percent in 1979 to 67 percent in 1984.[196]

James Kushner has characterized the term "federal fair housing enforcement effort" as an oxymoron, like such terms as "military justice" and "honest lawyer."[197] Criticism of fair housing enforcement has focussed principally on the meager number of cases and complaints dealt with by HUD and the Civil Rights Division by the Justice Department[198] and on the statutory limit imposed on HUD to resolve disputes by using "informal methods of conference, conciliation, and persuasion" only instead of being able to case "cease and desist" orders.[199] The structural inappropriateness of the Fair Housing Act's relying so heavily on private enforcement to attack systematically the broad patterns of discrimination and segregation has also been properly criticized.[200]

On September 13, 1988, President Reagan signed new legislation, the Fair Housing Amendments Act of 1988, effective 180 days from that date (i.e., March 12, 1989).[201] These statutory changes substantially strengthen HUD's enforcement powers and extend the Act's coverage to prohibit discrimination on the basis of handicap and on the basis of familial status.[202]

HUD's conciliation process is still primary, but now HUD has the power to recommend that the Department of Justice bring a civil suit to enforce any conciliation agreement breached. Should conciliation fail, HUD has the power to seek injunctive relief in federal court or to file an administrative complaint to be heard before an administrative law judge (ALJ). If the respondent is found to have engaged in or is about to engage in a discriminatory housing practice, the ALJ can issue injunctive relief as well.[203]

Moreover, the ALJ can impose penalties up to $10,000 in cases of first violation to $50,000 in cases of two or more violations during a seven-year period from the filing of the present change.[204] Also, in cases brought by the Attorney General's office, penalties can be sought up to $50,000 for a first violation and up to $100,000 for any subsequent violation.[205]

Finally, the new amendments require HUD to report annually to Congress, and to make available to the public statistical data on the race, color, religion, sex, national origin, age, handicap, and family characteristics of persons and households who are beneficiaries or potential beneficiaries of programs under HUD's administration. Moreover, HUD is required to report on the progress made nationally in eliminating, discriminatory housing practices, including recommendations for further legislative or executive action.[206]

For Black America, the expanded fair housing coverage to families with children is a significant development because blacks are disproportionally affected by housing policies that exclude children.[207] Female-headed households, a significant group among blacks, are similarly affected.[208] As *Betsey v. Turtle Creek Associates* indicates, discrimination against families with children can also serve as a pretext for racial discrimination.[209]

Indirectly, the Title VIII amendments also support the substantial majority of federal court decisions holding that a prima facie Fair Housing Act violation can be established if defendant's action had a discriminatory effect. The U.S. Supreme Court has recently affirmed a decision permitting an effect standard to prove a

Title VIII violation.[210] When the President signed the bill, he stated that the amendments should be construed to require discriminatory intent, rather than effect, in order to demonstrate a violation of the fair housing prohibition.[211] Senator Edward Kennedy, the amendments' principal sponsor, said in the next day's *Congressional Record* that Congress did not contemplate any such intent requirement.[212]

Without doubt, the struggle culminating in these new amendments should be applauded, but no false security should result. The primary dangers are that the new tools will not be employed effectively by the government and that the nation will see this legislation as sufficient to do all that needs to be done.[213]

ONCE MORE: THE GOAL OF SPATIAL EQUALITY

Three years ago in my article for *The State of Black America 1986*, I argued that efforts to improve life for poor blacks must now be redirected to create spatial equality in the sense that, *even under conditions of segregation,* the setting where blacks live should be improved so that blacks are not unjustly disadvantaged because of where we live.[214] Actually, at the heart of the argument is a position urged in 1975 by Kenneth Phillips and Michael Agelasto:

"If the deterioration patterns of central city hardcore poverty areas are to be reversed and marginal neighborhoods restored and conserved, realistic, cost effective, broad scale, job-creating, participatory program approaches must be found. Downtown renewal projects, benign neglect, and suburban bypass strategies have not met these criteria. The criticisms and suggestions put forth in this article are offered in the hope that a pro-cities commitment will be made and coordinated and feasible programs will be developed to restore urban communities."[215]

In this article I have again presented the case for spatial equality. After eight years of the Reagan administration the argument is even more necessary and proper today than it was in 1986. Indeed, it is a desperate argument that forces one to let go of certain assumptions about the commitment of America even to incorporate blacks into the national community as full citizens. In some ways, the argument revives the plight of Homer Plessy and the doctrine of separate but equal.[216] But at least Homer Plessy was on the same train as whites. With respect to housing and other basic needs today, we are not. Trying to board that train has only established a clear need to catch another one.[217]

Black America must recognize that integration at best has resulted in tokenism and "non-economic liberalism."[218] Fair housing must transcend its antidiscrimination principle and instead adopt an antisubjugation principle which strives to dismantle legally created or legally reinforced schemes of subordination that reduce some people to second-class citizens. As Professor Tribe states:

"The Constitution may be offended not only by individual acts of racial discrimination, but also by government rules, policies or practices that perennially reinforce the subordinate status of any group. Mediated by the antisubjugation principle, the equal protection clause asks whether the particular conditions complained of, examined in their social and historical context, are a manifestation or a legacy of official oppression.''[219]

When the housing predicament of Black America is thus evaluated, the legacy of official oppression clearly reveals itself.

Can a right to fair housing provide redress? Morton Horwitz asserts that "[t]he most promising way to ensure that rights may be used on behalf of the socially weak . . . is to ground rights theory in a substantive conception of the good society.''[220] Along this line, for blacks, the task of using rights involves, initially, avoiding co-optation and avoiding being employed to legitimate the present order of things.[221] We use rights in two related, but very different ways. First, we employ the language of rights to facilitate our access to a variety of legal norms and enforcement mechanisms by which we try to vindicate, in a particular case or controversy, important claims. Second, we invoke the ideology of rights "to mobilize people in support of a particular agenda."[222] As convincingly argued by Barrington Moore, until the subjugated group feels a sense of moral outrage, until it comes to say "we have a right to that and you can't take it away from us," the group will almost certainly not move into a position to resist the injustice which is oppressing them. The group must obtain justice for itself. The language of rights is used to provoke within the oppressed group the sense of outrage necessary to mobilize the group in a just cause.[223] It is in this regard that a right to fair housing, as manifested in spatial equality, can be most effectively utilized.

One development that African-Americans need to consider carefully is the incorporation of black neighborhoods into cities as a means to group improvement and local control. Perhaps a right to spatial equality will direct mobilization to that end. The incorporation of black neighborhoods has been recently addressed in a 1988 student comment, "Black Neighborhoods Becoming Black Cities: Group Empowerment, Local Control and the Implications of Being Darker than Brown."[224] The general idea is illustrated by recent movements to incorporate East Palo Alto, California, and the Roxbury section of Boston. Neighborhood incorporation is presented as a new civil rights concept. Unlike traditional civil rights strategies which focused primarily on racial discrimination and obtaining equality through access to the dominant white culture and institutions, neighborhood incorporation addresses this and, additionally, the problems of political powerlessness and economic deprivation.[225]

In the student comment, the Fair Housing Act has been criticized because "there was no provision for enabling people to pay for new housing, and only middle-class blacks were able to take advantage of the fair housing laws. While these laws were undoubtedly justified in breaking down the barriers of mandatory enforced segregation, they ignored the economic status of the majority of blacks and failed to help those blacks who were not in the upper strata of the black communities. The integrationist emphasis spoke of equality only in the sense of ending separation and argued that legal access to any community would be equality."[225]

While this represents an over simplification, the observation is generally true.[227] When we analyze fair housing, vis-a-vis poor blacks, we find that the governing law is inherently inadequate to further housing for those who cannot afford it; that fair housing has always meant something very different to poor blacks than it has to the upwardly mobile or middle class blacks; and that the larger problems of housing deprivation, disproportionately affecting blacks while at the same time transcending racial discrimination, are largely unrecognized, unappreciated and unaddressed by too many of us.[228] As indicated by then-Senator Mondale, supporters of fair housing recognized early on that the Fair Housing Act would primarily eliminate discrimination against those "otherwise able to purchase a home."[229] More tellingly, William L. Taylor, then Staff Director, United States Commission on Civil Rights, in testimony before the Senate Subcommittee on Constitutional Rights, declared that the Act would "benefit primarily . . . those who have the means to afford middle income housing."[230] Now, with virtual elimination of federally assisted and subsidized construction housing programs, even the once helpful efforts to challenge exclusionary zoning have become rather academic. And low-income dispersal policies have been a disaster.[231]

Critics of neighborhood incorporation contend that the strategy is racially divisive, that it goes counter to the integration imperatives of fair housing, that it is economically infeasible, that it is racist. In spite of this, the strategy has found support among black leaders who are "stressing equality of results and testing new approaches and alternate solutions to address the issues of political and economic empowerment."[232] While separatist, the orientation is not a matter of furthering segregation, which is imposed from the outside and to perpetuate inequality.[233] Instead, the separateness stems from cultural identity and group pride having the objective to promote local control and responsiveness to the needs of the blacks community, to resolve issues not adequately addressed by traditional civil rights initiatives.[234] Neighborhood incorporation goes beyond mere decentralization of government decision-making as it establishes an independent local government entity. It also gives blacks control over land use, an important factor given the incidence of gentrification and displacement traditionally sited in black urban areas.[235]

As the commentators state: "While attention shifts to the challenge of implementation, the idealistic and philosophical criticisms of the strategy should cease."[236] Neighborhood incorporation and other community equalizing strategies provide a legitimate basis for the exercise of group rights and present opportunities to awaken the sense of injustice over what I term the present "analogous apartheid" in both the victim and the victimizer.[237] It recognizes the Report of the National Advisory Commission on Civil Disorders' prescription for the future of the cities: "Enrichment must be an important adjunct to integration, for no matter how ambitious or energetic the program, few Negroes now living in central cities can be quickly integrated. In the meantime, large-scale improvement in the quality of ghetto life is essential."[238] True in 1968, more clearly true in 1989.[239]

CONCLUSION

In 1968, the Report of the National Advisory Commission on Civil Disorders recognized that the nation was rapidly moving toward two separate Americas and that within two decades, "this division could be so deep that it would be almost impossible to unite.[240] The societies described were blacks concentrated within large central cities and whites located in the suburbs, smaller cities, and on the periphery of large central cities.

While today's division seems to be that of three separate societies, as some suburban middle-class, black entry has occurred, but still within segregation, we nonetheless really have moved very near to a point of division that is beyond uniting.[241] America will not make wrong right until it provides for spatial equality. As Paul Gewirtz asserts:

"We need not accept an idea of collective guilt for our racial past to recognize a collective responsibility for purging our country of the continuing effects of that past. It is an obligation that derives from something as simple as the acceptance of citizenship in a nation whose glories have so long and so often been interwined with racism. We have a duty to act as a society, through institutions of government and through a shared recognition of the common bonds of citizenship."[242]

Future society may be color-blind where disadvantageous racial distinctions have been eradicated. Presently, however, we must not only overcome the lingering effects of racial discrimination, but we must also achieve a society "plural, but equal" to use Harold Cruse's terms.[243] Or as Lawrence Tribe says, we must achieve "racial pluralism and diversity without racial domination."[244] Presently, America is not moving in any such direction. In order to get on the proper track, fundamental transformation must be achieved in the orientation of Black America and in the responses of the national body politic.

In a detailed historical study, James Kusher analyzed (1) how the federal government facilitated suburban development; (2) how it has administered federal housing and community development programs; (3) how local land use regulations have been applied; (4) how state regulations of real estate and banking have been applied; and (5) how federal and state taxation policies have been applied.[245] According to Kushner, "As we stalked the elusive goals of decent housing and neighborhoods, quality education and municipal services, employment and other economic opportunities, what became clear was that public policy, as it dictated the patterns of community development in America, created the racial division which marks this nation."[246] As such policies were seldom accidental or inadvertent, Kusher found that apartheid in America reflected disturbing similarities with the segregation policies in South Africa. An obstacle to overcoming the present situation "is that the population of this nation is cognizant neither of the extent of this deterioration nor the causes of the segregation pattern."[247]

The principal necessary and proper aspiration of fair housing is to *disestablish* American analogous apartheid. The federal government must take a lead in this effort given its responsibility in creating and perpetrating the situation. As Eric Schnapper points out: "When governmental discrimination creates continuing social or physical conditions, each injury caused by those conditions is a fresh constitutional violation. The appropriate remedy in such cases is not merely to redress specific injuries, but also to disestablish whatever ongoing state of affairs produced those injuries and threatens future harms."[248]

President George Bush's choice for Secretary of HUD, former Congressman Jack Kemp, is quoted as saying "I have an audacious faith that together we can recapture the American dream for our distressed inner cities."[249] Secretary Kemp promised that he wanted to wage war on poverty. He stated: "And I don't believe we're going to balance the budget by cutting housing. I don't think we're going to balance the budget by letting unemployment go up. I don't believe that we're going to solve the budget problem unless we have healthy cities. I want it known that you cannot balance the budget off the backs of the poor."[250] In pledging to fulfill Bush's campaign promise of a "kinder, gentler nation," Kemp was described as using language reminiscent of President Lyndon B. Johnson's "Great Society" promises.[251] For the sake of the nation at large as well as that of the black nation within, one must hope that President Bush and new HUD Secretary Kemp can rise to the occasion:

"The challenge that confronts this country involves the task of arriving at conditions that allow blacks and whites to live equitably. Clearly we are closer to such equality now than we were 30 years ago, yet vast differences persist in the quality of the life experienced by Americans due to racial and economic stratification. In a society dedicated to the norm of equality, significant deprivation in the midst of prosperity represents a constant potential for explosion, since a failed promise is like a time bomb ticking."[252]

The challenge almost overwhelms, but we must offer visions or aspirations.[253]

If parity in terms of housing opportunity and spatial equality is to be approached — it cannot be achieved — we must adopt a fair housing vision which, like the mythical Janus, simultaneously looks back to recapture perspectives from the 1960s and forward to reorient present policies related to achieving fair and decent housing and a suitable living environment for all.

From the 1960s, however, impolitic, I would urge adoption of the Model Cities vision (aspiration), which focused on the eradication of opportunity-denying circumstances.[254] The program called for locally developed plans to eliminate obstacles to decent housing, good jobs, and quality education. Specific objectives were ambitious, but appropriately so:

". . . to rebuild or revitalize large slum and blighted areas; to expand housing, job, and income opportunities; to reduce dependence on welfare payments; to improve educational facilities and programs; to combat disease and ill health, to reduce the incidence of crime and delinquency; to enhance recreational and cultural opportunities; to establish better access between homes and jobs; and generally to improve living conditions for the people who live in such areas . . . ."[255]

As the nation has moved from urban renewal to urban revitalization, the elimination of slums and blight has also displaced black people disproportionately and eliminated the supply of low- and moderate-income housing, either by leveling such housing or rehabilitating it and pricing it beyond reach of low- and moderate-income households. Renewal activity simply has not been offset by increased supply.[256] The Model Cities legislation had intended to avoid such a result.[257] Alas, however, the Model Cities program was underfunded and misdirected before its vision (aspiration) could take hold.[258] In principle and policy, it deserves about another chance.

A consideration of the reorientation through a forward-looking vision must be deferred. This article cannot directly help Janus there, but its concluding thought may indirectly help each of us:

"[I]n all this striving for justice, we resemble a man walking with his backside into a storm. Under the circumstances, it is useful to turn around and assess the full force of our condition."[259]

On Parity and Political Empowerment

Charles V. Hamilton, Ph.D.

INTRODUCTION

At his first press conference on the morning after his victory, President-elect George Bush was asked the following question: ". . . you campaigned hardly at all in black neighborhoods and didn't receive very many black votes. Specifically, what are you prepared to do to assure these Americans that the next four years will not be a continuation of the last eight? And what would you try to do to reduce the number of racial incidents that have occurred in recent years?"[1]

Mr. Bush rejected the implication that the previous recent years had been "eight years of bigotry," and then he suggested that he hoped to use the White House as a "bully pulpit" against racial incidents. He conceded, however, that his campaign was focused not so much on the inner cities. He said: ". . . in a campaign you obviously have to be sure you get *your* vote out. And that doesn't mean you don't want the votes of others, but you have to turn out *your own* people and reach out to as many people as you can."[2]

Clearly, the President-elect was saying that he understood that his campaign did not perceive the black vote as part of its base or strength. Thus, in consolidating his base, appeals had to be made, issues had to be addressed, and attention had to be paid first to those most likely to support the Republican candidate. (Blacks voted 87 percent for Dukakis, 12 percent for Bush.) This was a candid recognition of political reality in the 1988 presidential election. The important point, of course, for the Bush camp was *what* would be required to make "sure (that) you get your vote out." Herein lay the essence of the accusations of "racism" that pervaded this presidential campaign. The political advertising depicting a black convict, furloughed by Governor Dukakis, who had raped a white woman while temporarily out of jail had all the nuanced messages of crime-race-sex, calculated, some people believed, to appeal to the racist instincts of white Americans. The seeming lack of public enthusiasm, after the Atlanta Democratic convention, on the part of the Dukakis campaign to become too publicly identified with Reverend Jesse Jackson fed fears that the Democrats wanted to put as much distance as possible between themselves and what Jackson represented in terms of issues. They wanted his voters, but not their visibility. Earlier, during the Democratic primaries, there was the subtle, latently racist, gnawing question (especially after Jackson's impressive victory in the Michigan caucus): "What does Jesse Want?" translated to mean: "Obviously, he cannot get enough white votes to be seriously considered as the Democratic nominee. So, what is necessary to placate him and his supporters?"

One syndicated columnist bluntly defined the situation just two weeks before the election in an article entitled: "The Dirty Little Secret":

"Class, it has been said, is the dirty little secret of American society. In the 1988 Presidential campaign, race is the dirty little secret: a highly significant factor that no one mentions out loud.

To say it right out, white fears have a good deal to do with George Bush's strong showing — white fears and white feelings about the Democratic Party's commitment to blacks. Race is a pre-eminent factor in the South. It also matters greatly in many Northern cities.

William Schneider, the eminent political analyst at the American Enterprise Institute in Washington, put it bluntly when I asked him about the significance of race in this campaign.

'Someone asked me recently,' he said, 'what groups Michael Dukakis was having the most trouble with. I thought for a moment and answered: white people.'[3]

In sum, the recent presidential campaign was one of the most racially sordid campaigns in the post-World War II period — one that makes a discussion of black political empowerment and parity that much more important, if, albeit, problematic.

Last year's *The State of Black America 1988* listed 10 recommendations. The first dealt with "Empowerment."

"Active citizenship participation is the first step toward empowerment. Black people must step toward empowerment. Black people must use the power of the ballot in their own self-interest.

. . . In this election year, voting must be our primary agenda; those officials we elect or allow to be elected by others shape our future. . . ."[4]

Certainly, electoral behavior is a major criterion for measuring political empowerment. In a political system governed by people elected to office, those who do not participate in that process can hardly be considered as having influence. This is especially the case if few other resources (financial, being the most important) are available. Voting becomes one important aspect of the first criterion for measurement. It is a yardstick of "Political Participation," with observable results manifested in various ways: registration and turn-out rates; favorable candidates elected; the kinds of offices to which they are elected.

A second criterion is "Public Attitudes." Those citizens who are able to get more people to believe the way they do about what government ought (or ought not) to do are going to be more politically important — empowered. Therefore, we should pay close attention to this factor in our discussion. It will tell us a lot about the road that has to be traveled toward "parity."

There is a third factor: "Public Policies." Elections (and other forms of political behavior such as lobbying, litigation, and protests) and attitudes are not ends in themselves. They constitute means, and they describe the context. Ultimately, if we *really* want to know how empowered a group is at any given time, we must examine the extent to which that group's policies are, in fact, enacted and implemented. It matters little if registration and turn-out rates are at a maximum, and "nothing ever happens," or if societal attitudes are closely in sync with those of the particular group, but actual programs do not come forth, and real lives are not improved. Therefore, an assessment of 'political empowerment' requires attention to what actually transpires in the political system in terms of concrete results.

In last year's *The State of Black America* recommendation on empowerment, there is a specific item for measurement:

"Because we believe that every reasonable effort must be made to enable citizens to vote, we also urge Congress and the president to support the Universal Voter Registration Act of 1987, which would establish mail-in registration and election day registration for federal elections."[5]

Other specific recommendations were listed and, to be sure, there will be "agendas" issued by other organizations. These various proposals, some more specific than others, provide a means for measuring in a concrete, empirical way the extent to which we can talk about and accurately assess the phenomenon of "black political empowerment." This takes us beyond the well-meaning (and, frankly, easily acceptable) rhetoric of egalitarianism, liberty, and social justice. It gives us a way to evaluate developments and stipulate goals.

POLITICAL PARTICIPATION

One thing we know about American electoral behavior is that Americans are, in presidential elections, voting less than before. Only 50.16 percent of the eligible (voting-age) population voted in 1988, the lowest turnout since 1924. This downward trend has been occurring since the 1960 Kennedy-Nixon election, when 62.8 percent voted. One national post-election poll indicated that blacks constituted 11 percent of the 1988 non-voters. They were also 11 percent of those Americans who voted.[6] An overwhelming majority — 67 percent — of *all* non-voters indicated that if they could have registered on election day, they would have voted. This signals clear support, from this group at least, for the proposed Universal Voter Registration Act.

One important study has shown that "legal barriers have a strong influence upon the level of black turnout."[7] This certainly is the history of southern enfranchisement. Over a forty-year period, from 1940 to 1984, the black registration rate in that region increased from 3.1 percent to 66.9 percent. In terms of parity, we have seen substantial changes. In the South, black turnout increased from 13 percent in 1952 to 85 percent in 1984.

An important fact is that when socio-economic status is held constant, blacks tend to vote as much as whites.[8] This has been true in the North and South over the last two decades. In fact, in 1984, blacks *reported* that they turned out five percentage points higher than reported white turnout, when other factors were held constant. An interesting (and important) fact is that black women "who are heads of households are 11 percentage points more likely than similarly situated white men to vote."[9] Overall, survey data from various on-going studies are beginning to suggest that blacks are as likely to vote as their white counterparts, and in some cases more so. The problem, however, is that the overall turnout rates are down, and what is happening is blacks are reaching parity in a shrinking area of activity! The goal in voting should not be, it seems, to aim for "parity," but to seek the goal of maximum registration and turnout.

Clearly, when properly mobilized and motivated, blacks are even more likely to vote in some circumstances than whites. This suggests that registration mechanisms are important in influencing turnout rates. It is also the case that black turnout is heavily affected by such variables as the identity of the candidate (especially if a popular black is running) and the saliency of the office (for example, for the mayoralty or a Jesse Jackson presidential primary contest). In addition, as could be expected, black electoral participation is higher when there is a perceived possibility that the favored candidate has a chance of winning. More often than not, this perception is highly correlated with the size of the black population.

"Empowerment" and political participation are also frequently, and understandably, measured by the number of black elected officials. We have seen a dramatic increase in this category over the last two decades, although the *rate* of increase has slowed recently. In the mid-1960s, prior to the passage of the Voting Rights Act of 1965, there were approximately 280 black elected officials in the United States — at all levels of government. Today, the figure stands around 6,200 (6,016 in 1985, according to the Joint Center for Political Studies). We are constantly reminded, however, that as dramatic as these figures are, they still represent only a tiny fraction of all elected officials in the country — namely, 1.2 percent in 1985.[9] This particular fact should not be especially important if one considers "parity" in other than sheer numerical terms.

Political reality is that some positions are simply more influential and can accomplish much more for larger numbers of people than other positions. Thus, in calculating "empowerment," it is necessary to evaluate the nature of the office held, with all its powers and constraints. Some things we know, for instance, about politics and positions, and this knowledge is sufficient to conclude that it is better to occupy a particular elective office than not, even if that office is minimally important. Congressperson William Gray, formerly as Chairman of the House Budget Committee or in his more recently elected role of Chairman of the House Democratic Caucus, is a positive — even though it is not possible to calculate precisely how much "power" he will have. Chairpersons of congressional committees — gained through seniority — continue to be important legislative figures, even if we cannot stipulate exactly how that influence (empowerment) will function in every case. Likewise, with mayors of cities, important state legislative leaders (California State Assembly Leader Willie Brown, for example), and strategically placed people on local boards of education and other decision-making bodies. Such offices are part of a complex political system, with many checks and balances, but people in such roles are at least in the game as potentially important players.

The point is that, although the overall "black elected official" (BEO) figure is comparatively low, parity is oftentimes a matter of *what* positions are held as it is of *how many* are held. The sheer number of such officials will likely remain low. This, nonetheless, need not suggest that the impact of such people need be minimal. In fact, it may indicate just the contrary. As long as "political empowerment" is so variable, and some positions are more potentially influential than others, it is wise to strive for them in any case. Holding the position per se might not translate into "empowerment," but the lack of having the office (or of having the position in the hands of one perceived as unfriendly) can hardly be considered worthwhile. Such a calculation, in addition, puts a premium on continuity in office. Very many positions in politics, especially in the legislative arena (state and national), carry with them more power as the incumbent gains seniority. This means that persons seeking such jobs ought to plan on a rather long tenure. Only in this way will cherished positions of institutional leadership come, and with them, more power. (There are at least three black congresspersons in 1989 who ought to be poised in the near future to be seriously considered for House Speaker and Democratic Party Majority Leader.)

An important factor in such deliberations, and one that should concern those interested in parity and political empowerment, is that it is still the case that most blacks are elected to office mainly when there is a sizeable black constituency. The more blacks there are in the particular district's or city's electorate, the greater the likelihood that blacks will be elected to office. This means that, for the most part, white voters still prefer white candidates over black candidates. In this realm of analysis, one cannot say that blacks have reached political parity until a black candidate can run in an election in a majority white district and have an equal chance of being elected. For this reason, we will continue to see attention paid to various structures and forms of electoral arrangements: district versus at-large elections; run-off primaries; partisan or non-partisan elections. It is known, for example, that blacks fare better when contesting for office in a district system than one based on at-large elections.[10]

It is also the case that there have been and will continue to be situations where a black is elected to serve a predominantly white constituency. But as a general proposition, this condition does not prevail. Black candidates must rely heavily on black voters in order to contest seriously for office.

It is virtually impossible in today's environment to "prove" that race is the motivating factor in one's vote, but survey data are useful (if limited) sources to consult. In a real sense we cannot expect significant political empowerment of blacks if the attitudes of whites and blacks on a range of important issues are not shared. Black Americans are a distinct minority, thus, what white Americans believe — and how they proceed to behave based on those beliefs — is very important. Here we find rather striking dissimilarities.

Political Attitudes

What is readily apparent in examining a plethora of survey studies is that black Americans are far more inclined than white Americans to favor government spending for social welfare programs. To the extent that labels such as "liberal" and "conservative" have meaning (and in a general way, they do), blacks are one of the most liberal groups in the society, in terms of socio-economic issues. At the same time, blacks accept the basic tenets of a market-economy, but they are much less optimistic than their white counterparts that such an economy will operate fairly and without racist consequences. Blacks perceive a wider gap between democratic theory of equality and justice on the one hand, and actual practice on the other.

Another crucial attitudinal point is found with black and white elected officials. One study asked the officials to agree or disagree with the following statement:[11] "True democracy is limited in the United States because of the special privileges enjoyed by business and industry." Seventy percent of black officials agreed with this statement, but only 26 percent of white officials. And in the same vein, the following proposition was put: "It is the responsibility of the entire society, through its government, to guarantee everyone housing, income, and leisure." Seventy-six percent of black officials subscribed to this view; compared to 30 percent of white officials agreed. Clearly, one could suggest that generally the attitudes of blacks (at the mass and leadership levels) on the proper role of government in the economy vis-a-vis the poor are at substantial variance with those of whites. Given such disparity in views, one has to be realistic about the limits to black political empowerment.

At the same time, one should not be overly pessimistic. Recent survey data — taken after the presidential election — would indicate stronger support for liberal programs than might be expected. The following questions were asked:[12]

During the next four years, do *you want* the federal government:

a) to pay more attention, less attention, or the same amount of attention to the concerns of blacks?

More	Less	Same	DK/NA
32%	10%	51%	7%

b) to spend more money on education, spend less, or about the same amount of money on education?

More	Less	Same	DK/NA
71%	3%	24%	2%

Some sharp and important attitudinal differences show up on questions asked in a nationwide survey dealing with race and public policies:[13]

Overall, do you think blacks and other minorities have the same opportunities as whites in the United States, or not?

	All	White	Black	Hispanic
	%	%	%	%
Yes, same	54	58	28	27
No, do not	42	37	69	69
Don't know	4	5	3	4

In the past 25 years, do you think the country has moved closer to equal opportunity among the races, or farther away from it, or has there been no movement?

	All	White	Black	Hispanic
	%	%	%	%
Closer	84	87	63	73
Farther away	5	4	11	18
No movement	7	5	18	9
Don't know	4	4	7	—

Do you think it is possible to achieve equal opportunity among the races in the United States, or not?

	All	White	Black	Hispanic
	%	%	%	%
Yes, possible	71	72	71	63
No, is not	24	23	25	37
Already have	—	—	—	—
Don't know	5	5	3	—

Do you think blacks and other minorities should receive preference in hiring to make up for past inequalities, or not?

	All	White	Black	Hispanic
	%	%	%	%
Yes	15	10	48	31
No	79	85	44	64
Don't Know	6	6	9	5

Do you think blacks and other minorities should receive preference in college admissions to make up for past inequalities, or not?

	All	White	Black	Hispanic
	%	%	%	%
Yes	18	14	44	46
No	76	81	47	55
Don't know	5	5	10	—

There have been some changes over time. Note the following:[14]

Do you think the United States government is paying too much attention, too little attention, or about the right amount of attention to the needs of blacks?

	Oct. 1980	Oct. 1988
	%	%
Too much	24	14
Too little	30	36
Right amount	36	41
DK/NA	10	9

Essentially, what these kinds of surveys reveal is a sense of the environment in which one is operating. In talking about empowerment, it is advisable (especially for a minority group) to be aware of the context. There are several ways of analyzing this, and no one particular interpretation should be relied on. Reading accurate meaning into trend data or into snap-shot, timebound polls is problematic at best. But, with intelligent caveats, understanding political attitudes can be important to a discussion of the various dimensions of the subject of parity. Opinion polls at best provide signals. They might reveal areas of policy opportunity. They by no means should dictate action completely. (*Brown v. Board* probably would not have resulted if the NAACP Legal Defense Fund had decided to file law suits based on poll data in the 1930s, 1940s, and 1950s.) But, they can indicate likely preferable strategies at a given time. The civil rights movement has a long illustrious history of ability to understand the possibilities and limits of such data at any given moment — and over time. At the same time, one should not reject the possibility, slight or great, of changing unfavorable attitudes. Attitudes stem from values and interests, and these have been known to change over time.

The discussion thus far has not dealt with the role of the courts, but the judiciary should not be overlooked. Indeed, as is certainly known by readers of *The State of Black America*, this branch has been fundamentally instrumental in civil rights law over the decades. If the Supreme Court in the near future — to the year 2000 — does not appear to be very like the Warren Court of the 1950s and 1960s, it is not necessarily the case that this spells irreparable doom for black political empowerment. The United States Constitution constructed a three branch "separation of powers' system, with each branch capable in different ways of checking the others. Last year's *The State of Black America* correctly called attention to the relationship between black empowerment and the Senate's rejection of the Robert Bork nomination to the Supreme Court. Senators from southern states, where once, not too long ago, blacks could not register to vote, voted against Bork, and to protect the seats an enfranchised black electorate helped them to win. *That was black empowerment!* There *are* checks in the system that have to be utilized. If a court decision is unfavorable, it need not be irrevocable. The Civil Rights Restoration Act passed by Congress is an obvious case in point.

Precisely because the political system is fragmented in many ways, and offers several points of access, this facilitates a group's quest for empowerment. It means that there are optional routes. For years, the executive and legislative branches were unresponsive to demands for justice and equality. Litigation had to be pursued, and the federal courts led the way with landmark decisions. (While other groups in the society were mobilizing mass electorates and capturing political offices of institutional power, blacks had to file protracted lawsuits, debate the meaning of the Constitution, and literally prove they were human beings. Thus, seriously delaying the route to political empowerment.) As the current judicial orientation of the Supreme Court tends to lean away from the direction established by the Court under Chief Justice Earl Warren, this means that other avenues must be pursued. This puts added emphasis on using the franchise in concerted, specific, self-interested ways. It means voters can ask candidates very specific questions, the answers to which they can use in holding them accountable.

This is, indeed, an acceptable and an expected form of democratic governance. It is, in fact, the first way a group can tell whether it has even a modicum of power — namely, does it have control directly over its elected representatives? If the answer is negative, the remainder of the discussion becomes moot. If affirmative, then the process of gauging a group's strength — empowerment — can begin. But first, the elected representatives must be subject to reward or punishment directly by the group, without any intervening variables. This leads to the third, and final, aspect of the subject — Public Policies. Organizing, voting, protesting, suing, even changing attitudes, are all fundamentally important factors in the empowerment equation. But they are all prelude.

Public Policies

Ultimately, the best and simplest test of political empowerment is in the results: Did you get what you wanted?

The clearest way to begin that assessment is to focus on the agenda: What did you try to get?

This means that black political empowerment is to be measured by clear and specific objectives. Last year's recommendations in *The State of Black America* contained reference to several specific pieces of legislation — the Universal Voter Registration Act; the Family Welfare Reform Act of 1987 (H.R. 1720); the Civil Rights Restoration Act; the Fair Housing Amendments. Presumably, this year's

119

recommendations will be no less specific. The more specific, the easier to hold accountable and the easier to assess strength. Broad general language will be less than useful; it provides too much latitude for decision-makers to reinterpret and to evade.

This emphasis has other important implications. We know there will be several organizations setting forth various "black agendas." This might serve the cause of pluralism and healthy diversity, but hardly the goal of certainty and accountability. The onus, at first, is on those groups with discernible, identifiable black constituencies to come together and fashion a reasonably coherent, unified policy agenda — the National Urban League, the Congressional Black Caucus, the NAACP, the Rainbow Coalition, and any others that perceive themselves as legitimate representatives of a black constituency. Here, of course, we talk about "coalitions," but this has to have concrete meaning in terms of specific targets. And this means beginning with quite specific actionable proposals. To be sure, they might have to be modified — exactly how much modification, given the level of political participation and the attitudinal environment already discussed, will help answer: What did you get?

A final point should be made on the subject of "empowerment." No group, and certainly not a minority group, is ultimately and permanently empowered. It is a fluid, evolving matter, but it is discernible. And its discernibility begins with the definition — that is: What did you seek?

The State Of Black Higher Education: Crisis and Promise

Reginald Wilson, Ph.D.

INTRODUCTION

The circumstance of blacks in higher education in America represents both crisis and promise. The crisis is detailed in dismal statistics in the sections of this report that follow. The base outline of the crisis can be succinctly summarized: high dropout rates from high school; declining college enrollments; low participation in science and mathematics; low participation in teacher education; overrepresentation in the armed forces; overrepresentation in proprietary schools; and high unemployment for undereducated teenagers. The circumstances for blacks reveal a national crisis that affects the social and economic viability of the black community; the economic viability of the nation; and diminishes the national competitiveness of America in world society.

This crisis is related to the decline in leadership by the executive branch of the federal government in matters affecting civil rights and equal opportunity programs to overcome past discrimination. Indeed, the decline in leadership has not been a passive phenomenon, but has been characterized by an active assault on education funding, affirmative action, and social welfare programs.[1] The clarity of this negative leadership has not been lost on the general populace which has responded with overt acts of bigotry and a retreat from a commitment to social justice that had not been experienced in this country for over 15 years.[2]

With a new administration assuming office on January 20, 1989, there is the possibility of, if not totally reversing, at least halting the decline of black participation in American society. That is the promise. If the new president chooses to take such affirmative steps, he will not be alone. The American Council on Education and the Education Commission of the States in 1987 formed a National Commission on Minority Participation in Education and American Life to address what it saw as an alarming decline in minority involvement in society's universities and in the economy. That Commission issued a clarion call statement, "One-Third of A Nation," on May 23, 1988, calling on American institutions, particularly higher education, to renew their commitment to equal opportunity and to redouble their efforts to accomplish this achievement during the next 20 years.[3]

Various colleges and universities have begun to respond to that challenge, and in the 1986 and 1987 higher education enrollment figures we are witnessing a modest, but real, halting of the decline in enrollments for the first time in the decade of the 1980s. The question before the 41st president, the 101st Congress, and the nation, is do we have the will to sustain and expand those tentative gains to accomplish, unlike the 1960s, a *permanent* state of progress for blacks in American higher educationl? The initiatives of 1989 will begin to give us an answer to that all important question.

ENROLLMENT TRENDS IN HIGHER EDUCATION

Between 1976 and 1986, "the percentage of young people completing high school in the 18-to-24-year-old age cohort has improved more for blacks than for any other racial or ethnic group (see Table 1)."[4] The high school completion rate increased from 67.5 percent in 1976 to 76.4 percent in 1986. Black females completed high school at a higher rate than black males throughout this period. However, black males experienced a larger gain. The gap between black completion rates and those of whites narrowed during this decade (whites remained relatively stable at 82.4 percent in 1976 and 83.1 percent in 1986). Nevertheless, nearly one-fourth of all blacks continue to leave school without a diploma, and the dropout rate in inner-city schools is even higher.

Studies of black participation in the Scholastic Aptitude Test and the Advanced Placement Test show promising increases both in numbers and higher score attainment.[5] Similar successes have been noted in the American College Test and the National Assessment of Educational Progress over the past five years. Despite unacceptable dropout rates, nevertheless, it can be said that the 1988 cohort of black high school graduates is the largest and best prepared of any black group in history.[6] The foregoing fact, therefore, makes it even more paradoxical that, as this improvement in high school graduation rates and academic preparation has been accomplished, during the same decade, 1976 to 1986, black college enrollment steadily declined until 1986.

The participation rate being discussed is the "enrolled-in-college" rate, which identifies the percentage of high school graduates who are actually enrolled in college in October of any given year. As Table 2 indicates, blacks had equal enrolled-in-college participation rates to whites in 1976, which makes false the myth that when given the opportunity and the resources blacks do not desire to attend college. We must look elsewhere than simple motivation to explain why 10 years later the black participation rate had slipped disastrously from 33 percent in 1976 to 28 percent in 1986. However, as mentioned earlier, the *number* of blacks enrolled increased slightly from 1984 to 1986 by about 5,000 students. However, this increase did not make up for the loss of over 30,000 black students from the peak of 1980. Moreover, this increase was almost entirely at the graduate level. Blacks in undergraduate school showed no appreciable increase between 1984 and 1986.

The black enrollment decline is compounded by the particular loss of blacks in four-year colleges (see Table 3), while every other minority group showed increases in these key institutions to baccalaureate degree attainment and the pathway to graduate and professional school. Between 1984 and 1986, black four-year enrollment declined by 2,000 students.

Table 1

High School Completion Rates and Enrolled-in-College Participation Rates of 18-to-24-Year-Old High School Graduates in Institutions of Higher Education by Race/Ethnicity, 1976 to 1986

Total Population

	Total Population (000)	High School Graduates (000)	High School Completion Rate(a) (Percentages)	Enrolled in College (b) (000)	Enrolled-in-College Participation Rate (Percentages)
1976	26,919	21,677	80.5	7,181	33.1
1977	27,331	22,008	80.5	7,142	32.5
1978	27,647	22,309	80.7	6,995	31.4
1979	27,974	22,421	80.1	6,991	31.2
1980	28,130	22,745	80.8	7,226	31.8
1981	28,965	23,343	80.6	7,575	32.5
1982	28,846	23,291	80.7	7,678	33.0
1983	28,580	22,988	80.4	7,477	32.5
1984	28,031	22,870	81.6	7,591	33.2
1985	27,122	22,349	82.4	7,537	33.7
1986	26,512	21,766	82.1	7,397	34.0

White

	Total Population (000)	High School Graduates (000)	High School Completion Rate(a) (Percentages)	Enrolled in College (b) (000)	Enrolled-in-College Participation Rate (Percentages)
1976	23,119	19,046	82.4	6,276	33.0
1977	23,430	19,292	82.3	6,209	32.2
1978	23,650	19,526	82.6	6,077	31.1
1979	23,895	19,614	82.1	6,119	31.2
1980	23,975	19,786	82.5	6,334	32.0
1981	24,486	20,123	82.2	6,548	32.5
1982	24,206	19,944	82.4	6,593	33.1
1983	23,899	19,644	82.2	6,464	32.9
1984	23,347	19,374	83.0	6,526	33.7
1985	22,632	18,917	83.6	6,501	34.4
1986	22,008	18,280	83.1	6,239	34.1

Black

	Total Population (000)	High School Graduates (000)	High School Completion Rate(a) (Percentages)	Enrolled in College (b) (000)	Enrolled-in-College Participation Rate (Percentages)
1976	3,316	2,238	67.5	748	33.4
1977	3,387	2,287	67.5	722	31.6
1978	3,451	2,340	67.8	695	29.7
1979	3,511	2,356	67.1	696	29.5
1980	3,555	2,480	69.8	688	27.7
1981	3,779	2,680	70.9	749	27.9
1982	3,872	2,743	70.8	767	28.0
1983	3,865	2,741	70.9	742	27.1
1984	3,863	2,885	74.7	786	27.2
1985	3,716	2,809	75.6	734	26.1
1986	3,665	2,801	76.4	801	28.6

Hispanic (c)

	Total Population (000)	High School Graduates (000)	High School Completion Rate(a) (Percentages)	Enrolled in College (b) (000)	Enrolled-in-College Participation Rate (Percentages)
1976	1,551	862	55.6	309	35.8
1977	1,609	880	54.7	277	31.5
1978	1,672	935	55.9	254	27.2
1979	1,754	968	55.2	292	30.2
1980	1,963	1,054	53.7	315	29.9
1981	2,052	1,144	55.8	342	29.9
1982	2,000	1,153	57.7	337	29.2
1983	2,025	1,110	54.8	349	31.4
1984	2,017	1,212	60.0	362	29.9
1985	2,223	1,396	62.8	375	26.9
1986	2,513	1,506	59.9	443	29.4

(a) The number of high school graduates was calculated by adding the numbers of individuals in this age group enrolled in college as of October of that year and the number of high school graduates not enrolled in college; these rates include individuals who enrolled in college without receiving a high school diploma or a GED. Several states do not require entering junior college students to have a diploma or GED. Therefore, these high school completion rates will be slightly higher than figures that do not include this relatively small population.

(b) Totals differ from those shown in other tables. These figures came from sample surveys of households rather than surveys of institutions of higher education. The Current Population Survey samples are derived from the decennial census of the U.S. population.

(c) Hispanics may be of any race.

Table 2
Total Enrollment in Institutions of Higher Education by Type of Institution and Race/Ethnicity of Student, biennially, Fall 1976 to Fall 1986 (a)

Type of Institution and Race/Ethnicity of Student	1976 (000)	1978 (000)	1980 (000)	1982 (000)	1984 (000)	1986 (000)	Percentage Change 1984-1986
All Institutions	10,986	11,231	12,087	12,388	12,235	12,501	2.2
White, non-Hispanic	9,076	9,194	9,833	9,997	9,815	9,914	1.0
Total minority	1,691	1,785	1,949	2,059	2,085	2,243	7.6
Black, non-Hispanic	1,033	1,054	1,107	1,101	1,076	1,081	0.5
Hispanic	384	417	472	519	535	624	16.6
Asian	198	235	286	351	390	448	14.9
American Indian	76	78	84	88	84	90	7.1
Nonresident alien	219	253	305	331	335	344	2.7
Four-year Institutions	7,107	7,203	7,565	7,648	7,708	7,826	1.5
White, non-Hispanic	5,999	6,027	6,275	6,306	6,301	6,340	0.6
Total minority	931	975	1,050	1,073	1,124	1,195	6.3
Black, non-Hispanic	604	612	634	612	617	615	–0.3
Hispanic	174	190	217	229	246	278	13.0
Asian	119	138	162	193	223	262	17.5
American Indian	35	35	37	39	38	40	5.3
Nonresident alien	177	201	241	270	282	291	3.2
Two-year Institutions	3,879	4,028	4,521	4,740	4,527	4,675	3.2
White, non-Hispanic	3,077	3,167	3,558	3,692	3,514	3,575	1.7
Total minority	760	810	899	987	961	1,047	8.9
Black, non-Hispanic	429	443	472	489	459	466	1.5
Hispanic	210	227	255	291	289	345	19.4
Asian	79	97	124	158	167	186	11.4
American Indian	41	43	47	49	46	51	10.9
Nonresident alien	42	52	64	61	53	53	0.0

It is important to point out that declines in participation rates affected both black women *and* men. The decline in black male participation was so much more dramatic that some education commentators made the erroneous assumption that black women were doing fine. However, Table 2 illustrates that black women's rate declined from 32 percent to 29 percent during the 1976-1986 decade. It is only in *comparison* to black men that black women seem to be doing better. Our concern, while recognizing the more precipitous decline of black men, should be with the educational attainment of *all* blacks.

As mentioned, black graduate enrollment increased by 5,000 students in 1986, which brought those enrollments back up to the 1976 peak of 72,000 students.[7] Despite this improvement, and including the 1976 peak, blacks have always been underrepresented in graduate schools, and they constitute only five percent of the total students. Creating the faculty of the future will require substantial increases in black enrollment, particularly in Ph.D. programs.

Black enrollment in professional schools is the only index that has shown steady improvement from 1976 to 1986. Yet, we are discussing only 14,000 students who represent only 5.2 percent of the total enrollment. Thus, despite the improvement, blacks are underrepresented in professional schools as in all other institutions of higher education.

THE HISTORICALLY BLACK COLLEGES

The historically black colleges and universities (HBCU) were the backbone of black higher education for over 100 years. As recently as 1965, the majority of blacks in college attended the HBCUs. However, with the availability of Pell grants in 1972 and the desegregation order of white colleges in 1973, blacks flocked to colleges with Federal money in hand, reaching a peak of over a million students in 1980. In 1988, only 16.8 percent of black students attended HBCUs.[8] Between 1976 and 1986, black enrollment in HBCUs, as elsewhere, declined considerably (Table 3). However, 1987 enrollment figures show a slight increase of 4,000 students in these schools. Despite the perception of some analysts that "black students are coming home," it is safe to predict that over 80 percent of black students will continue to attend predominantly white schools in the future, and it is at those institutions that the primary solution of the problem of black under-representation will be accomplished.

Nevertheless, black colleges, like women's colleges, and religious colleges, will continue to play an important and successful role in the education of black and other race youth (12 percent of HBCU enrollments are "other race" students). Despite enrolling only 17 percent of black youth, they award 34 percent of the degrees blacks attain. Moreover, 50 percent of black faculty in research universities obtained their BA from an HBCU. Not only are these institutions more successful in educating black students but also their graduates evidently have higher academic aspirations as a result of that education.[9]

Although 80 percent of black students attending HBCUs attend public colleges, these colleges will be most affected by the present and future consequences of

Table 3

Enrollment in Historically Black Colleges and Universities by Race/Ethnicity, Fall 1976 to Fall 1987

Race/Ethnicity	1976	1980	1982	1984	1986	1987	Percentage 1986-1987	Percentage 1976-1987
Number of HBCUs	105	102	100	104	104	100		
Total	212.120	222.220	216.570	216.050	213.093	217.367	2.0	2.5
Black, non-Hispanic	185,820	185,780	177,000	175,110	176,596	182,019	3.1	-2.0
White, non-Hispanic	18,390	21,480	23,040	23,450	22,651	23,225	2.5	26.3
Asian	610	1,340	1,050	1,350	1,237	1,187	-4.0	94.6
Hispanic	460	1,030	1,070	1,560	1,485	1,588	6.9	245.2
American Indian	180	400	570	240	552	519	-6.0	187.2
Nonresident alien	6,660	12,200	13,840	14,340	10,572	8,829	-16.5	32.6

Note: Details may not add to total because of rounding.

Source: Hill, Susan T., *The Traditionally Black Institutions of Higher Education, 1860 to 1982*. (Washington, D.C.: Government Printing Office, 1984.)

National Association for Equal Opportunity Research Institute, staff analysis of the U.S. Department of Education, Office of Civil Rights unpublished data, fall 1984, 1986, and 1987.

the *Adams* case. This decision, handed down in 1973 by Federal District Judge John H. Pratt, eventually ordered 17 states to dismantle their previously segregated public systems of higher education. This decision has had greater impact on the black public colleges, where non-black enrollment is 12 percent, than on the white public colleges, where black enrollment is only five percent.[10] Indeed, five public black colleges now have more than 50 percent white enrollment. It is likely that more public historically black colleges will be incorporated into their state systems in the future and become predominantly white in their bodies and faculties. Over 30 percent of the faculties of these institutions are now already white.[11]

Yet, the stronger of these institutions will survive as predominantly black and continue to play a critical, though smaller, role in the education of black Americans. It is unlikely, however, that these institutions will gain the laboratories and physical plant facilities to excel in science and technology, which is the wave of the future in careers and professions.

CAUSES OF DECLINE

It is one thing to document the decline of black participation in higher education, but quite another to explain it. Nevertheless, some lines of inquiry do offer compelling arguments. For example, the most clearcut explanation of black decline is a combination of forces in the 1980s which saw the declining value of Pell grants accompanied by an alarming increase in tuition costs and a lessening economic viability of the black community in being able to afford college education.

Between 1976 and 1986, college tuitions nearly doubled while Pell grants did not keep up with inflation.[12] This made the cost of education more prohibitive for low income families which are disproportionately present in the black community. Eighty-five percent of blacks in college require some form of financial aid. Moreover, while the "Reagan revolution" was increasing the income of middle and upper class whites, more blacks were below the poverty line in 1986 than in 1976, and "between 1973 and 1986, average real annual earnings for black males . . . fell by 50 percent."[13] Thus, the ability of black families to send their children to college was considerably diminished by economic considerations.

The volunteer armed services established after the Vietnam War were the most "equal opportunity" employer of all American institutions. Blacks are over one-fourth of the U.S. Army and are overrepresented in the other branches of service as well.[14] Black recruits are more likely to be high school graduates than whites and are more likely to stay in service longer. Nevertheless, the black presence in the more technological fields and in the upper command ranks is not proportional to their numbers. Yet, studies of high school students who say they definitely plan to join the military after completing school show the highest proportion of such students to be black.[15]

As one recruiting device, the military boasts of the availability of the new GI bill, which, they promise recruits, can be used for college after completing their tour of duty. There has not been enough experience with this benefit to determine if, indeed, blacks are going to college after they leave the armed services. If they are not, then the services are, in fact, taking college-eligible young blacks out of the educational pipeline with little likelihood of their return. That, then, represents an overall loss of potential educated leaders for the black community and the nation.

Similarly to the military, proprietary schools have aggressively recruited black students. These for-profit institutions, with their TV and newspaper ads, literally bombard potential students with promises of a quick education and lucrative jobs at completion. A study done for the Association of Independent Colleges and Schools documented that over 30 percent of proprietary enrollments consisted of minority students.[16] As with the military, there is concern as to whether the educational promises of these institutions equal their occupational payoff. There is concern in the educational community about the quality of education offered by these institutions such as to raise doubts about many of them being viable educational alternatives for black high school graduates.[17]

Finally, it must be said that other societal trauma, although this report is not prepared to detail them, impact on black declines in higher education participation. High unemployment of black youth, increasing crime rates, rampant drug abuse, and teenage pregnancies all reduce youth opportunities to pursue higher education. Certainly these circumstances must be addressed by the black community and by the nation if additional progress in education is to be made. Nevertheless, it must be said that if our higher education institutions even did a better job with those it enrolls, the black degree holders would dramatically increase. Measures taken six years after freshman enrollment shows that only 25.6 percent of blacks have attained a baccalaureate degree.[18] Obviously, the productivity of our academic institutions is shameful in getting such a minuscule proportion of blacks through the educational pipeline.

AFFIRMATIVE ACTION

The signing of Executive Order 11246 by President Lyndon B. Johnson in 1965 required all entities, public or private, with 50 employees or more receiving at least $50,000 in Federal contracts, to file affirmative action plans specifying "goals and timetables" to correct under-utilization of minorities and women in their workforces. In addition, Judge Pratt's order desegregating Southern colleges also required those institutions to examine their workforces for increased employment of blacks in faculty and administrative positions. Under the onus of these orders, collegiate institution began to make progress in correcting the minimal representation of blacks on staffs and faculties of higher education institutions.

Between 1975 and 1985, minorities as a whole increased their employment in higher education by 34.3 percent (See Tables 4 and 5). Half the workforce was female in 1985, up from 46 percent in 1975. Women held 59 percent of non-faculty positions, 35 percent of administrative positions, and 27 percent of all faculty positions.[19] Minority women made more gains in higher education employment than their male counterparts. Black females increased employment by 23

Table 4
Full-time Employment in Higher Education by Race/Ethnicity and Sex, 1975, 1983, and 1985

Race/Ethnicity and Sex	1975 Number	1975 Percent	1983 Number	1983 Percent	1985 Number	1985 Percent	Percentage Change 1975-1983	Percentage Change 1983-1985	Percentage Change 1975-1985
Total	1,388,406	100.0	1,588,151	100.0	1,623,145	100.0	14.4	2.2	16.9
Male	749,579	54.0	815,417	51.3	819,256	50.5	8.8	0.5	9.3
Female	638,827	46.0	772,770	48.7	803,889	49.5	21.0	4.0	25.8
White	1,155,794	83.2	1,297,929	81.7	1,310,736	80.8	12.3	1.0	13.4
Male	642,897	46.3	686,313	43.2	681,823	42.0	6.8	-0.7	6.1
Female	512,897	36.9	611,616	38.5	628,913	38.7	19.2	2.8	22.6
Black	167,990	12.1	193,047	12.2	197,213	12.2	14.9	2.2	17.4
Male	70,160	5.1	75,874	4.8	76,238	4.7	8.1	0.5	8.7
Female	97,830	7.0	117,173	7.4	120,975	7.5	19.8	3.2	23.7
Hispanic	35,252	2.5	48,926	3.1	54,028	3.3	38.8	10.4	53.3
Male	19,861	1.4	25,120	1.6	27,426	1.7	26.5	9.2	38.1
Female	15,391	1.1	23,806	1.5	26,602	1.6	54.7	11.7	72.8
Asian	24,709	1.8	41,550	2.6	53,136	3.3	68.2	27.9	115.0
Male	14,074	1.0	24,159	1.5	29,307	1.8	71.7	21.3	108.2
Female	10,635	0.8	17,391	1.1	23,829	1.5	63.5	37.0	124.1
American Indian	4,661	0.3	6,735	0.4	8,032	0.5	44.5	19.3	72.3
Male	2,587	0.2	3,951	0.2	4,462	0.3	52.7	12.9	72.5
Female	2,074	0.1	2,784	0.2	3,570	0.2	34.2	28.2	72.1

Note: Details may not add to total because of rounding.

Source: U.S. Equal Opportunity Commission, "EEO-6 Higher Education Staff Information" surveys. 1975, 1983, and 1985.

Table 5
Full-time Non-Faculty in Higher Education by Race/Ethnicity and Sex, 1975, 1983, and 1985

Race/Ethnicity and Sex	1975 Number	1975 Percent	1983 Number	1983 Percent	1985 Number	1985 Percent	Percentage Change 1975-1983	Percentage Change 1983-1985	Percentage Change 1975-1985
Total	941.576	100.0	1.102.412	100.0	1.134.346	100.0	17.1	2.9	20.5
Male	413.217	43.9	458.838	41.6	465.043	41.0	11.0	1.4	12.5
Female	528.359	56.1	643.610	58.4	669.303	59.0	21.8	4.0	26.7
White	745.847	79.2	857.488	77.8	870.969	76.8	15.0	1.6	16.8
Male	330.604	35.1	360.142	32.7	360.854	31.8	8.9	0.2	9.1
Female	412.243	43.8	497.282	45.1	510.115	45.0	20.6	2.6	23.7
Black	148.244	15.7	173.376	15.7	176.930	15.6	17.0	2.0	19.4
Male	59.266	6.3	65.333	5.9	65.185	5.7	10.2	-0.2	10.0
Female	88.978	9.4	108.143	9.8	111.745	9.9	21.5	3.3	25.6
Hispanic	28.929	3.1	41.470	3.8	45.941	4.0	43.4	10.8	58.8
Male	15.288	1.6	19.880	1.8	21.743	1.9	30.0	9.4	42.2
Female	13.641	1.4	21.590	2.0	24.198	2.1	58.3	12.1	77.4
Asian	14.946	1.6	24.651	2.2	34.032	3.0	64.9	38.1	127.7
Male	6.244	0.7	10.482	1.0	13.984	1.2	67.9	33.4	124.0
Female	8.702	0.9	14.169	1.3	20.048	1.8	62.8	41.5	130.4
American Indian	3.610	0.4	5.427	0.5	6.474	0.6	50.3	19.3	79.3
Male	1.815	0.2	3.001	0.3	3.277	0.3	65.3	9.2	80.6
Female	1.795	0.2	2.426	0.2	3.197	0.3	35.2	31.8	78.1

Note: Includes the following non-faculty employment categories: executive, administrative, managerial, professional, non-faculty, clerical, secretarial, technical, paraprofessional, skilled craft, service and maintenance. Details may not add to total because of rounding.

Source: U.S. Equal Opportunity Commission. "EEO-6 Higher Education Staff Information" surveys, 1975, 1983, and 1985.

131

percent while black males only gained eight percent from 1975 to 1985. In non-faculty positions, black females increased by 25 percent while black males increased only by 10 percent. In fact, between 1983 and 1985, black males declined somewhat (see Table 5).

In faculty positions, during that same decade, the growth of both black males and females was so low as to be negligible (see Table 6): black males 1.5 percent and females 4.3 percent. Indeed, faculty growth was so minimal compared to other groups that actual black percentage representation in the total faculty dropped from 4.4 percent in 1975 to 4.1 percent in 1985. Blacks are minimally represented in the ranks of full professors (2.2 percent) and mostly concentrated in the lower ranks of assistant professors and lecturers. In tenure attainment, blacks fall over 10 points below whites (61 percent versus 72 percent).[20]

The picture that emerges is a precarious one. Blacks declined in graduate school enrollment until 1986 when, not advancing, they simply regained losses. The limited production of Ph.D.s is reflected in the minimal growth of black faculty. Nearly half of the current American faculty are expected to retire by the year 2000. If blacks are to make significant strides in faculty numbers, they must be available with requisite degrees when those vacancies occur. However, given the limited graduate school enrollment, it is doubtful if sufficient black Ph.D.s will be produced to replace the current black retiring faculty, not even considering future faculty needs. Graduate schools have lessened their active recruitment of black graduate students, unlike the activities of the 1960s and 1970s in response to real threats of Federal action. In the "benign" 1980s, institutions feel little pressure for affirmative action compliance and, thus, make minimal efforts to recruit students.

Institutions and the Executive branch of the Federal government must be convinced to provide leadership in developing aggressive programs to produce black scholars for future faculty positions as acts of national and institutional self-interest. We are wasting potential talent that could enrich the nation. That message must be heard soon as the cost and programmatic effort to halt the current national malaise will be prohibitive.

Despite the modest representation of blacks in faculty position, the myth is still prevalent that less qualified blacks are displacing qualified whites in academic slots. For example, in a study by the Institute for Social Research at the University of Michigan that asked white respondents "What do you think the chances are these days that a white person would be denied a promotion or a job in favor of an equally or less qualified black?" Seventy-five percent answered "very likely" or "somewhat likely."[21] However, a study by the Carnegie Commission revealed, after controlling for degree attainment and scholarly productivity, the black faculty members systematically achieve tenure and promotion at lower rates than whites.[22] Indeed, although whites held only 78 percent of the doctorates, they occupied 87 percent of the tenure-track faculty positions.[23]

Maintaining the myth of unqualified blacks displacing qualified whites tends to retard the efforts of white academics to work for increasing black representation

Table 6
Full-time Faculty in Higher Education by
Race/Ethnicity and Sex, 1975, 1983, and 1985

Race/Ethnicity and Sex	1975 Number	1975 Percent	1983 Number	1983 Percent	1985 Number	1985 Percent	Percentage Change 1975-1983	Percentage Change 1983-1985	Percentage Change 1975-1985
Total	446,830	100.0	485,739	100.0	488,799	100.0	8.7	0.6	9.4
Male	336,362	75.3	356,579	73.4	354,213	72.5	6.0	-0.7	5.3
Female	110,468	24.7	129,160	26.6	134,586	27.5	16.9	4.2	21.8
White	409,947	91.7	440,505	90.7	439,767	90.0	7.5	-0.2	7.3
Male	312,293	69.9	326,171	67.1	320,969	65.7	4.4	-1.6	2.8
Female	97,654	21.9	114,334	23.5	118,798	24.3	17.1	3.9	21.7
Black	19,746	4.4	19,571	4.0	20,283	4.1	-0.9	3.6	2.7
Male	10,894	2.4	10,541	2.2	11,053	2.3	-3.2	4.9	1.5
Female	8,852	2.0	9,030	1.9	9,230	1.9	2.0	2.2	4.3
Hispanic	6,323	1.4	7,456	1.5	8,087	1.7	17.9	8.5	27.9
Male	4,573	1.0	5,240	1.1	5,683	1.2	14.6	8.5	24.3
Female	1,750	0.4	2,216	0.5	2,404	0.5	26.6	8.5	37.4
Asian	9,763	2.2	16,889	3.5	19,104	3.9	73.0	13.1	95.7
Male	7,830	1.8	13,677	2.8	15,323	3.1	74.7	12.0	95.7
Female	1,933	0.4	3,222	0.7	3,781	0.8	66.7	17.3	95.6
American Indian	1,051	0.2	1,308	0.3	1,558	0.3	24.5	19.1	48.2
Male	772	0.2	950	0.2	1,185	0.2	23.1	24.7	53.5
Female	279	0.1	358	0.1	373	0.1	28.3	4.2	33.7

Note: Includes full-time faculty who are in non-tenure earning positions, tenured faculty, and faculty who are non-tenured, but in positions which lead to consideration for tenure. Details may not add to total because of rounding.

Source: U.S. Equal Opportunity Commission, "EEO-6 Higher Education Staff Information" surveys, 1975, 1983, and 1985.

in the faculty. Holding such mythical beliefs, despite strong evidence to the contrary, allows such inaction to be rationalized without guilt. It is the responsibility of university and graduate school leadership to speak out strongly against such myths with convincing arguments to persuade white faculty and deans that it is in their institutional self-interest to make strenuous efforts to increase the number of black graduate students and to recruit them for the considerable faculty vacancies expected to occur in the next few years.

THE PROMISE

The crisis of black underrepresentation in education and American life spelled out in the previous pages is dismal in its litany and real in its impact. However, increasingly the higher education community is being made aware of its responsibilities and much discussion in legislatures, state capitols, and Congress is being focused on the crisis. The academy, with leadership from the American Council on Education, the Education Commission of the States, the American Association of State Colleges and Universities, and other higher education entities, is beginning to ask itself what it must do to marshall its resources to respond to this crisis. That is the promise. However, so far, much of the activity has been in workshops, seminars, conferences, publications, etc.

It is now time to act to fulfill that promise. It is now time to implement strategies that we know will work from years of experience with a number of projects and programs that are not sufficiently replicated or wide-spread to have an impact on the declining numbers of blacks in many areas of higher education. We do know what to do, as a higher education community, and we, in a small part, are doing some exemplary things.

For example, in undergraduate recruitment and retention: Eastern Michigan University has a College Day program targetted to junior high school minority students and their parents. Successful participants in the program are guaranteed admission to one of several public and private Michigan colleges. In California, 22 public and private colleges participate in a consortium that emphasizes engineering, mathematics, and science projects for minority students.

In graduate schools: the Woodrow Wilson National Fellowship Foundation established in 1987 a Black Scholars program to inspire and assist black students to enter graduate study to prepare for college teaching careers. Ohio State University brings to campus each year approximately 200 students from 60 historically black colleges to be oriented and counseled toward graduate and professional study. The McKnight Black Doctoral Fellowship provides generous stipends and tuition to promising black scholars to attain the Ph.D. in arts, science, business, and engineering.

For faculty: the state universities in Michigan are provided stipends by the legislature to invite a number of Martin Luther King-Cesar Chavez-Rosa Parks Visiting Professors to campus for periods from a week to a semester. Several of these visiting faculty are later recruited for permanent faculty positions. The University of North Carolina offers five post-doctoral research fellowships for periods of up to two years for minority scholars to pursue full-time research while being required to teach not more than one course per year.

All of these programs are innovative and exciting. Suffice it to say that despite their promise — five fellowships here, six students there — they are insufficient to halt the dismally declining statistics. Therefore, what is needed is not small, campus-restricted programs, as welcome as they are, but a national effort of serious magnitude. In 1945, at the end of World War II, with Europe devastated, the United States mounted the Marshall Plan, sending millions of dollars, technical assistance, and food to aid the recovery of England and Europe. Similarly, when we fell behind in space with the Russian launching of Sputnik, we passed the National Defense Education Act and poured millions of dollars into the training of scientists and engineers that ultimately resulted in landing a spacecraft on the moon. We now need a Marshall Plan for America to save itself, or the escalating problems of the one-third of our nation trapped at the bottom will drain all of our ability to prosper. It is in the self-interest of all Americans to see that that does not occur. The question is do we have the will as a society to regain the sense of commitment to social justice and equal opportunity that sparked our national momentum in the 1960s and, through our higher education institutions, develop the black leadership and professionals that will truly make us the equalitarian society our Constitution promised us we would be. We have had the crisis and the promise. We await the fulfillment.

Knowing the Black Church:
What It Is and Why

C. Eric Lincoln, Ph.D.

INTRODUCTION

The independent black church movement is generally recognized as the first black stride toward freedom and responsibility. The Black Church as a distinctive communion traces it ancestry to the Free African Society which was formed in Philadelphia in 1787 to escape the segregation and denigration in the white churches of that day. The Free African Society was not itself a church, but a sort of transitional fellowship designed to sustain the faith, encourage moral responsibility, and provide mutual aid for its members until a more satisfactory solution could be found. Two local churches were eventually spun off by the society: The African Protestant Episcopal Church of St. Thomas and Bethel African Methodist Episcopal Church. Both churches were dedicated in July of 1794. St. Thomas remained within the existing Anglican (Episcopalian) communion; Bethel eventually severed all connections with the white Methodists and went on to become the "Mother" of the first black denomination.

THE BIG SEVEN

The Black Church is usually understood to mean the historic black communions or denominations which are independent of white control, and which maintain their own structures of governance, finance, ritual, worship, and out-reach. Because segregation remains an entrenched phenomenon in religion in America, black churches or congregations, even when affiliated with white communions, are with rare exceptions all black, and the spiritual and ritual ambience observed there is rarely different from the norm in the independent black churches. In consequence, the "Greater Black Church," or the GBC refers to black congregations collectively, while "Black Church" is reserved for the churches of the historically independent black communions.

Seven national communions of the Black Church account for about 84 percent of the black Christians in this country. Three of the communions are Methodist; three are Baptist, and the other one is Pentecostal, The Church of God in Christ. The remaining 16 percent of black Christians are distributed among the white Protestant and Catholic communions and a scattering of smaller independent black churches with limited local or provincial representation. The Islamic communions are not included in this breakdown of black churches, but it should not be overlooked that the Muslims constitute a growing presence in this country, and their impact upon the black estate and the country at large must be a consideration wherever religious interests are seriously addressed.

THE BLACK METHODIST CONNECTION

The first independent black denominations were Methodist, although the first independent black local churches were Baptist. There was a black Baptist church established at Silver Bluff, South Carolina, sometime between 1750 and 1773, and led by David George and George Liele. This was a slave church, of course, and closely monitored by the prevailing slave interests. There were a handful of other unitary black Baptist churches in Georgia and Virginia before the outbreak of the Civil War, but under the rigid strictures of the slave system, there was no option for the establishment of a unified black communion or denomination. Nevertheless, Charles H. Wesley, the late church historian estimated that by 1790 there were 18,000 black Baptists and 12,000 black Methodists in America. By far the overwhelming majority of these held a kind of auxillary status in white churches of the South. It remained for the free blacks in the North to make the historic departure from the established tradition in which whites assumed spiritual leadership over blacks as a routine part of their alleged property rights.

Large numbers of blacks were identified with the Methodist Church from its inception. John Wesley baptized the first black Methodists in 1758. Ten years later blacks figured prominently in the establishment of the John Street Church in New York City, the first Methodist Church in America. By 1796, fully one-fifth of the membership of the Methodist Episcopal Church was black. One of the catalysts to the extraordinary black interest in Methodism was the strong anti-slavery stand of the early Methodist Church. Another was the uncomplicated doctrine and ritual which lent itself to the needs of a people unexposed to formal education. But among the most effective attractions of all was the Methodist acceptance of black preachers such as Richard Allen (who was permitted to hold services at five in the morning at St. George's Methodist Church in Philadelphia) and "Black Harry" Hosier. Hosier, who has been identified as one of the greatest preachers America has produced, traveled the countryside with Bishop Asbury in the early days of Methodism preaching to large, enthusiastic mixed crowds in the towns and cities, and playing a significant role in helping to anchor the new faith on the American frontier.

The ever-increasing number of blacks in their churches began to create problems for the racially sensitive white Christians of *whatever* denomination, and the physical segregation of the races inside the churches, denial of common participation in church rituals and an ever-increasing schedule of demeaning denigration wherever possible eventually broke the pattern of relationships established for blacks in white churches, and the Black Church emerged in consequence.

The African Methodist Episcopal Church (AMEC)

The first black denomination originated when the representatives of several independent black Methodist churches along the eastern seaboard met at Mother Bethel in Philadelphia in April of 1816 and formed "an Ecclesiastical Compact, one body under the name and style of the African Methodist Episcopal Church."

Richard Allen, the pastor of Mother Bethel, was elected bishop of this first black denomination. The Rubicon of black spiritual independence had been crossed, and the first organized commitment to black spiritual responsibility had been made. Under Allen's leadership, the Negro Convention Movement begun in 1830 brought together the combined efforts of black Christians of whatever persuasion on behalf of abolition and freedom. The Convention Movement may well be counted as the direct descendent of the Free African Society, and the first political expression of the Black Church.

The AME Church from its inception maintained a strong interest in education and trained clergy. It founded Wilberforce University, the first black college founded by black people, in 1856. Other AME schools are Morris Brown, (Atlanta); Paul Quinn, (Waco, Texas); Allen, (Columbia, South Carolina); and Edward Waters, (Jacksonville, Florida). *The AME Review,* founded 1881, is the oldest journal in the world owned and published by black people. The AME Church is the largest of the black Methodist communions, claiming a current membership of about three million, with more than a million members in 2200 churches in Africa and the Caribbean. The annual budget of the AME Church is about $7 million. It has no centralized national office or chief administrative officer. Between General Conferences which meet every four years, the business of the church is carried on through a General Secretary. The AME Publishing House is located in Nashville, Tennessee. In addition to its five colleges, the church supports a junior college, two seminaries, and two Job Corps Centers.

The African Methodist Episcopal Zion Church (AMEZ)

In the late eighteenth century, despite the popularity of Methodism among black believers, the problems of racism and segregation in the white churches of all denominations were quite general. But, there was a growing unwillingness on the part of black Christians to submit to the undignified separatist practices a segregated church demanded. The notion that God was "not a respecter of persons," and that when God called you to discipleship He called you to freedom and responsibility was a basic tenent of black religion then, and remains so to this day. As the rebellion against segregation became more pervasive, the withdrawal of blacks from white congregations to form independent black churches became common wherever a black church would be tolerated.

By 1793, the black membership of the John Street Methodist Church in New York City stood at about 40 percent, and the continuing efforts to maintain effective segregation in that church soon precipitated a racial crisis in the congregation. In addition to the routine segregation in seating and in the celebration of the eucharist, blacks were refused ordination as preachers and denied membership in the church's Annual Conference, without which they could not participate in the governance of the body of which they were members. In 1796, under the leadership of Peter Williams, a black caucus in the John Street Church organized an "African Chapel" which met in a cabinet-maker's shop until a church house was completed in 1801. The new church was incorporated as the "Zion Church." The charter of the "Zion" church required that its property be owned by a board of trustees, and that only trustees of African descent could act on behalf of the church. Here the Zionites were no doubt instructed by the unhappy experience the AMEs of Philadelphia had had with the white Methodists there who unsuccessfully laid claim to Mother Bethel and all its property. However, ecclesiastical oversight, including the appointment of pastors remained in the hands of the John Street Church from which they had fled.

In October of 1820, Zion Chapel and a sister independent black church, Asbury African Methodist Episcopal adopted their own discipline. On June 21, 1821, a second black denomination was born when church representatives from Long Island, New Haven, and Philadelphia met with Zion and Asbury to form the African Methodist Episcopal Zion Church. This new African communion was invited to merge with the original AME Church led by Bishop Richard Allen, but declined to do so preferring its own separate identity. In 1822, James Varick was elected the first bishop of the AME Zion Church.

The "Zionites," like their counterpart "Allenites," were strongly opposed to slavery and deeply involved in the abolitionist cause and the Underground Railroad. Traditionally known as "The Freedom Church," Zion counted among its early members such historic figures as Harriet Tubman, Frederick Douglass, and Sojourner Truth.

The most recent statistics credit the African Methodist Episcopal Zion Church with about 500,000 members including 100,000 in Africa and the Caribbean. In 1984, the church claimed 3,000 clergy serving 2,700 churches in the United States and 200 overseas.

Its current budget is estimated at more than three and one-half million dollars. The church has no centralized headquarters and no chief administrative officer, but the offices of the General Secretary and the publishing house are located in Charlotte, North Carolina. The administrative body of the Church is the *Connectional Council,* which meets once each year. The Board of Bishops exercises supervision of the church between quadrennial sessions of the General Conference.

The Christian Methodist Episcopal Church (CME)

The Christian Methodist Episcopal Church is a relative late-comer to the ranks of black Methodism, having completed the transition only after the Civil War. Unlike the two "African" churches, the CME church had its origin in the South and in the Southern branch of the Methodist Episcopal Church which split from the national body over the issue of slavery in 1844. Because blacks in the South were subject to the rigid condition of bondage, their determination to assume responsibility for their own spiritual destiny could not come until their emancipation was secure, but it was set in motion even before the war had ended.

One of the classic features of the African churches was their strong, competitive effort in the recruitment of black Christians who held membership in white congregations. Theirs was a "missionary zeal" in the most literal sense as they campaigned to bring black Christians into black churches, which they felt would be more compatible with their interests and welfare. The Southern white church was alarmed at the fervent defection which was rapidly depleting its black membership, but it was hardly disposed to change the practices blacks found offensive. At its General Conference of 1866, the Southern Methodist Church decided that if by the next General Conference (four years later), there was "sufficient interest" demonstrated within its black constituency for separation, it would bless and assist its black members in forming a separate communion of their own. In consequence of this arrangement, representatives of black churches met in Jackson, Tennessee, in 1870 to found a third black communion which took the name of "Colored Methodist Episcopal Church in America." (This historic name was modified to Christian Methodist Church in 1954.) The senior Bishop of the Methodist Church South presided over the proceedings, and the new black denomination was launched with the general good will and support of the white church, out of which it came, on December 15, 1870. William H. Miles and Richard Vanderhorst were elected bishops five days later.

The Christian Methodist Episcopal Church is the smallest of the three major black Methodist bodies. Its national membership is approximately 850,000 with an overseas constituency of about 75,000 (1984). Like the AMEs, the CMEs have more churches (3,000) than clergy (2,400). The General Conference is the legislative body, and it is presided over by the College of Bishops. The Judicial Council, made up of four ministers and five lay persons, serves as a court of appeals. The church supports five colleges — Lane, Texas, Paine, Miles, and Mississippi Industrial. It also supports Phillips School of Theology, a constituent of The Interdenominational Theological Seminary in Atlanta. Its national headquarters is in Memphis, Tennessee, as is its publishing house. The CME national budget is estimated at about $52.7 million.

Other black Methodist communions include the Reformed Methodist Union Episcopal Church, the African Union First Colored Methodist Protestant Church, The Union American Methodist Episcopal Church, and the Free Christian Zion Church of Christ. All of these are small but independent black denominations.

THE BAPTIST CONVENTIONS

The first independent black Baptist church emerged in the final half of the 18th century. Today, there are at least eight black Baptist denominations identifiable in the United States. The three principal ones are well known and national in scope. Less well known and more regional in outreach are smaller groups such as the National Primitive Baptists (250,000), The Free Will Baptists (100,000), the National Baptist Evangelical and Soul Saving Assembly (50,000), and the Free For All Missionary Baptists (10,000). Another 75,000 black Baptists are in the (white) Southern Baptist Convention, and perhaps 150,000 others belong to the predominantly white American Baptist Convention. All in all, the Baptists have by far the largest black affiliation of any church in America, and their impact upon American religious life from Nat Turner to Martin Luther King, Jr., has been in keeping with their members and their zeal.

NATIONAL BAPTIST CONVENTION, USA/INC. (NBCI)

The earliest black Baptists whose churches dotted the Southeastern slave states before the Civil War were the first black Christians to try to find their own religious identity in America. However, the strictures of the slave security system and the independent nature of Baptist polity delayed the effective formation of denominational structures until after the Civil War. In the white churches blacks often out-numbered the whites in the congregation. In 1846, for example, the Baptist church in Georgetown, South Carolina, had 33 white members and 798 blacks. A similar situation prevailed in Natchez, Mississippi, where 62 white Christians shared a church with 380 blacks. But in every instance the white contingent, whatever its numbers, was in complete control of church polity, and blacks were subject to humiliating patterns of rejection and prejudice. So wherever possible the blacks formed their own churches. The roster of historic black Baptist churches is an impressive one. There was a black Baptist church at Petersburg, Virginia, as early as 1776; and First African Baptist at Richmond organized in 1780. In 1785, black Baptist churches were established at Savannah, Georgia, and in Williamsburg. By the end of the first decade of the 19th century, the Joy Street Baptist Church in Boston, Abyssinian Baptist in New York, and the First African Baptist Church of Philadelphia had all been established as strong beacons of spiritual freedom.

The first attempts to bring the scattered, independent black Baptist churches into some kind of organizational framework began with the organization of regional "associations" in Ohio in 1834 and 1836. In 1840, the American Baptist Missionary Convention was organized, presaging perhaps the three major conventions of today.

In 1867, the Consolidated American Baptist Missionary Convention met in Nashville, Tennessee. This meeting represented the first attempt to create a national convention. By 1868, the ABMC reported a constituency of 100,000 black Baptists with 200 ministers. The consolidated Convention was composed of six "district conventions" and it survived until 1879 when it fractured into autonomous regional conventions. Other efforts at Baptist unification were made from time to time, but all foundered for one reason or another until the American National Baptist Convention was organized in St. Louis on August 25, 1886. The Convention claimed a constituency of a million members with 4500 ministers in 9,000 churches. In Atlanta, Georgia, on September 28, 1895, the American National Baptist Convention was successfully merged with the Baptist Foreign Mission Convention, USA, (organized in 1880). The resultant organization, the National Baptist Convention, USA/ Inc. became, and remains, the largest black Protestant organization in the world. Reverend E. C. Morris was elected first president of the Convention.

The NBCI was supporting nearly 100 schools and colleges by the turn of the century, and it was prominent in the various efforts to deal with racial violence and segregation. It formally endorsed Booker T. Washington's program in 1909, but was from its inception a strong supporter of the NAACP. Under the leadership of Dr. J. H. Jackson (1953-1982) the Convention adopted a more conservative stance.

NBCI reports a membership of 7.1 million, accounting for about one-fourth of the officially estimated black population of the United States. It has an overseas constituency of about 100,000. The Convention has an annual meeting each September. Officers headed by the president serve for one year. A Board of Directors is the governing body, and with the Executive Committee, the Board conducts the business of the Convention between sessions. The 1984 budget was about $3 million, prior to an upsurge in membership and programs since then. Dr. T. J. Jemison, who was the first General Secretary of the Southern Christian Leadership Conference has been president since 1982. The Convention has no permanent headquarters, but its $9 million World Baptist Center being built in Nashville is scheduled for occupancy in June of 1989. National Headquarters will be located in the Center.

The support of colleges and seminaries overlap among the various Baptist constituencies, but well-known black institutions supported in part by the black Baptist Conventions include Morehouse, Benedict, Spelman, Shaw, and Virginia Union colleges and universities; Turner Theological Seminary in Atlanta, and the American Baptist Theological Seminary in Nashville.

The National Baptist Convention of America (NBCA)

The National Baptist Convention of America, sometimes called the "unincorporated convention," grew out of a schism occurring in 1915 in the National Baptist Convention, USA founded 20 years earlier. The dispute was a complicated one involving the publishing house, and it culminated in the establishment of the NBCA at a meeting in Chicago on September 9, 1915. Reverend E. P. Jones was elected first president of the new Convention.

NBCA is the second largest of the black Baptist denominations reporting a membership of around 2.5 million. It has about 7800 local churches served by a clergy of approximately 3,000. The NBCA meets annually and delegates or "messengers" are received from its local churches, associations, and state conventions. A president is elected annually, and the president of the state conventions along with the moderators of the General Associations are *ex-officio* vice presidents. An Executive Board carries on the business of the Convention when it is not in session. E. Edward Jones of Shreveport was elected president at the 1988 convention. The NBCA does not have a national headquarters. The publishing house is in Nashville, Tennessee.

The Progressive National Baptist Convention, Inc.

The Progressive National Baptist Convention, Inc., separated from the National Baptist Convention, Inc., in 1961. The rupture came over long-standing disagreements with the policies of Dr. J. H. Jackson who was president of the Convention for 19 years until he was finally unseated by Dr. T. J. Jemison in 1982.

The 1961 revolt was led by Dr. Gardner Taylor, Dr. Benjamin Mays, Martin Luther King, Sr., Martin Luther King, Jr., Ralph Abernathy, and others opposed to President Jackson's conservative policies which they considered inimical to the black freedom movement underway in America. At the regular Annual Meeting of the NBC, Inc., held in Kansas City in September of 1961, dissident delegates were removed from offices they held, including the Board of Directors. At a "rump meeting" in Cincinnatti, Ohio, two months later, delegates of the dissident group organized the Progressive National Baptist Convention, Inc., which is the third largest of the black Baptist communions. The first annual meeting was held in Philadelphia the following year, and the Reverend T. M. Chambers was elected president.

The PNBC was deeply involved in the civil rights movement from its inception. Its membership is made up predominantly of younger, more liberal pastors with more college and university experience. PNBC was prominent in the opposition to the war in Vietnam, and in recent times it has emphasized black political and economic development. Some PNBC pastors maintain second affiliations with one of the white Baptist Conventions.

The convention claims about a million members in a thousand churches serviced by a thousand pastors. Its congregations tend to be quite large, and they are located primarily in major metropolitan areas. The Convention is divided into four "Regions" representing thirty-five state conventions. The PNBC Convention meets each year in August, and receives a number of "messengers" from each church depending upon its size. Each State Convention and each Fellowship is also entitled to send messengers, as are Associations. Since 1967, Presidents of the Convention and most of its other officers have been limited to consecutive one-year terms. An Executive Board of 60 members oversees the business of the Convention between sessions. The General Secretary is a full-time employee responsible for day-to-day administration, and national headquarters with a full-time staff is in Washington, D.C. PNBC has no publishing house of its own. Reverend Fred Lofton of Memphis was elected president of the Convention in 1988.

THE PENTECOSTALS

The Pentecostal movement grew out of the radical preaching of William Seymour, a black Holiness minister who led the famous Azusa Street Revivals in Los Angeles from 1906 to 1908. To the traditional Holiness doctrine of "salvation" and "sanctification" Seymour added a "third blessing" identified as "baptism in the spirit," which was evidenced by "*glossalalia*," or "speaking in tongues" (as occurred at the Feast of Pentecost following the resurrection of Jesus). Thousands of people, white and black from every section of the country within and outside the Holiness tradition, flocked to hear Seymour and to subscribe to his new doctrine. Many came to be ordained by Seymour. In short order the movement spread to all parts of the United States, to Europe, Africa, China, India, South Africa, and South America. Today, there are about 35 million Pentecostals world-wide, with large concentrations in the Third World. In the United States the first Pentecostal churches tended to be interracial, but soon split along color lines giving birth to a multiplicity of derivative denominations ranging from the (black) Church of God in Christ to the (white) Assemblies of God. Some Holiness churches embraced the new order by simply adding "Pentecostal" to their names and discipline; others vigorously resisted the Pentecostal identification. In recent times elements of Pentecostalism under the guise of a newly recognized "charismatic movement" have become entrenched in many churches of other denominatons, including the Catholic church.

Pentecostalism is the only major black Christian communion which did not have its origins in a white church. To the contrary, William Seymour in Los Angeles, and later Charles H. Mason in Mississippi, ordained hundreds of white preachers who in turn founded churches or denominations which planted the flag of Pentecostalism throughout the world. Ironically, ecumenical Pentecostal bodies in the United States, such as the Pentecostal Fellowship of North America and the National Association of Evangelicals, have been closed historically to black membership.

THE CHURCH OF GOD IN CHRIST (COGIC)

The Church of God in Christ was founded in Memphis, Tennessee, in 1897, by Charles Harrison Mason, formerly a Baptist pastor in Arkansas. Mason's experience of "santification" in 1893 brought about his dismissal from his Baptist church and from the Baptist Association to which he belonged. He subsequently founded "The Church of God" in Mississippi, and later incorporated it in Memphis as "The Church of God in Christ." Ten years later at the Azusa Street Revival in Los Angeles, Mason experienced the "gift of tongues" and embraced the doctrines of William Seymour. His church in consequence made the transit from Holiness to Pentecostal.

At the first General Assembly of the Church of God in Christ representatives of twelve churches convened in Memphis in November of 1907, the official founding date of the new communion. Mason was named General Overseer and Chief Apostle (later changed to Senior Bishop). The church which was already established in Tennessee, Arkansas, Mississippi, and Oklahoma soon expanded into Texas, Missouri, and California. COGIC was the only incorporated Pentecostal body from 1907 to 1914, and hence the only ecclesiastical authority to which independent Pentecostal churches, white and black, could appeal for ordination and other matters.

COGIC is currently the fastest growing of the black denominations. Second only to the National Baptist Convention, Inc., in numbers, the Church of God in Christ has a national membership estimated at more than three million in about nine thousand local churches serviced by some 10,000 clergy. It has another 80,000 members in 43 foreign countries where it maintains more than a hundred schools, clinics and orphanages in Africa, India, Sri Lanka, and other Third World areas. There are 100 COGIC churches in Haiti alone.

The General Assembly is the administrative authority of the Church and its supreme judicial body. The assembly includes the members of the General Board (Bishops elected by the General Assembly), all jurisdictional bishops, all pastors, elders, etc. The Assembly meets twice a year at the National Convocation, which is held in April, and the International Convention held in November. The General Council of Elders, made up of all the elders in the Church, serves as an ecclesiastical council and hears all matters referred to it. But the General Assembly is the supreme judicial body. The presiding Bishop is elected from the Board of Bishops by the General Assembly for a four-year term. There is no limit on successive terms. The Presiding Bishop is the chief executive officer, and he administers the affairs of the Church between meetings of the General Board. COGIC has 134 active bishops, including eight overseas. The Reverend J. 0. Patterson holds the office of Presiding Bishop.

COGIC sponsors 70 bible colleges, and one junior college,in Lexington, Mississippi. Charles H. Mason Seminary is a unit of the Interdenominational Theological Seminary in Atlanta. All Saints University is scheduled to be built in Memphis where the church maintains its headquarters.

Smaller black Pentecostal denominations include the United Holy Church of America, The United House of Prayer for All People, The Fire Baptized Holiness Church of God of the Americas, and the Sought Out Church of God in African Universal Church.

THE IMPACT OF THE BLACK CHURCH

These are the institutions, the pastors, and the people who are the primary shapers of the black sub-culture in America, and who impact the spiritual, economic, social, educational, and political life of the country at large. The Black Church is by all odds the dominant symbol of the African presence in the United States, and were it to suddenly suffer eclipse, it would be extremely difficult to gather convincing identifying marks of that presence from the void. It was the Black Church which was the nurturing mother of black freedom, black pride, black ambition, music, education, oratory, politics, and self-respect. Out of it came our first fraternal orders, savings institutions, insurance companies, educational institutions, and the first glimmer of hope that tomorrow could be better than yesterday; and that tomorrow begins where today makes its decisions. In the midst of its competitiveness the Black Church has been the matrix of black solidarity, for when all is said and done, competition is the best hedge against lethargy, just as solidarity is the final focus of any effective strategy for change.

There has been wide-spread concern in recent decades over the continuous splintering of traditional religious bodies, and the even more phenomenal emergence of new religions. Whether or not the concern is justified, the "phenomenon" is undebatable, for since World War II, the proliferation of recognized religious bodies in America has soared past 1,500, more than half of which were not in existence a mere two decades ago. We used to call these new entities "cults" and "sects" for the most part, but in the context of today's religious revolution those typologies are probably as outdated as they are misunderstood. What we are experiencing is a massive restructuring of spiritual values and inspirations that reflect new needs and new insights as we confront a post-war world with a bewildering spectrum of new experiences. It is precisely on the understanding of this principle that the predictions of the rapid demise of the Black Church have foundered. The Black Church is thriving because the traditional black experience is essentially intact. Whatever else it may be, religion is the deepest response of which man is capable of making to the exigencies and the excellences of past and future experiences. The holding tenacity of the Black Church suggests that despite the blips and pips in the panaroma of social change, there has been insufficient substantive variation in the underlying fabric which determines the basic quality of the black experience to precipitate a radical change in black religion. The values, interests, and aspirations remain constant because the index of black reality is essentially the same.

Except for the Muslims, the Black Church has experienced no serious challenge to the spiritual hegemony it has enjoyed for almost 200 years. The Roman Catholic Church and the United Methodist Church claim by far the largest segments of "affiliated" blacks outside the independent Black Church, but neither of those communions represents a black commitment of substantial consequence. The Presbyterians and the United Church of Christ are very distant contenders. Beyond that, the "eccumenical" hopes that the Black Church would merge itself into mainline white Christianity become increasingly unrealistic the more the dynamics of religious expectations are understood. As for the "new religions" of the post-war proliferation, they have attracted almost no black adherents beyond a very thin fringe of habitual spiritual transients who in effect serve as sensors for the larger black community.

We may safely conclude that in 1988, the Black Church was engaged in doing what it was doing a hundred years ago, but with significant new emphases. The Church has always been a spiritual refuge with a social consciousness which has at some times and places been more pronounced than at others. While this unevenness exasperates those who have a one-dimensional perspective of the Black Church, its inherent genius is that it recognizes man as *both* spirit and body with a *duality* of needs which must be addressed, because both are constantly at risk in this society. (Effective mission is the ability to determine where the emphasis should be placed in the light of existing realities.) Contemporary needs are both deeply spiritual and agonizingly physical, and the resultant burden of the Black Church has never been more critical or more challenging.

The Church is moving to address these needs, not with perfect symmetry, but with persistence. The Black Church is after all, no more and no less than the black people who comprise it, and it mirrors the imagination, the interest, and the sense of urgency of the black community it serves and symbolizes.

Today's Black Church is struggling for relevance to today's black problems: racism; drug abuse; child care; health and welfare; housing; counseling; unemployment; teenage pregnancy; and the whole tragic malaise with which society in general is burdened. It must address all these social challenges without abandoning its distinctive mandate to assist man in his efforts to find conciliation and comfort with his Creator. There is no moratorium on the human need for spiritual and moral nurture.

CONCLUSION

The Rural/Urban Profile

The emphases of ministry in today's Black Church are varied from time to time and from place to place, but they are essentially a reflection of the urgencies perceived and the available facilities to address these urgencies. The rural church, for example, was once the backbone of black identity and commitment. Today, rural black churches hold on, but it is a vanishing phenomenon. The black population is now concentrated in the cities, North, South, East and West, and the rural churches, which survive in the Old South, survive in spite of the encroachments of urbanism, both physical and ideological. Today's rural church pastor almost always lives in the city. He may have as many as three or four "charges" or small churches among which he must divide his Sundays. And, he has a secular job on which he depends for the main income on which he and his family are dependent. This leaves the effective leadership of the rural church in the hands of the deacons or other church officers who live in the community. In consequence, the emphasis in the rural church tends to reflect more traditional concerns — like "good preaching," annual revivals, and occasions for fellowship — than the entrenched social problems which besiege the urban churches. Yet, the rural Black Church retains a resilience and a commitment which shame the crude appraisal of its critics. It was the rural Black Church which shared the brunt of the Civil Rights Struggle; which provided the facilities, the day-to-day resistence, the critical leadership in faith and practice that made black freedom possible, and made it magnanimous.

General Observations

Two general observations about today's Black Church will be helpful: the most visible urban churches are increasingly pastored by a "trained" clergy, and the phenomenon of the mega-church with memberships in the thousands is shifting from the North to the South and West. The counterparts to the historic "big churches" like Abyssinian in Harlem and Concord Baptist Church in Brooklyn, New York, are developing in Baltimore, Washington, Atlanta, Houston, and Los Angeles. It is the larger "institutional" churches that are better equipped with trained personnel and financial resources to address the social needs of the black community, and they are doing it. Churches like the Reverend Gardner Taylor's Concord Baptist Church in Brooklyn, the Reverend Floyd Flake's Allen AME Church in Jamaica, New York, are prototypes of effective Black Church involvement in social crises that range from poor academic adjustment to drug abuse, to family counseling, to child care, and the whole gamut of unattended needs incident to being poor and black in America.

At the ecumenical level, the Congress of National Black Churches (embracing five of the seven major communions) brings the combined weight of the Black Church into play against school drop-outs and related delinquency in an ambitious tutorial program in several citites across the country. CNBC, with headquarters in Washington, D.C., is also a major ecumenical effort in church-based black economic development. In Durham, North Carolina, The Church Connection is a collaboration of several interdenominational local churches with the local Lincoln Community Health Center in counseling and other activities and services aimed at better health and habits for teenagers. Ten churches in Chicago work with each other in Project IMAGE designed to retrieve and refurbish the image of the black male as a positive role model in the family and in the community.

In all of these examples offered here the chief significance is that the Black Church is alive, alert, and addressed to the realities of our times. Perhaps most significant of all is the fact that the black churches are not only cooperating with each other, they are increasingly willing to work closely with secular institutions in the struggle against the mundane challenges to the physical well-being of the black community. But the biblical maxim that "man shall not live by bread alone . . . ," remains intact. The *word* and the *spirit* have not been abandoned. Far from it. In Boston, the Reverend Warren M. Brown of Columbus Avenue AME Zion Church has built a loyal and thriving congregation in a church which has "no church-sponsored housing programs, no day care programs, and no social service programs, "and this in the heart of the black 'inner city.' " Explains Reverend Brown, "I see the church's primary function not as a social service agency, but as a religious worship center. . . . When people leave this church, we want them to have the inner fiber they need to go out and cope."

So goes the Black Church, 1989 — anchored in tradition, stretching for contemporary relevance; cautiously exploring new relationships; trying as it always has to meet, the diverse, the urgent and pervasive needs of a constituency in need of miracles.

Valuing Diversity: The Myth and the Challenge

Price M. Cobbs, M.D.

My examination of the state of Black America 1989 finds many unfinished and complex issues. These issues remain unfinished because our national leaders have placed a low priority on understanding and resolving them. They remain complex because this country has not yet come to gripe with deeply embedded attitudes, assumptions, and behavior regarding racial and cultural differences.

As a psychiatrist, my first task in conducting this examination is to determine how people are developing, growing, and faring in their inner lives. Is it the same as last year or 10, 20 years ago? How are they coping and surviving? In facing the world of 1989, what level of personal mastery is brought in managing fears, overcoming doubts, and realizing dreams?

Next, the task is to understand how people interact with others, especially observing relationships involving individuals most alike and most unlike. Again, has this changed from 1969 to 1979 to 1989? What present internal conflicts do people carry with them which enhance or inhibit interactions? What conscious and unconscious factors decide in a relationship who characteristically dominates and who usually submits? Why does one person assume the persona of perennial victim while another person, in similar circumstances, flourishes?

A third and equally critical task I assume is an analysis of the society in which people live. What dynamics are operative now and how do they compare to previous periods? How, for example, do social policies, economics, changing demographics affect power and resource distribution? These tasks dictate an ongoing scrutiny of people, policies, and institutions. Among other things, this is the focus I bring in preparing this article.

Elsewhere in this volume scholars will shed light on the drug epidemic ravaging this country and especially its impact on black communities. They will write about the ever-rising rate of teen age pregnancies and the subsequent human cost of single parent homes and family instability. Information will be given about the effects of double digit unemployment, homelessness, and the ever-widening economic gap between black and white.

In eight years of short-sighted national policies and priorities, African Americans have witnessed an abrupt shift of concern from benign neglect to hostile indifference. As one result of this shift, I see many segments and regions of the nation doing quite well in my travels around the country. At the same time, I see most black communities and inner cities not sharing in the prosperity which they see all around them.

Regardless of one's politics, the present administration, however much it manipulates statistics, has ignored and neglected people at the bottom. Since African

Americans have always been overrepresented at the bottom, they cannot view the eighties as having brought the prosperity experienced by their fellow Americans at the top. In addition, the Reagan revolution has co-opted the themes of patriotism, morality, and family values and has declared racism officially dead.

In my work throughout the nation, impinging on the above issues, are several overarching themes I find intellectually challenging and emotionally seductive. These themes are incorporated in words like *diversity*, *pluralism*, and *inclusion*. What do they mean and why are they appearing now and so frequently? Are they describing cosmetic and superficial shifts in the complexion of the country or do they speak to a series of issues black people should be aware of in preparation for the year 2000?

Until quite recently such words and themes might be only discussed in obscure academic journals or an arcane doctoral dissertation. Quite suddenly, they are becoming staples of newspaper articles, magazines, T.V. shows and business journals. Practically every day one reads accounts or hears analyses of the changing demographics of the United States and the implication of these changes on everything from the workforce to marriage rates. As an example of how rapidly they have emerged and are being discussed, I find that an increasing number of national conventions and conferences have invited me to address these and similar themes.

Thus, to write about the themes of diversity and differences is to focus on a major tributary of contemporary thought and discussion. Moreover, in exploring the implication of these themes, I sense possibilities of a powerful shift occurring in how many Americans view themselves and define their individual identity and therefore how they want to be viewed by others. Further, if my notions about these possibilities are correct, America could be at the dawn of a major transformation in how it defines itself and will be defined by the world in the twenty-first century.

However, before further exploration of these themes, we, the reader and I, have a preliminary piece of work. We must conduct a brief historical analysis to help us understand more fully how our country has arrived at this particular place.

Throughout this country's history the attainment of the American dream has assumed a certain, if rarely spoken about, homogeneity. The metaphor for attaining this desired homogeneity has been labeled the melting pot theory. Even without a precise meaning of the melting pot theory, Americans who did not fit its unspoken definitions have been quite clear that they did not "fit."

Where the cultural expressions and practices of an individual or a group were different from the idealized image of an American, such differences have been diminished, changed, or obliterated. This was the price to be paid in the on-going process of Americanization.

Until the last decade, individuals could speak languages other than English and observe old country rituals. They could engage in practices at variance with the norms of the country, even if they did so comfortably only in the privacy of one's home. Where people lived in an ethnic or racial enclave, a ghetto, then their cultural differences could be expressed within the boundaries of these enclaves or behind the walls of a sanctuary.

With few exceptions, to celebrate cultural differences in seeking success in this country was to chart a path counter to the all-encompassing myth of the melting pot. The few exceptions we have seen to this myth only serve to remind us that they were just that, exceptions.

Only in the past 10 years has one been able to read street signs, election ballots, and advertisements for upscale boutiques printed in a language other than English. Now, in cities and work places around the nation, signs and ballots are sometimes printed in no fewer than four languages in addition to English.

Accompanying these visible changes the country is deluged with words like *workforce diversity*, *cultural pluralism*, and *valuing differences*. In many organizations people are challenged to prepare for the year 2000 when these words will be the order of the day and the ideas implied will be standard operating procedure. In order to emphasize the magnitude of these changes, I ask the reader to remember the last time a serious article was read or a television documentary was seen in which the subject was the benefit of the melting pot.

The vicissitudes of my life have made me sensitive to new ideas involving elements of psychological and social development linked with increased racial and cultural awareness. When such ideas shape how people define themselves or involve possible changes in the social order, my psychiatric antennae go up. It was just such a powerful shift in internal and external factors that allowed William Grier and me to define and write *Black Rage* and to accurately predict the ensuing urban riots.

History informs us that people who understand ideas first and are able to act on their meaning are best able to capitalize on changes resulting from them. Ideas, particularly those involving how people see themselves, have a unique time in history. They provide a fleeting window of opportunity, for aware individuals to grasp and exploit them.

The reader need do no more than trace the recent evolution of the words colored, Negro, black and African American. The group being described has continued to look the same. As words, therefore, they are merely shifting descriptions. However, as ideas they highlight profound shifts in the psyche of a group of people struggling mightily to define themselves rather than be defined by others. Therefore, if encompassed in the words and themes of diversity are ideas whose time has come, what unique lessons do African Americans need to learn or teach? In short, how do black people who have laughed silently and painfully about the lie of the melting pot inform themselves and seize leadership?

Words like *workforce diversity* and *valuing cultural differences* sound good, but underneath what do they really mean? Are they extensions of passive and well-meaning concepts like brotherhood and tolerance? Are they new code words designed to take the focus away from the conflict, tension, and pressure inherent in eliminating prejudice, discrimination, and racism?

In grappling with these ideas, what ought to be the posture of Black America — to embrace and co-opt these themes or to stand aside and risk again the possibility our issues and concerns will be made secondary? At bottom, what is the individual and group self-interest of those Americans who are at once the most like and most unlike the idealized image of an American?

DEFINING KEY TERMS

Before making a determination about the self-interest of black people regarding these issues, we must first define the several terms most commonly used in today's organizations. *Workforce diversity* is probably the term most widely used. It refers to a future state for organizations in which different groups of the population of the United States are represented at all levels of an organization. The term also refers to the placement of women who, until recently, were mostly consigned to lower level clerical functions.

Workforce diversity in any meaningful way is still an unattained goal for the great majority of American institutions.

Representation in key line positions and at the top continues to remain a prerogative of white men. Therefore, when the term is used, there should be an acknowledgment of the need for active efforts in recruitment, retention, and upward mobility. Implicit and therefore less acknowledged or even understood is the more risky goal of *power sharing*. This will be touched on more fully in the next section.

Cultural pluralism is another term used and is also a description for a desired future state rather than the characterization of a present condition. Most globally, it speaks to a time in this country where all groups — minority and majority — participate fully in the dominant society yet maintain and celebrate their cultural differences. As the reader can readily grasp, the meaning of cultural pluralism is the polar opposite from the meaning of the melting pot.

Valuing differences is an offshoot of both workforce diversity and cultural pluralism. It postulates placing a neutral or positive value on differences be they racial, gender, cultural or differences in lifestyle. Where it is used in organizations it means allowing people more opportunity to be themselves within the framework of organizational effectiveness. For many people it is a liberating thought to know they can be more of themselves at work.

We can better determine how and why these terms have arisen in the last several years after digesting some of the following statistics.

- Blacks, Hispanics, and Asians will be 25 percent of the population of the United States in 10 years.

- By the year 2000, 80 percent of the new entrants to the labor force will be minorities, women, and immigrants.

- In California, English will be the second language for the majority of the population by the end of this century.

154

- Sometime in the 21st century whites will become the minority population in the United States.

- By the year 2000, 47 percent of the workforce will be women and 61 percent of all women will be employed. (Black women have traditionally worked and will comprise a higher percentage of women employed.)

- Black women will comprise the largest share of the increase in the non-white labor force by the turn of the century.

- Black women will out number black men in the workforce by the year 2000.

In reviewing the statistics listed above, one can easily see the attainment of workforce diversity by most organizations is driven by necessity and self-interest. Words like fairness and equality may be used, but institutions with good strategic planning know they will be less competitive if they do not plan for a diverse workforce. In my experience, those employers and institutions who understand these figures and prepare for their implications, will achieve competitive advantage.

They will be able to attract and retain the best and brightest from all groups because representatives from diverse groups will be present in the workforce and in the hierarchy. Also, such organizations will find themselves more motivated to tap and exploit new markets both domestically and internationally.

Implications

If a logical consequence of my work is to assist in the development of a healthy self-identity, then my recommendation is for black Americans to embrace these ideas openly and enthusiastically. They can be another tool in attaining greater self-esteem and more fully defining individual and group identity. If the ideas are rejected and resisted, I think an opportunity will be lost in taking further steps along the journey of self-determination.

Black people in America must never forget several painfully learned lessons. Central to these lessons is one historical fact. Throughout the history of this country most things — intellectual, emotional, or spiritual — associated with darker skin or African heritage are assumed to have less value than those of white people. In other words, African Americans and their culture has been consistently devalued. Whatever different, unique, or special expressions of community or culture, whether it is language, art, music, dance, or religion, all have been assigned a lesser worth compared with the same white or European expression.

In a project conducted at an elite private institution in this country, I find Asian, Hispanic, and Native American students arriving at this same conclusion. They too, speak of devaluation of their cultures and how this occurrence has been another barrier in the healthy development of all Americans. They are demanding changes in the core curriculum and methods of instruction in addition to wanting more equitable distribution of non-whites in faculty, staff, and administration.

Even today, all but the most racially healthy Americans at some point in their lives have an assumption African Americans are somehow tainted or otherwise inferior. Even after many years of experience, I remain fascinated as I watch new immigrants in the process of Americanization adopt negative assumptions and prejudices against black people.

However, even more important is for black people themselves to understand these dynamics. Throughout my lifetime I have observed individuals struggling to resolve the historical duality of being black and American. It was a struggle accompanying the first African slave who arrived on these shores in 1607, and it remains an issue for most blacks as they ponder the State of Black America 1989. This all encompassing struggle was first depicted so prophetically by W.E.B. DuBois when he wrote *The Souls of Black Folks* (1903). The anxiety and tension resulting from this inner conflict are no less present now than they were at the turn of the century.

Because of this historical duality, black parents in their desire to raise kids with healthy doses of pride and realistic views of racial identity assume a task of heroic dimensions. It remains a monumental task to achieve this against a backdrop of devaluation. Deep in every black soul who has lived in this magnificent country there is a balancing act; a rarely resolved ambivalence reconciling being black with being American, whatever that means. This balancing act remains a singular dynamic in shaping the psychological development and outlook of an entire group of people.

Individuals describe in vivid details the paradoxes, contradictions, dilemmas, and grand opportunities which occur as a by-product of this dual life. Its healthy resolution determines how effectively most black people will manage their ever-present rage. A vivid manifestation of the on-going nature of this struggle occurs when a black person is asked whether things are better off now than before. Whatever the logical answer, the inevitable pause is an unconscious acknowledgment the battle goes on for a healthy self-identity.

A current demonstration of the dual life dilemma is a fear expressed to me by many black men and women working in predominately white organizations. They express a fear that in pursuit of career success they will gradually and inexorably become a white Anglo-Saxon protestant clone. Whatever the chances are of this phenomenon occurring, the fear is there. Further, many people state an outcome of this cloning process is a psychological and cultural never-never land—isolated and estranged from all groups including one's own and alienated from self.

Thus, the perception that to be different from white America is to be inferior is no recently arrived at formulation heralding a worsening state of race relations. It has been there in good times and bad, through periods of civil rights advances and conservative revolutions. For black people, it is a central and constant dynamic to be understood and mastered. In my view, a most powerful tool in combatting the fear of success is a deeper understanding and acceptance of one's individual and group cultural differences.

Analyzing and embracing the themes inherent in workforce diversity and valuing differences also helps individuals shed the deficit model view frequently accompanying affirmative action programs. In this view, black people and sometimes other non-whites are regarded as incomplete white people and therefore deficient in ways usually unvoiced or unspecified.

A further discussion of the melting pot theory is appropriate here. When the playwright, Israel Zangwill, first spoke in 1908 of the melting pot, he meant explicitly melting the races of Europe. Black people were thus excluded in this initial formulation of a concept so rooted in American mythology. It therefore comes as no surprise blacks were the first to challenge this mythology and protest their exclusion.

There are of course many risks associated with a mindless embrace of this theme. Most importantly, this country like most others around the world has yet to confront racism in any fundamental way. As a country we have progressed along many dimensions in solving the American dilemma. However, the country has not reached a fundamental understanding of the etiology of personal and institutional racism. Until this occurs, black progress, however arrived at, will continue to meet resistance. For black Americans to lose sight of demanding the end of racism in all its pernicious forms is shortsighted at best and culturally suicidal at worst.

Racism continues to be a major factor affecting the quality of life of black and whites alike. Events of the past several years in places like Howard Beach, New York and Forsythe County, Georgia serve to remind us of the presence of racial hatred, the manifestation of which is once again socially acceptable in some quarters. No individual or group ought to embrace the themes of diversity without at the same time keeping the above issues in the forefront.

CONCLUSIONS

After assessing the risks and opportunities mentioned in earlier parts of this article, we must deal with several remaining questions. If one is to embrace enthusiastically ideas and themes of diversity, a core question deals with the intellectual and emotional preparation required. The reduction of tension and anxiety is central in achieving the level of mastery needed in order to take leadership around these issues.

A vital part of achieving mastery around these issues is for the individual to adopt a mindset which fosters receptivity to cultural and other differences. In this context mindset means striving for a more disciplined and strategic way of thinking and adopting an attitude and disposition to bring this about. With these and other issues an appropriate mindset means the ability to ask the right questions rather than necessarily possessing the correct answers. It means attaining personal empowerment through a fundamental understanding of an idea or concept.

In the interest of personal empowerment the reader is encouraged to participate actively in readings, discussions, and other activities exploring diversity. This means intellectual curiosity about others and actively listening to them with a specific focus on understanding that which is most different from one's own life experiences.

Individuals must bring a high level of personal honesty, openness, and candor into discussions about differences if they are to result in further empowerment. Lacking this insight most discussions about individual and cultural differences end up in a recitation about similarities.

Another important component of the mindset of diversity is to avoid making quick and thoughtless value judgments based solely on not understanding differences. In my experience nothing so quickly shuts down learning about oneself and others as a premature and sweeping value judgment. A major reason why people know so little about other individuals and groups is they substitute value judgments for learning.

In the two decades of studying about these issues, I have developed a technique designed to help people, especially African Americans, achieve more empowerment. The technique involves helping people achieve clarity in their perception of themselves and others. The more clarity about who and what one is, the more free one is to value the specific elements of personal and group identity.

In a recent book, *Walking on the Edge of the World*, George Leonard, the celebrated author writes movingly of his experiences as a leader of the first encounter groups involving blacks and whites. The first group was held in California in 1987 at Esalen Institute. These early groups involving volatile confrontations between black rage and white fear served as laboratories for my work with diversity.

Starting with these groups, collecting different and exciting clinical material, learning from and working with others, exploring new ideas and experiences resulted in the development of the technique called *ethnotherapy*. A basic outcome of ethnotherapy is to help people engage in self-study and make healthier determinations about various elements of their identity. This involves an examination of one's thoughts, feelings, and behaviors and how they result in victimhood.

A further outcome of ethnotherapy is assisting individuals to build personal and communication skills so legitimate discussions of differences can occur. In these discussions important work can be accomplished in getting individuals to examine their assumptions about others. The purpose of these discussions is to eliminate stereotypes and force people to engage in the crucial task of individualizing others.

An important task of ethnotherapy is for individuals to understand the world in which they live and work to probe the ideas of diversity and cultural differences and explore the concept of power. How is power gained, used, and shared? Who has it, who doesn't, and why are parts of the many questions asked.

As we approach the year 2000, African Americans must take leadership in further developing and refining the language and imagery which describes differences. We must actively challenge the notion that there is something called colorblindness. At present, most visible symbols and most of the language describing success or power relates to white people. Repeatedly in my work I hear successful black people groping for words to describe themselves and ending up saying they function "like a white boy."

Such descriptions must be changed as black people define themselves and their successes beyond a comparison with whites.

The turmoil of the sixties resulted in an identification and channeling of black rage. Promoting "black is beautiful" was an attempt to go beyond the rage and to remove generations of self-hatred. As we approach the year 2000, we must find the words and images to complete the realization of the dream.

The black experience in this country has been a complex one. While it has involved the differences of race and skin color, it has also involved cultural differences. Honoring and valuing these differences remains an unfinished task for leaders in government, industry, academia and all other walks of life. How they champion the ideas of workforce diversity and cultural pluralism will define the society of the next century.

Drugs In The African-American Community: A Clear and Present Danger

Wade W. Nobles, Ph.D.
and
Lawford L. Goddard, Ph.D.

Over the last several years drug use has emerged as an extremely critical problem affecting young people in America today. Former First Lady Nancy Reagan's interest in this problem undoubtedly gave the issue greater public attention. However, in many ways, because this problem was regarded as the first lady's and not the president's, it lost much of the urgency to see it as a threat to national security, which was more immediate and probable than missiles from Russia. Accordingly, the need to openly and radically address the problem of drugs and youth was relegated to sloganizing and pomp. The problem of drugs and youth is, nevertheless, a long-standing one. Its understanding has, in fact, been approached from many different perspectives (i.e., educational, legal, health, etc.), including the opinion that the introduction of drugs in the African-American community was allowed and encouraged in order to derail the growing militancy, political nationalism, economic independence, and cultural integrity of the African-American community.

Substance abuse is the single major leading social, economic, and health problem confronting the African-American community. In addition to being implicated in deaths from cancer, strokes, hypertension, cirrhosis of the liver, and heart diseases, substance abuse is a major factor in the increase in crime, family violence, the growing rate of violent deaths among African Americans and the depletion of the future resources of the African-American community. Substance abuse further leads to an erosion of life chances, an erosion of family life and the erosion of the cultural traditions and sense of community life for African Americans.

THE IMPACT OF SUBSTANCE ABUSE IN THE AFRICAN-AMERICAN COMMUNITY

The question of substance abuse in the African-American community has been linked to three general processes (Goddard, 1988). The primary process that impacts upon the African-American population involves the issues of economic deprivation, racism, and stress. The psychiatrist, Chester Pierce (1974), has indicated that life in the urban ghetto is often characterized by an extreme mundane stressful environment. By "extreme mundane stress" Pierce refers to stress that results when actors perceive no rewards or relief from their constantly stressful quest to survive on a day-to-day basis. Living in the urban environment is an extremely stressful situation for the African-American population in general and particularly for African-American adolescents. In addition to the difficulties of lack of adequate employment opportunities for adolescents, the urban environment is characterized by high levels of noise and environmental pollutants, lack of open space, and limited recreational facilities. The extreme environment of the ghetto is loaded with "offensive put-downs," which Pierce classified as social trace contaminants which promote acceptance of (1) a devalued state and (2) hope-lessness. In this condition people require accessible escape mechanisms in order for the human organism to continue to function at a level of minimum survivability.

In an earlier work, Pierce (1970) noted that the African-American population, and particularly adolescents, is constantly bombarded by "microaggressions" in which they are hindered in their society. This repeated bombardment produces a cumulative impact on the personality of the urban ghetto which is structural in nature and long-term in its duration. This constant bombardment, he contends, produces a condition of "status dislocation" wherein the individual cannot effec-tively function in society and seeks escape mechanisms (i.e., substance abuse) to enable him to survive. He notes in this regard that the twin interactional and mutually reinforcing effects of racism and stress condition those so victimized to opt for addictive escapism.

It should be noted here that the restructuring of the American economy has affected the African-American population to such an extent that it has created a permanent underclass. The benefits of the Civil Rights struggle have been severely eroded through the massive retrenchments and cut-backs in the basic industries, automobile, steel, and rubber, in which African Americans had made significant inroads in the 1970s. These effects are manifested in the high levels of unem-ployment and underemployment among the African-American population, the increase in the proportion of persons living in poverty, and in the general sense of despair and hopelessness experienced by many African-American youth as indicated by the increase in suicide.

The underclass has swelled by an increasingly large number of African-Amer-ican males who are experiencing extensive periods of unemployment as well as those who have dropped out of the labor market completely. Operating at a very basic level of survival, the underclass, in many significant ways, is isolated from society. Lacking appropriate marketable skills, lacking information about oppor-tunities in the labor market, and symbolically separated from the wider society, the members of the underclass survive at a minimum level. Within this context, they find it relatively easy to opt for those "escape mechanisms" which Pierce had suggested. Participation in drug-related activity represents an attractive alter-native to poverty and despair. It offers escape to users and quick profits to dealers. For others of the underclass, participation in a drug-related lifestyle is part of their normal routine of living. This is the lifestyle in which they have grown and it is difficult for them to imagine anything different. The small area around their homes represents the extent of the world for the African-American underclass.

Lacking the resources and the inclination, few have ventured outside of their immediate surroundings to explore the wider society.

The second process is the general availability of alcohol and drugs in the African-American community. The research literature clearly indicates that in the African-American community, liquor stores are the most common form of small businesses. The corner liquor store flourishes within the urban central city and is the prime source of availability of alcoholic beverages for African-American youth. The spatial geography of these communities reveals an excessive amount of retail liquor outlets. Along the major expressway that runs through any of the large urban African-American communities on almost every other block an alcohol retail outlet is found. The presence of these outlets, in addition to the visible ads, would seem to reinforce the pressures to engage in drinking behavior.

In this vein, it should be noted that the alcohol industry has embarked on a vigorous campaign to market and distribute wine coolers. Wine coolers represent the "magic elixir" for which the alcohol industry has been searching for years. Sweet to the palate, with a rich bouquet, it lacks the harsh, bitter taste characteristic of all alcohol. It is easily accepted by youth and is rapidly replacing beer as the initial entry-level drink for young people. The success of the wine cooler can be seen in the rapid increase in sales. Wine cooler sales increased from 150,000 cases in 1982 to 40,000,000 cases in 1986.

Illicit drugs have become commonplace within the urban environment with drug sales being conducted on almost every corner and at all times of the day. The salesmen, guards, and lookouts in this process are generally impoverished, angry kids who are willing to take up arms and lay down their lives for a piece of the lucrative drug market. Lacking any remorse or sense of moral obligation, they carry on their business with utter disdain for legal authorities and engage in open warfare for control of the trade. Drug trafficking has become a highly rewarding economic activity for poor, impoverished inner-city youths, providing them with the vestiges of material wealth. Drug dealers boast openly of the vast amounts of money they can make plying their trade.

The third general process is the impact of the media. Our society is a media-oriented society, and there is no doubt that the media have helped to project the image that the way to solve a problem or to feel good is to take something — a pill or a drink. In terms of alcohol advertising, the general image the media project is that alcohol is associated with success, wealth, and having fun. Similarly, when we watch "Miami Vice," we see the glamour, the wealth, and luxury associated with drug-related behavior. We do not see the poverty, the filth, and the squalor of the drug addict. We see the beautiful homes, the fancy cars, and the fancy parties. We do not see the misery, human suffering, and pain associated with drug use.

In addition, the urban community is inundated with billboards proclaiming the message that drinking is fashionable and offering high-priced alcohol as the standard against which to measure one's worth. These ads all advocate the purchase of dark-colored, heavy-bodied alcohol which has a much higher ethanol content than the distilled, light-colored alcohol. Further, the use of athletic heroes as marketing representatives in commercials for alcohol impacts heavily upon the susceptibility and impressionability of the African-American adolescent, in particular. When his favorite hero appears in a commercial or on a billboard drinking a particular brand of beer, wine cooler, or hard liquor the impressionable adolescent is likely to emulate the behavior of the hero as a role model and to engage in that behavior. Vast amounts of money are also spent in magazines targeted to the African-American community (e.g., *Ebony, Jet, Essence*) on alcohol advertisements each year.

SUBSTANCE ABUSE IN THE AFRICAN-AMERICAN COMMUNITY

The problem of substance abuse is a long-standing one which has been approached from many different perspectives (i.e., educational, legal, health, etc.). Across the nation, city after city and community after community are reporting on the ever-increasing involvement of people with drugs, particularly young people. Drug abuse has reached epidemic proportions in America. The people who are actually involved in drug use represent the mere tip of the iceberg. For every one person identified in drug-related activity there are approximately 3-5 persons directly connected to that individual (c.f., Nobles, 1985). The extent of the substance abuse problem reaches far beyond the actual number of users and abusers. At all levels, national and local, drug abuse among minority populations continues to be disproportionately worse than other segments of the society.

Alcohol Use and Abuse: In regard to the epidemiology of substance abuse, alcohol use and abuse, for instance, is so common in the African-American community that it has become acceptable behavior with little or no stigma attached to it. The research literature indicates that African Americans tend to be group drinkers, drinking in a social context with friends and relatives as opposed to drinking alone. African Americans also tend to drink more frequently and heavily during the weekend. Their "heavy drinking" tends to begin in the age group 20-24 and reach a peak in the age group 35-39. The consequence of this is that African Americans tend to drink more and for a longer period of time and hence are more likely to suffer from the negative consequences of long-term heavy drinking as reflected in high mortality rates due to cirrhosis of the liver. In many communities, street drinking has become a social custom with many African Americans drinking on the street corner, outside liquor stores, in automobiles, and in front of homes and stores. As a group, African Americans have higher rates of abstainers and heavier drinkers than whites. African Americans are status conscious drinkers, paying more attention to brands of liquor and prices. Although African Americans represent only 11 percent of the national population, they purchase 30 percent of the scotch sold in this country. It is estimated that African Americans spend $11-12 billion annually on alcohol.

In a recent report prepared by the Fanon Research and Development Center part of the Charles R. Drew University of Medicine and Science in Los Angeles, it was indicated that approximately 16 percent of the African-American population are alcoholics. Alcohol use has increased over 86 percent since 1979 with 65 percent of African-American youth engaging in regular weekly use, with first drinks being taken between the ages of 8 and 10 years, and girls trying almost as often as boys. The health effects of alcohol use is devastating. Alcoholism is a secondary diagnosis in 65 percent of hospital beds; it is implicated in 61 percent of job absenteeism; 84 percent of traffic deaths; 70 percent of suicides; 80 percent of homicides; 90 percent of stabbings; 70 percent of all violent crimes; and 60 percent of automobile accidents. The incidence of cirrhosis of the liver for urban African-American males under 35 years old is 12 times higher than with any other comparable group. In 1983, the death rate for cirrhosis of the liver for African-American males was 23 per 100,000, almost double that of white males of 13 per 100,000. The African-American female death rate for cirrhosis of the liver was 11 per 100,000 as compared to six per 100,000 for white females.

In light of these hard data relative to the effect of alcohol on the African-American community, it is important to note that the African-American community is still less likely to view alcoholism as an illness and has been slow in confronting excessive drinking as a social problem requiring professional help. Consequently, the involvement of African Americans in the treatment process occurs very late in the onset of alcoholism and is often at the order of the legal system. (Williams, 1982; Lipscomb, 1981).

Drug Use and Abuse: In regards to drug use/abuse, official data (National Survey of Drug Abuse, 1982, 1985) indicates that the overall incidence of drug abuse in the African-American population is about the same as that for the white population. Data from these studies show that about 32 percent of each group had used drugs illicitly at some time in their lives. In terms of current usage the pattern remained substantially the same with 13 percent of African Americans and 12 percent of whites reporting having used illicit drugs in the past month. These data, while they point to the magnitude of the problem, should be taken with some caution since they are generally based on samples in which African Americans are underrepresented and people are less likely to implicate themselves in an illegal activity, such as drug use. Consequently, it is highly likely that these data represent a significant undercount of the incidence of drug abuse in the African-American community.

There can be little doubt that drug use and abuse has reached epidemic proportions within the African-American community. The primary drug in the African-American community has traditionally been marijuana and heroin, with cocaine being seen as the drug of the rich and powerful. However, within recent years there has been a dramatic shift in the drug of choice in the community. While the incidence of marijuana and heroin use appears to have stabilized, cocaine use has skyrocketed with the emergence of crack. In Oakland, for example, it is estimated that 90 percent of the drug trafficking is in cocaine. The emergence of this drug has brought the more expensive and addictive cocaine into the reach of the poorer sectors of the community. Crack is cheap. It is easy to hide, easy to use, deadly, potent, and highly addictive. While everything else in the society has been increasing in cost, crack cocaine is becoming increasingly cheaper to buy. For example, in California, crack can be bought for as little as $5. And reportedly, in New York, crack is available for only $1. In fact, six months ago a jumbo vial of crack cost $40. Today, that same vial will cost $15. The cost of a vial of the most deadly drug known is equivalent to the cost of a cheap tie or a pair of sun glasses. The consequence of this is that a wider segment of the community with the least resources for remediation is involved with this drug. In this regard, data from the latest National Survey of Drug Use (1987) reported that one out of every 25 high school seniors (4.1 percent) reported having tried crack in the past year. Usage rates were substantially higher among the non-college bound (5.2 percent) than the college bound (2.8 percent); and in the larger cities (5.9 percent) than the smaller cities and non-urban areas (3.5 percent each). It is important to note that dropouts who are possibly more inclined to drug use were not included in the survey.

The main danger with crack is its potency. One shot is never enough to satisfy the feelings of euphoria experienced. Crack users have said that the high obtained from crack is so high that there is no desire to come down and the low is so low that they never want to experience that low feeling. Consequently, most crack users lose self control as they seek to experience that feeling of euphoria over and over. They lie, steal, cheat; sell their bodies, their belongings, and their property all in quest of another "hit" from the crack pipe. Crime, violence, and prostitution have become by-products of the crack epidemic sweeping the African-American community. It should also be noted that the crack epidemic has led to the emergence of a more serious health problem in the African-American community in that a significant number of babies are being born affected by cocaine. This is such a new phenomenon that the medical community has no baseline knowledge on the developmental disabilities that this would have on the infant.

The ultimate danger of crack cocaine is that it is affecting the very young members of the African-American community who lack the knowledge and refusal skills and, hence, are unable to make appropriate decisions about participation. With its low prices, ease of use and storage, and affordability, more and more young people are becoming caught in its web of entrapment. Available data indicate that the recent upsurge in drug abuse, in fact, has been concentrated mainly among the younger population.

The context of drug use in the African-American community is especially problematic in that most children learn about drugs and are offered drugs the first time by social peers and sometimes relatives. The consequence of this is that children are exposed at early ages to the presence of drugs; are capable of identifying the behavioral modalities associated with drug use; and become quickly acclimated to a drug-infested environment.

While we have discussed alcohol and drugs separately, it is important to point out that the prevailing pattern of substance abuse in the African-American community is one of polydrug use. The Institute's study (c.f., Nobles et al., 1987) indicated that for the African-American community, alcohol serves as the gateway drug to more addictive drug use. Recent data from the national Drug Abuse Warning Network (DAWN, 1985) system indicated that many of the patients presenting themselves at emergency rooms in hospitals across the country were polydrug users and that the most common pattern was alcohol in combination with another drug. In fact, of the top 10 drug combinations reported in 1984, eight of the 10 involved alcohol in combination.

AIDS: Acquired Immunodeficiency Syndrome (AIDS) is the newest and most frightening danger to emerge from the presence of drugs in the African-American community. According to latest official statistics, as of April 6, 1987, a cumulative total of 83,231 cases of AIDS and 46,667 deaths had been reported. No one knows the exact extent of the disease. It is estimated that between 1 and 1.5 million Americans have already been infected with the AIDS virus. Although the overwhelming majority of these individuals are presently asymptomic, given the long incubation period (up to five years) of the disease, they may unknowingly transmit the infection to others by sexual intercourse, by sharing hypodermic needles, and by in utero transmission from mother to child. Recent data now suggest that intravenous drug users and heterosexuals with multiple partners represent the bridge to the other segments of the population.

The high-risk groups for AIDS are as follows: gay and bisexual men, with and without a history of intravenous drug use; heterosexual drug users; heterosexual contacts of people with AIDS; babies of women with AIDS; and sexually active people with multiple partners. However, until recently, in the African-American community, AIDS had been considered a disease affecting white homosexual and bisexual men and some African-American intravenous drug users. At the current time African Americans represent 27 percent of AIDS cases, but only 12 percent of the national population. However, among children and women, the situation is even worse. Currently 52 percent of women with AIDS are African American; and 53 percent of children with AIDS are African-American (Health, United States, 1987). Almost all of these children have been infected in utero; 89 percent of diagnosed children have at least one intravenous drug-using parent. The disproportionately high rates of infection of the virus by peoples of African descent have led several people to speculate that Africa and/or Haiti was the origin of the virus. However, Kanter and Pankey (1987) have indicated that the virus had been endemic to the U.S. population and that it was through sociocultural changes in society (sharing of IV needles and risky sexual practices), not importation from Africa, that the infection has become epidemic and has subsequently been exported.

There is little doubt that the incidence of drug use has placed the African-American population at great risk of contracting this deadly virus. In reality, AIDS is a non-discriminating killer which is now spreading beyond the original high-risk groups into the heterosexual population. Given the prevailing pattern of drug use in the African-American community, the sharing of needles, common among heroin users, represents the primary mode of transmission of the virus in the

167

African-American community. Similarly, the increase in teenage prostitution associated with "crack houses" is placing a large proportion of young women at risk of contracting the virus through sexual intercourse with multiple partners.

Without a doubt, the primary effects of substance abuse in the African-American community are death, devastation, and destruction as lives are lost, careers are destroyed, families are torn apart, and the future resources of the community are depleted.

The Issue of Drug Testing: Due to the high concentrations of serotonin and melatonin in people of African descent, Carol Barnes, a brilliant young chemist, has repeatedly warned against random and "for cause" drug testing of African-American people. In reviewing the natural laws of chemistry, Barnes (1988) notes that upon physical or electromagnetic contact, if two chemicals have similar structures, they will dissolve into, or chemically react to, each other. He then explains that cocaine, marijuana, alcohol, and LSD have alkaloids and ring structures that are very similar to melanin and its precursors (p. 82). Environmental herbicides, like agent orange (Dioxin) and paraquats, also have similar structures to melanin. It is believed that the chemical binding of melanin with these elements is irreversible and that the new chemical mixture remains in the life system of the host body forever and can cause harm to the body, and even death.

Given the affinity of amino groups, Barnes further points out that a toxic chemical, like cocaine, also has the potential to co-polymerize into the melanin structure. Once the co-polymerization is complete, it (the cocaine) can remain intact within the melanin centers throughout the body for an indeterminate period. Any significant event (e.g., stress, dietary changes, environmental shifts, climatic flux, etc.) can trigger the melanin molecule to release unknown amounts of cocaine into the blood stream which, in turn, can cause delayed "trips," spontaneous highs, seizures, and even sudden death.

The implication these facts have for drug use addiction and drug testing is not fully appreciated. One should recognize, however, that due to the "melanic capacity" of African people, African Americans will become addicted (due to the binding nature and structural similarity of the melanin) faster and have greater difficulty (takes longer) in becoming drug free. The Barnes analyses also suggest that people of African descent have greater likelihood of testing positive for the presence of drugs when, in fact, they are drug free. That is to say, given the similarity of the melanin structure and the structures of toxic alkaloids, the natural pineal producing alkaloids like seratonin and melatonin in African-American people may fool the test into thinking it has identified a toxic alkaloid or chemical structure. Hence, African Americans may have greater incidences of undetected "false-positives" with current drug testing practices. Clearly, more research and study in this area is needed if we are to prevent the new interest in drug testing from becoming another tool in the victimization, discrimination, and domination of African-American people.

THE IMPACT OF DRUGS ON AFRICAN-AMERICAN FAMILIES, CHILDREN, AND COMMUNITIES

Across the nation, city after city and community after community are reporting that drug use and drug-related activity have resulted in traditional youth delinquency and crime (i.e., petty theft, truancy, etc.) taking on the countenance of more serious life-threatening activity (i.e., assault, murder, extortion, etc.). In fact, with the eruption of the so-called drug wars in urban communities throughout the nation, the central city has earned the reputation of being an unsafe place. In a 1981 survey of serious crimes in the Bay Area cities, Oakland, California, (the city with the 16th largest African-American population in the United States) was ranked as the third "meanest" city to live in with a serious crime rate of 128 per 1,000 population. (Data will be provided for the city of Oakland, California. However, the conditions found in Oakland are generalizable to any central city in the United States with a large black population.) It should be noted that almost half (48.3 percent) of the families in Oakland are African-American and six out of every 10 (59.4 percent) of the children in this city are African-American children. Given the 1984 report of 6,608 drug arrests, we can estimate that between 18,000 and 30,000 people are being directly affected by drug-related activity in this city alone.

Analysis of the crime data for 1984 points to an alarming trend in the pattern of crime. This trend, some believe, is linked to an increase of (drug and drug-related activities). For example, in 1984, there were 115 homicides in the city, an increase of 16 percent over the 1983 total. Thirty-two percent were drug-related. This figure represented a 39 percent increase over the 1983 total. Similarly, there was a 5.5 percent increase in burglaries spread throughout the city but being most serious in mid-East Oakland. This increase might be reflective of the increase in drug and drug-related activities with addicts looking for a quick and easy dollar to feed their habit. The increase in drug-related activities is reflected in a corresponding increase in arrests for drug offenses. There was a 19 percent increase in arrests for drug offenses in 1984, compared to 1983. The alarming trend in this statistic is that there was an 11 percent increase in arrests for heroin and cocaine sales and a seven percent decline in marijuana sales. These data reflect a shift in the pattern of drug activities to the more addictive drugs of heroin and cocaine. Across the nation, drug cases are smothering the criminal justice system.

For example, in this year, New York city police made over 20,000 drug arrests for crack alone. Drug arrests are up across the board by 24 percent. Understandably, the issue of drugs and drug-related activities has captured the public's attention as a criminal justice issue or a drug-abuse treatment issue.

The mind-set or group psychology surrounding drugs and criminal activity in the urban community presents an especially complex climate. In many ways drug dealers are revered, feared, respected, and despised all at the same time. The picture this creates for African-American children is understandably confusing. For instance, the killing of a young African-American man in Oakland who was involved in drug trafficking and drug-related criminal activity received national press coverage. Prior to his death the local media gave his life and rise to "Kingpin" of the drug culture a kind of "Robin Hood" aura or mystique. Reports of his illegal activities were almost always juxtaposed with the fact that he often fed hungry families, took groups of kids to amusement parks, tossed basketballs out to needy kids from his white Rolls Royce, etc. Upon his death, no other issue occupied the minds of the community. Partly due to the attention his death received from the press, an inordinate amount of discussion centered around the life and death of a convicted criminal and known drug-dealer. Consequently, hundreds, if not thousands, of youths witnessed the power and importance of drug-related criminal activity when the casket of a criminal and deviant drug dealer was literally carried across the entire city by a horse-drawn glass hearse, followed by five white Rolls-Royces, a grey Rolls-Royce, a Silver Cloud, five grey Cadillacs, two white Lincoln Stretch Continentals, a black Lincoln Limousine, and numerous other signs of prestige and importance.

In the lives and minds of thousands of people, the life-style and meaning of this drug dealer had, and still has, greater personal significance and importance than the lives and deaths of men like Martin Luther King, Jr., Lt. Col. Ronald McNair, or Malcolm X. Hence, drugs, drug related behavior, and the images of power, prestige, and privilege associated with them are combining to create a peculiar psycho-social phenomenon for African-American children and families.

It is important for us to understand the social, cultural, and psychological, as well as political and economic, impact of drugs in the African-American community. Early in 1986, the Institute for the Advanced Study of African-American Family Life and Culture was awarded a grant from the Alcohol and Drug Abuse Services Agency of Alameda County to undertake a formal investigation of the Effects of Drugs and Drug Trafficking on the Mental Health of African-American Children and Families in Oakland (cf. Nobles et al, 1987a & b). The aim of this research effort was to specifically study the influence that drug-related behavior (i.e., drug trafficking, lifestyle, and culture) has on the functioning of African-American children and families and determine the extent to which drug-related behavior (as distinct from drug use/abuse) is affecting human service delivery systems.

Under the leadership of Supervisor John George, The Alameda County Board of Supervisors supported this unique study. The Board, through George's influence, were able to see that the "War on Drugs" could not be won with more police, treatment, and slogans. As evidenced by their support of this study, The Board took the position that the solution to the drug crisis was to be found only in accurately understanding the emerging drug climate and culture. Supervisor George, up to the time of his death, recognized that the emerging drug culture exacerbated all other county problems and had the greatest permanent danger to the well being and welfare of the African-American community as well as the larger county-wide communities.

In a very real sense, this study represents the only attempt to understand the emerging influence of "the drug culture" on African-American family dynamics and its consequence for the behavior of children and parents. In this study we were able to develop a data base which revealed a link between drug-related activities and the family's difficulty in determining and reinforcing proper conduct/ values and the positive development of its children. This relationship also suggests, in turn, that the emerging drug culture may be associated with the increasing involvement of African-American youth in criminal behavior.

From the perspectives and testimony of former participants in the drug lifestyle and consultants, experts, and observers of drug related activity, the staff at the Institute for the Advanced Study of African-American Family Life and Culture was able to explicate the features of the emerging drug culture. In contrast to

---

CHART 1

SHIFT IN AFRICAN-AMERICAN CULTURAL ORIENTATION

BLACK FAMILY VALUE ORIENTATION	DRUG CULTURE VALUE ORIENTATION
I. Cultural Themes	I. Drug Culture Themes
• sense of appropriateness	• anything is permissible
• sense of excellence	• trust no one
II. Cultural Value System	II. Drug Cultural Value System
• mutual aid	• selfish
• adaptability	• materialistic
• natural goodness	• pathological liars
• inclusivity	• extremely violent
• unconditional love	• short iused
• respect (for elders)	• individualistic
• restraint	• manipulative
• responsibility	• immediate gratification
• reciprocity	• paranoid
• interdependence	• distrustful
• cooperativeness	• non-family oriented
	• not community-oriented
	• self worth = quantity

African-American culture, the general design for living in the drug culture is (1) trust no one and (2) anything is permissible. The subsequent rules by which one lives and the value system guiding one's behavior in the drug lifestyle emphasize selfishness, individualism, violence, hostility, impulsivity, etc.

It is especially worth noting that the behavioral patterns (i. e., persistent pattern of dishonesty, irresponsibility and callousness without signs of remorse, personal responsibility or motivation to change) consistent with the features of the emerging drug culture are in fact reflective of the most devastating psychiatric malady, the psychopath. The drug culture is, in fact, creating a "psychopathic" environment wherein "effective family functioning" is determined not by the rules or moral values of one's socio-cultural group, but by the dictates of a system of deviancy and chaos. Essentially, the drug culture is one that emphasizes immediate gratification, a sense of hedonistic pleasure, and lack of concern for others. For individuals and families involved in the drug culture, the drug-related behaviors and the pursuit of the means necessary to sustain the drug-taking lifestyle become the central life interests and the primary determinants of all social relations. As the producer of a psychopathic environment, the emerging drug culture and the subsequent cultural shift are the most powerful dangers which African-American children and families must confront on a daily basis. To the extent that families experience this cultural disalignment, there is tension and potential conflict within and between families. Hence, with the emergence of the drug culture as the dominant environmental influence in the lives of African-American families and children, we are witnessing a shift in cultural orientation of the African-American community (See Chart 1). As more and more African-American families and children begin to internalize the laws and rules of the drug culture, we are beginning to see a permanent, and possibly irreversible, change in the nature of African-American families and children.

The impact of the drug culture is that parents have to compete with a culture that provides immediate gratification and material possessions to its participants. The glamor, glitter, and material possessions of the drug dealers serve as a powerful attractant, seductively enticing more and more African-American children to enter into the web of self-destructive behavior. The drug dealer emerges as a model of someone who has been able to create an alternative economic activity that gives the material vestiges of power. In the presence of high levels of unemployment, limited educational attainment and the adoption of a materialistic value orientation, drug dealing and drug-related activity emerge as a viable economic alternative for urban African-American youth.

In this vein, African-American families are confronted by a phenomenon which is simultaneously aberrant, addictive, and economically viable. On the one hand, in response to economic impoverishment, participation in drug trafficking appears to be the only option for family economic viability and hence becomes reasonable and acceptable; while on the other hand, the same act of participation represents behavioral dysfunctioning and social deviancy. The Institute's drug study suggests that the conflict associated with an illegal activity that also benefits the family was a precipatory basis for the expression of severe feelings of psychological stress/trauma in African-American children. The climate of drugs has resulted in families who are simultaneously victims and representatives of an emerging drug lifestyle.

It is not solely the drug-using population that is being affected by the spread of drugs throughout the community. The non-drug-using population is being severely affected by its very presence and the emergent drug culture. The random violence and the drive-by shootings that take place as dealers struggle to maintain control of their "turf" create in residents a deep sense of fear for their own safety. In this vein children are unable to venture out into the community to engage in those developmental activities that instill in them a sense of confidence and pride in their ability to master some new activity. Parents are afraid to allow their children to go to the corner store on an errand or even to go outside to play for fear of some violence that might be perpetrated on them by being in the wrong place at the wrong time. The primary environmental socialization experiences that African-American children face, given the presence of drug-related activity in the African-American community, are violence, fear, hostility, tension, criminalization, and community disunity.

The sense of apathy and helplessness that is felt by African-American families is exacerbated with the advent of decreased efficacy among service delivery systems. Mental health service providers are seeing behavioral and emotional disturbances among their clientele that they have not seen before, and consequently, they are having difficulty in being able to effectively identify and provide treatment to African-American families.

In response to the pervasive presence of drug-related activity and/or behavior, service providers reported feeling inadequate and ineffectual. This inadequacy is clearly understandable in as much as the service provider, regardless of the specialty; is confronting new phenomena which are simultaneously aberrant, addictive, cultural, and economic. The difficulty in addressing the issue of drug-related activity/behavior and the provision of services can be found, in part, in not having a prior knowledge base dealing with the problem. In terms of "practice," there are very few agencies which have treatment and intervention strategies designed to deal with the special health problem of drug activity and drug-related behavior in the communities in which they serve. For example, with the spread of cocaine use, doctors are seeing more and more cocaine-affected babies. In one urban hospital, it is estimated that on the average 25 cocaine-affected babies are born each month. This is such a new phenomenon that there is little or no medical evidence about the long-term health problems or the developmental growth patterns of these babies. Thus, the practitioner has no body of knowledge on which to base his diagnosis and treatment. S/he is essentially operating in "virgin" territory. Similarly, general practitioners are unknowingly treating cocaine abusers for their primary symptoms, for example, nasal sores, rhinitis, problems in swallowing, hoarseness, nausea, vomiting, hypertension, etc., and fail to diagnose the cocaine dependency. It is only through a long period of contact and treatment with the patient that the general practioner is able to begin to identify the cocaine dependency. It should also be noted that health practitioners report seeing maladaptive behaviors in the non-drug using population and in general believe that health disorders associated with drug-related behaviors are often misidentified as purely "psychiatric." Given the high percentage of drug-related maladaptive behavior seen by service providers and in the absence of a clear way of diagnosing such problems, one can assume that many people are not currently being accurately assessed or treated. The perceived inadequacy of those charged to help the weakened and the sick is understandable given the special aberrancy and acclimation emerging from a drug culture, its blending of the problems of mental health and drug abuse, and its creation of a "new normalcy" which is deviant.

The results of our investigation suggest that the emergence of a "drug culture" which threatens to destroy the very fabric of the African-American culture" is even more dangerous than the actual incidence of drug use/abuse.

THE COST IN ACHIEVING PARITY

It is clear that drug use and drug-related activities are exacting a heavy toll on the African-American community—in many ways directly depleting the community's economic resources. Equally significant, however, is the fact that the future (non-replaceable) resources and life-chances of the African-American community are also being eroded and/or destroyed.

Drugs and the drug culture are making it extremely difficult for the African-American population to attain parity on economic and social levels. African Americans spend on the average $11-$12 billion annually on alcohol. The cost of illicit drugs is equally staggering. It is estimated that the average crack user spends $100 per week on crack. Assuming one percent of the African-American population is using crack, at the average cost of $100 per week, the African-American community is losing $655 million (126,000 x $5,200) a year to crack alone. These are conservative estimates, but they pinpoint the enormity of the economic burden that the African-American population is carrying in the drug epidemic. When we look at the economic value of the goods seized in drug raids we see the extent of the profitability in drug trafficking. In Oakland alone, in 1986, for example, the police seized one million dollars in cash from people involved in drug trafficking. Another $300,000 in assets, cars, and houses were also seized. This does not include the actual drugs that were seized that were reported to have a street value of $6.8 million. In 1987 alone, Federal enforcement agencies seized approximately 70 tons of cocaine, 1,400 pounds of heroin, and 2.2 million pounds of marijuana (cf, Herrington, 1988). These illicit drugs have an estimated street value of $11.2 billion. The drain of the economic resources of the African-American community can be easily extrapolated from these data.

Beyond the actual money spent on drugs, there are the related costs of treatment for drug addicts and the criminal justice costs for prosecution and incarceration of offenders. We can project the tremendous economic burden that the community and society is suffering from the drug culture. It is estimated that it costs $20,000 per annum to keep one prisoner incarcerated. In Oakland alone, in the period January-April, 1987, there were 1,687 arrests for possession of cocaine, heroin, and other dangerous drugs. If we assume a 50 percent conviction rate, then, it would cost this metropolitan area $16.8 million to incarcerate 843 people for one year. The projected criminal justice costs are staggering. Assuming that drug trafficking remains the same, Oakland will spend $84 million during the next five years to incarcerate drug offenders alone. This is a heavy drain on the resources of any city. Given the attractiveness data from the Institute's drug study, which found that two out of every three youth surveyed felt that their peers were attracted to the lifestyle and material wealth of drug dealers, it is easy to see that the above is a rather conservative estimate of the potential costs associated with drugs.

When we factor in the cost of treatment for substance abuse, the figure becomes even higher. At present, there are approximately 9,000 drug treatment centers throughout the country (Herrington, 1988). It is estimated that outpatient care cost $4,000 per year per slot, while residential slots average $15,000 per year. Other estimates place the cost of residential care at approximately $25,000 per month for the most expensive care (cf, Herrington, 1988). If we use the Fanon Center's 16 percent ratio of alcoholism as the lowest level of substance abuse addiction, the African-American community could expect to spend between $16 billion and $61 billion in substance abuse treatment alone per annum.

The economic drain of substance abuse on the African-American community could be better seen if we were to project it in terms of alternate resource allocation. For example, the low estimate of substance abuse treatment cost ($16 billion) could provide full four-year scholarships to Spelman or Morehouse College for 451,773 African-American children per year. In fact, the low estimated substance abuse treatment cost could provide each of the 101 Historically Black Colleges with an annual endowment of $5 million for the next 30 years. For the estimated nine million African-American persons living in poverty, this low estimated treatment cost could provide full health coverage annually in a Health Maintenance Organization. Applying the process to housing, the low estimated treatment cost could purchase 200,000 four bedroom homes (at $80,000 per home) annually for use by the homeless.

In terms of issues of parity, the glamor, glitter, and allure of the drug culture serve as powerful attractants that are seducing large numbers of African-American youth away from productive efforts in traditional areas of social life. It is increasingly difficult to encourage African-American youth to continue their education when they see educated African Americans unemployed or working in occupations for which they are overqualified and underpaid and, on the other hand, high school dropouts involved in drugs having all the material trappings of success in the society. African-American youth are openly questioning the value of education, the work ethic, and delaying gratification. They are surrounded by the vestiges of material success which they can potentially have immediately and with little work. The impact of this is that African-American youth are more likely not to see higher education as a goal to which they should aspire. As more and more youth succumb to the allure of the drug culture, the proportion of African-American children with the motivation, discipline, and desire to complete high school, let alone attend college, is declining accordingly. The problem of African-American children dropping-out and/or being pushed out of school is further compounded by the presence of drug-related activity in our communities. The long-term consequence of the drug culture is that the African-American population is in danger of not being able to reproduce its current middle class. Thus, it is difficult for the African-American population to maintain its current comparative social and economic position, let alone attain parity.

Drug use is a primary contributory factor to the lower life expectancy of the African-American population at present. The behavioral lifestyle associated with drug use increases the probability of early death through several preventable causes. Data from the Secretary's Task Force on African-American and Minority Health (1985) indicate that six causes of death — cancer, cardiovascular disease and stroke, chemical dependency, diabetes, homicide and accidents and infant mortality account for 80 percent of the mortality observed among African Americans. Utilizing the concept "excess death" the Task Force reported that 42 percent of all African Americans who die before age 70 could be considered excess deaths. The concept of <u>excess death</u> *"expresses the difference between the number of deaths actually observed in a minority group and the number of deaths that would have occurred in that group if it experienced the same death rates for each age and sex as the White population"* (Secretary's Task Force Report (1985). The Task Force further reported that the six causes previously mentioned account for 80 percent of the "excess deaths" among African Americans. Recent data (Health, United States, 1987) indicate that homicide is the leading cause of death among young African-American men. In 1988, major cities including New York; Newark; Atlanta; Los Angeles, and Miami have reported record numbers of drug-related homicides. Indeed, the Secretary's Task Force estimated that homicide accounted for 38 percent of the male excess deaths and 14 percent of the female excess deaths below age 45. Given the violence, unpredictability, and volatile nature of drug trafficking and drug-related behavior, we can estimate that 80 percent of the "excess deaths" due to homicide are drug-related.

In addition, the life chances of the present and future generations are being affected as drug use, primarily crack cocaine, increases. Since crack use is associated with a generally young population, the contraction of sexually transmitted diseases will have a decidedly detrimental effect on the future well-being of the African-American population. AIDS is having a major effect on African-American women, both in terms of incidence and mortality rates. With the projected rate of infection, a significant proportion of African-American women may have already contracted the virus. Given the lower rate of survival for African-American persons with AIDS, many of these women would die before they are able to reproduce themselves in the population. In addition, those women who are affected with the virus and who do bear children are likely to transmit the virus in utero to their children. From a demographic perspective, the impact of drug-related behavior is two-fold. On the one hand, the fecundity of African-American women would be affected through exposure to, and contraction, of sexually transmitted diseases. On the other hand, fertility would be affected through the death of large numbers of women of child-bearing age and an increase in childlessness among sub-fecund women. In addition, infant and neonatal mortality would increase as a result of drug-related effects. The long-term consequence of substance abuse would be a reduction in the future stock of the African-American population.

Similarly, the emergence of crack-affected babies represents another danger to the future viability of the African-American population. The presence of crack-affected babies is such a new phenomenon that no one knows the actual developmental delays, the long-term psychiatric conditions, or later life developments associated with it. It should be clear, however, that with the associated brain damage that crack affected babies experience, those who do survive will represent a population who will be in need of extra-ordinary specialized services that will pose additional untold economic and spiritual burdens on our community.

The effect of drugs and the drug culture is that the African-American population is steadily losing social and economic ground and is in danger of suffering a permanent retrogression. The transformation of the American economy and the consequent shifts in the labor force have created a high level of unemployment in the African-American community and the creation of a permanent underclass. The ranks of the underclass are being swelled with large numbers of African-American youth who drop out and/or are pushed out of the school system. In a similar vein, drug use, particularly crack cocaine, is increasing the rate of serious medical and psychiatric problems in the African-American community and is, thereby, threatening the fundamental survivability (fecundity, fertility, morale, spirituality, etc.) of the African-American population.

WHAT CAN BE DONE

Obviously, when one honestly examines American cultural and social conditions relative to African-American people, the overwhelming quality of (African-American) its society has to be characterized by the twin forces of socio-political exploitation and racial and cultural dehumanization (domination). Hence, at the outset, the on-going debate regarding the proper governmental response to drugs via public policy has to be qualified by the historical and socio-political experience of the African-American community. For example, the issue of the proper role of government relative to the strategies of interdiction, prevention, and treatment has most often been couched in terms of the extent to which the public sector (i.e., government) vs. private responsibility (i.e., individual initiative) ought to be the basis of eradication efforts. In effect, the question becomes to what extent should command mechanisms (i.e., the authority of government) rather than personal mechanisms (i.e., the law of individual responsibility) be utilized or employed as the method for eradicating drug abuse. This debate seems reasonable and even though the current political climate favors private or personal responsibility, the question becomes complicated by the perception, and socio-cultural and geo-political position, of the African-American community (i.e., politically disenfranchised and subject of oppression).

The problem of substance abuse in the African-American community is, clearly, societal. If one looks at the fact that (1) African-American unemployment remains twice as high as white unemployment; (2) African-American people experience serious crime more often than their white counterparts; (3) only 51 percent of African-American youth in the United States complete high school and only 29 percent of African-American high school graduates are enrolled in college; (4) 13 percent of all births in the United States are to teenagers and 29 percent of the teen births are African Americans; and (5) the generalized health status of the African-American population is worse than that of the white population, then one is able to see that the problems experienced by the African-American community are systemic to the socio-cultural reality of America and that each of these social factors are linked to substance abuse.

In regards to substance abuse in the African-American community, as well as to most social issues and/or problems, the debate over public vs. private sector resources is somewhat specious. However, there is at least one concept that must be recognized if one is to see the pervasive and insidious nature of the drug problem for the African-American community. Though difficult to accept, that concept is the question of genocide.

The most common definition of genocide is that it is the deliberate and systematic killing of an entire people, race, or nation. In so defining genocide, the horror of the possibility results in almost every reasonable person dismissing the notion as unthinkable and impossible. However, when the concept is actually broken down, one is able to see that "geno" refers to the germ plasm (or life force) that transmits hereditary character or information and "cide" refers to the act of cutting or killing something. Hence, a more accurate conception of "genocide" is any deliberate and systematic act of commission or omission which results in the killing of a group's life force and the destruction of their ability to transmit its own hereditary character and/or information. Accordingly, if one can find that the prevalence and presence of drugs in the African-American community is resulting in the African-American group's inability to transmit its own hereditary character and information and, thereby, through its own sense of integrity and worth, create history and meet the prerequisite of life; and if one is able to determine that those mechanism (be they the laws of commerce or the authority of government) crucial to mastering life's challenges are withheld or available inequitably, then one could arguably perceive the genocidal implications of the substance abuse problem. For instance, it is now known that 60 percent of all illicit drugs produced in the world are imported and consumed in the United States (cf. Herrington, 1988). Many even suspect that the flow of illicit drugs from foreign lands has not been terminated because of the political expediency it offers domestically and internationally. While the production of illicit drugs has corrupted government officials world-wide, been suspect in the Iran-Contra affair, undermined the governments of many of our democratic allies in the Caribbean and Latin America, and placed in serious jeopardy the economic infra-structure of our own economy, the national response of this country has been overly dependent upon demand reduction strategies. This response is especially interesting, given that at the exact time of this writing, the United States is considering the invasion of Libya in order to militarily destroy what it "suspects" is a chemical weapons plant. Why not conclude that this, too, is a question of individual responsibility and tell Libya or its potential customers to "Just Say No." The drug-producing fields of Bolivia and Columbia are, in effect, "chemical weapons plants." The law of consistency would, therefore, suggest that if one is willing to militarily destroy one chemical weapons plant then one should also be willing to destroy any chemical weapons plant.

The point, of course, is that it is highly likely that through acts of commission and/or omission the command mechanism of government has allowed the drug problem to go unchecked and consequently, those communities with the least ability to resist the inevitable destruction are being systematically destroyed.

Given the implications of the above, one must be reminded that discrimination is an act designed to separate individuals or people for the purpose of allowing one group to receive preferential treatment and/or advantage; and, that in a system characterized by racism and oppression, almost every element or process managed by the racist system is designed primarily to continue and secure the status of the "advantaged" by guaranteeing in all arenas their preferential treatment. Substance abuse, in many ways, is becoming an American condition. However, in relation to the African-American community, substance abuse can immediately be judged as a phenomenon which, at best, will result in the African-American community becoming a "drug-dependent" socio-politically exploited and racially/culturally dehumanized community; and, at worse, an instrument of genocide in the African-American community.

Accordingly, the solution to the problems of substance abuse in the African-American community is, obviously, not to be found in individual therapy and programs targeted to the individual. Neither are the solutions to be found in campaigns based on individual responsibility when the structural constraints of the society prohibit and prevent individual initiative and advancement based on race.

The solution to the substance abuse problem does lie, however, in the area of national interest and, therefore, public policy. We believe that the solution to substance abuse in the African-American community must be prescribed in public policy which targets the cessation of supply (as contrasted to the reduction of demand) and which supports and guarantees the cultural realignment of African-American people and the revitalization of the African-American community.

Given the pervasiveness of the drug phenomenon as a cultural way of life, and the necessity of a national prevention agenda, it is our opinion that it is only those programs which are consistent with the traditional cultural orientation and precepts of African-American people that have the highest potential for successfully responding to the drug epidemic. Culturally consistent programming provides a spiritual base, a sense of connection, and a value system that is based on the intrinsic cultural orientation of the African-American population. It is imperative that we provide our youth with a solid value orientation if we expect to develop mature, responsible African-American adolescents.

The authors and several senior members of the African-American community (most notably, Mrs. Dorothy Pitts of Tennessee, Prof. John Henrik Clark of New York and Mrs. Queen Ester Thurston of Oakland) have discussed the corrective potential of a "National Council of Elders" who, in addition to providing culturally consistent guidance and historical wisdom would be charged with the responsibility of actively interpreting and understanding African-American cultural precepts and laws as well as protecting and monitoring the cultural integrity and direction of the African-American community.

Any program of prevention, intervention and treatment should, therefore, have three components that are of critical importance if the problem of substance abuse is to be solved by the African-American community reclaiming its inherent responsibility to satisfy its own human imperatives and cultural prerequisites. The first component or focus is to consciously re-claim, evaluate, apply, and institutionalize our own traditional techniques of development, socialization, and enculturation. In this respect and in response to the need to overtly and intentionally impact on the development of the African-American community and the need to eradicate the substance abuse problem, efforts should be made to (1) research and study (evaluate) traditional African and African-American cultural forms of human development via a systematic analysis of our formal and informal sets of rituals, ceremonies and practices; (2) create contemporary examples of those techniques without violating the traditional cultural core; and (3) develop methods and processes designed to allow and encourage societal institutions to "respect, reflect, and incorporate" the cultural integrity and expressions of African peoples.

This approach is currently enjoying some experimentation. Several programs have developed across the nation which attempt to create rites and rituals that would represent transitional stages in the development of a competent, confident, and conscious African-American community.

The Institute for the Advanced Study of Black Family Life and Culture has developed the HAWK Federation which is a national network of manhood training programs aimed at developing High Achievement, Wisdom and Knowledge in African-American males and therein impact on the revitalization of the African-American community. The Children of the Sun/Crime is Not a Part of Our Heritage Project developed by Garry Mendez, The Simba Project developed by Jawanza Kunjufu, The Bringing the Black Boy into Manhood Rites of Passage developed by Nathan and Julia Hare and the Urban League's Black Male Fatherhood Responsibility Program are all similar experiments. Several authors have developed rituals, programs and rites-of passage for both males and females. There are "experiments" being undertaken in Chicago, Seattle, New York, Washington, D.C., Florida, etc.

The staff at the Institute for the Advanced Study of Black Family Life and Culture has developed some theoretical ideas about what constitutes cultural immunology and what the community inoculation program should encompass. These are represented in the Institute's Community Inoculation Grid and the Institute's African-American Family Project's Blueprint. These are prototype developmental ideas that could form the basis for a national community inoculation through cultural immunology effort.

The second component or focus is to develop authentic Afrocentric theory and practice (therapy and education). This focus would require the establishment and support of African-American Think-Tanks and Research and Development Centers, charged with the responsibility for developing (1) Afrocentric theories of human development and transformation; (2) culturally consistent intervention, prevention and treatment methods; and (3) African-based development and training programs in response to the concrete conditions impacting upon the viability of African-American peoples.

The third and final component or focus would be to undertake a systematic program of "community inoculation through cultural immunology." The focus on community inoculation through cultural immunology would require that we develop and formally (re)introduce into the African-American community cultural mandates, functions, and expectations designed to stimulate the community's production of indigenous processes which have the capacity to resist negative agents and/or prevent the development of attitudes, ideas and/or behaviors antithetical to the African-American community's own well-being, welfare, and viability. This is a radically new and different perspective on what needs to be done in the African-American community. To our knowledge, there are few agencies or programs that are, in effect, attempting to inoculate the community against negative agents.

Clearly, the tremendous costs associated with substance abuse will, and are, depleting the resources of this nation and preventing the development of more positive life-enhancing activities that could improve the social and economic status and parity position of the African-American community. The African-American community individually and collectively must, therefore, read the "signs of the time" and assume the authority and responsibility for proactive self-vested policy, program and theory which will guarantee the positive development and transformation of the African-American community; and, thereby the good of the nation.

CONCLUSIONS AND RECOMMENDATIONS

Conclusions

The history of African Americans in this country reveals a constant struggle against racism and denied opportunity. However, in spite of grueling adversities, black Americans have continued to keep their eyes on the prize in an indomitable quest for equality and full participation in all sectors of American life.

The State of Black America 1989 comes at a critical juncture in our nation's history — as we begin the countdown to a new century.

The battle continues against indifference and ignorance; against discrimination; and insensitivity to black concerns; against a specious argument that those who confront racism somehow perpetuate it. Some leaders in this country proclaim their belief in brotherhood and equality, although their actions or inactions belie that claim. For some, racism is too difficult an issue to discuss; they would rather deny its existence.

The eminent psychiatrist, Dr. Price Cobbs, has written in this document about the "historical duality of being black and American" in an attempt to provide insight into the "paradoxes, contradictions, dilemmas" that make up the "central and constant dynamic" which affects the lives of all blacks in this country. But his is not a message of despair — nor is ours; the message is one of hope that Americans will learn to honor and value each other so that the dream of an open, pluralistic, integrated society will become a reality.

The pursuit of equal opportunity has been a clear and unequivocal goal of the National Urban League since our founding almost 80 years ago. Co-founders George Edmund Haynes and Ruth Standish Baldwin expressed hopes then that continue to have contemporary relevance. Mr. Haynes has stated that "Freedom is based upon the ideal of the infinite worth of every human being." His sentiment and the words of Mrs. Baldwin, who urged black and whites to work together for the "common good . . . of our common country," have been our guiding principles. From their vision, the Urban League has grown into a national movement which has resulted in improved social and economic circumstances for millions of people.

As we look toward the future, it is with a profound sense of urgency. The sobering realities described in the preceding pages serve to remind us of the tremendous tasks we face in completing America's unfinished agenda as we work toward our goal of Parity 2000.

The initial struggles are over; Jim Crow laws are gone; and there are no longer segregated drinking fountains and "separate but equal" schools. But, the war is far from won; the battles have simply taken on a new personality. The struggles today are in some ways more important, for they will decide whether blacks and whites will live in a harmonious and productive America or one convulsed by the divisive cancer of racism, suspicion, and ignorance. The fight at the back of

185

the bus 30 years ago is now centered over much more powerful issues — education, jobs, values, and money.

Much of the new struggle hinges on two things — higher education and how the federal government acts to foster change in the hearts and minds of all Americans.

When the Constitution was drafted, blacks were accorded only half-human status and in reality had fewer rights than other peices of "property."

America has not been a nation of fairness and justice and equality for a very long time. It was not until the great Civil Rights Movement of the mid-1960s that blacks began to come into their own.

The Voting Rights Act, The Fair Housing Act — the numerous measures designed to protect minority rights in this country — were simply "instruments" to control behavior. What they could not do was change the values of Americans. The notion then was that if you can get a nation behaving a certain way, then its attitudes would fall in line. Affirmative action, school desegregation, and other measures were gaining acceptance, and, people were learning to live with them.

In 1980, with the advent of the Reagan administration, government turned away from its advocacy of minority rights programs and began to slip slowly into an adversarial relationship with programs that previous administrations had conceived and supported. Affirmative action became reverse discrimination and busing became a tool that was against neighborhood schools.

What we have had is an administration saying that we are now a color-blind society with no racial problem.

While we have struggled to overcome much, many people have never seen blacks as real people, but as problems — problems that are burdensome — people who are not contributing. That created very harsh feelings over the years. Great Society programs today are argued by some to be programs that waste the taxpayers' money, programs that did not work, programs that did not call upon the self-help notion of people in the nation.

There is no doubt that great strides have been made. Thirty years ago in our southern cities the situation was not that such different than what we are seeing in South Africa today. From the bleak beginning, when the black poverty rate in 1959 was about 56 percent, the federal and state programs were primarily responsible for cutting it almost in half by 1979. (It is now back up to 33 percent.) There are now approximately 6,000 black elected officials in the country, compared to a handful in 1959, with a Congressional Black Caucus of growing influence and black mayors in several of the major American cities. In 1960, there were only 250,000 blacks in college, compared to more than a million today.

We acknowledge that there has been some improvement in the black condition over the years, but the issue of parity remains. Today, a third of all blacks live in poverty; half are children under the age of six. The jobless rate for blacks in an economically recovered nation is still at Depression levels. Both the income and wealth gaps continue to be significant. The wealth of a typical white family is 12 times greater than a typical black family.

The nation must further recognize, as the data show, that by the year 2000, the pool for workers will be primarily minorities and women — the most neglected groups today. To ignore this fact and its potential impact on the economy could prove devastating. We could find ourselves with people who need work and jobs that need people, and no match. The people who are being miseducated in the public schools today are the same people we will need as replacements in the work force of the future.

The federal government has tried to relinquish its role as provider and initiator of new programs by giving the responsibility to the private sector, which is not producing enough jobs for people who want to work. Of the three million jobs most recently created, half paid less than $7,000 annually.

Government cannot abdicate its responsibility to its citizens, just as the National Urban League cannot diminish its commitment to serve the needs of its constituency, especially poor and disadvantaged people.

The following recommendations speak to critical policy areas that must be addressed if we are to move toward the goal of racial parity in this society.

Recommendations

1. Race Relations

As America moves toward the twenty-first century we call on our national leadership – public and private – to make the improvement of race relations a national priority. Not only must racism be eliminated, but the aggressive improvement of race relations must be a national goal.

2. Economic Development

There is a need to develop a viable self-sustaining economic base in black communities. While full employment will ultimately help in closing the wage gap, we continue to urge a national program of black economic development, targeted to America's Central Cities and supported by the Federal Government and the private sector, that assists in creating jobs for the black community. There must be combined efforts on both the part of the private and public sector if blacks are to reach parity by the year 2000.

3. Education

The new president wants to be known as "an education president." We encourage efforts to expand programs targeted at black and minority students and preschool age children.

Though major studies were made in the 100th Congress, efforts to keep education as a number one priority must continue. Our schools must be strengthened and tailored to meet the demanding needs of our children and our nation.

4. Health

Parity in health for black and other minority Americans must be a national public health objective for the year 2000. Between 1985 and 1986, black Americans experienced a historic decrease in life expectancy for the second year in a row, to 69.4 years, the same level as in 1982, whereas whites experienced an increase in life expectancy to a record high of 75.4 years. This alarming disparity must be corrected and calls for public policy that ensures that the poor, the elderly, and the disadvantaged receive maximum parity in health coverage and access to care. The devastation of AIDS to the black community requires that every sector in the nation join in a commitment to halt this epidemic. Government and community-based organizations must work together to fully implement the newly enacted national AIDS policy and continue to explore new strategies for combatting the spread of this disease and other sexually transmitted diseases.

5. Empowerment

In 1988 we insisted that black institutions and black people increase their political potential by becoming active in voter registration campaigns and get-out-the-vote efforts. Further testament to our voting power is passage of the Fair Housing Admendments Acts and the Civil Rights Restoration Act by the lOOth Congress. We must continue our activism and our political involvement to help ensure that the political system produces public policy that is in the interest of Black America.

6. Labor/Employment

Black unemployment figures remained double digit throughout 1988. Every effort should be made to ensure that productive training and employment programs are adequately funded to provide opportunity for gainful employment. Most important, Congress should enact a new law bringing the "minimum wage" to a fair and equitable wage.

7. Housing

The housing crisis continues to be a national problem requiring a national solution. It dramatically demonstrates this by the increasing numbers of homeless people including families with children. It is also evident by the diminishing supply of affordable housing coupled with the mounting number of foreclosures that the social safety net has become unravelled. We urge immediate intervention to develop housing targeted to the central cities designed to alleviate homelessness and fill the gap of disappearing affordable housing for the poor. Homeownership is increasingly becoming only a distant dream for families as costs skyrocket and loans become more difficult to obtain. The attainment of parity in both the rental and ownership of housing will not be realized unless the federal government makes a serious commitment to bring housing within the financial reach of black Americans.

8. Child Care

The availability of affordable, quality child care is an essential component for economic self-sufficiency through employment. It is especially important for black families. Data reveal that of all mothers who worked in 1985, approximately 70 percent worked full time. In 1985, 84 percent of black working mothers and 69 percent of white working mothers worked full time, and 35 percent of women working part time or looking for work would work additional hours if they could find affordable quality child care. Having reached a national consensus on the need for child care, the National Urban League urges that Congress enact a comprehensive child care plan to assist families in securing affordable and safe child care systems.

9. Judicial Appointments

The President of the United States has the responsibility for judicial appointments. The possibility of controversial appointments will be a major issue for the protection and enforcement of existing civil rights laws. We entrust that not only the best qualified candidates are appointed, but that all candidates profess a fairness to all Americans regardless of ideological orientation.

10. International Affairs

While the House of Representatives passed a bill to enact stronger sanctions against South Africa in the 100th Congress, the Senate was not as supportive. It is anticipated that there will be efforts to push for passage of a South Africa sanctions bill in the Senate that will be acceptable to both the House and the new administration.

Chronology of Events
1988*

POLITICS

Jan. 8:   Jesse Jackson brings his presidential campaign to Osakis, Minnesota, a town of 1,326. Jackson was the first black that many residents have seen up close since 1963 when the "Inkspots" performed at the local high school.

Jan. 11:   Former Washington lobbyist Maurice Barboza launches drive to honor black soldiers in the Revolutionary War with a memorial. The drive under the arm of The Patriots Foundation is a fund-raising campaign to collect money to build the monument.

Jan. 11:   Federal obstruction of justice trial begins in Baltimore, MD, for former Maryland state senator Clarence M. Mitchell III. Mitchell charges that the Reagan administration is seeking to discredit black leaders through selective prosecutions.

Jan. 28:   Dr. Lenora Fulani of the New Alliance Party is the first black woman presidential candidate to receive federal matching funds for her campaign and is awarded $800,000.

Feb. 20:   After a credible finish in Iowa and New Hampshire, Rev. Jesse Jackson begins his presidential campaign in the south declaring that, "We meet in a New South," and further telling his audiences, "There is unfinished business. What good are civil rights without economic rights?"

March 11:   Rev. Jesse Jackson narrowly edges out presidential candidate Michael Dukakis by winning nearly 35 percent of the delegates selected at the Alaska Democratic Party precinct caucuses. Jackson also scores an overwhelming victory in the Democratic caucuses in his home state of South Carolina.

This chronology is based on news reports. In some instances, the event may have occurred a day before the news item was reported.

March 26: Rev. Jesse Jackson wins an easy victory in Michigan and deals a blow to the presidential candidacy of Gov. Michael Dukakis. Jackson received 42 percent of the votes and Dukakis received 35 percent of the votes with 74 percent of the precincts reporting.

April 5: Despite a landslide victory in Michigan, Rev. Jesse Jackson fails to translate the amount of good will he created among white voters in Wisconsin into votes needed to win that state's primary. Gov. Michael Dukakis defeats Jackson in the Wisconsin Democratic primary by a margin of more than 5 to 3.

April 10: Gov. Ray Mabus of Mississippi fails in his effort to oust the black chairman of the state's Democratic Party, Ed Cole, and replaces him with a handpicked white person.

April 13: President Reagan, responding to a question from a member of the American Society of Newspaper Editors, states that presidential candidate Jesse Jackson has been spared criticism of his policies because of his race and says that more attention is being paid to his color than what he is actually saying.

April 22: District of Columbia Mayor Marion Barry sounds an alarm for citizen vigilance and calls on residents to "form patrols" and "rise up against drug dealers." Barry also applauds the black Muslims' drive to run dealers out of the drug-ravaged Mayfair Mansions.

April 26: New York City Police Commissioner Benjamin Ward criticizes Mayor Edward Koch and calls on the mayor to apologize for attacks he made on the Rev. Jesse Jackson.

April 27: In a letter to the New York Times, New York City Mayor Edward Koch states: "I regret it if racial or religious friction resulted from my comments. It was never my intent to reject or insult the black community. I regret that my opposition and my voice sounded strident. In part, this was because no other voices were being heard on this issue." The apology was in response to an earlier criticism by Police Commissioner Benjamin Ward.

April 30: District of Columbia Mayor Marion Barry announces firing of Department of Human Services Director M. Jerome Woods. Woods had authorized the use of city funds to pay the rent for an apartment he had shared with a top aide.

May 3: Philadelphia Mayor W. Wilson Goode cleared by a grand jury of his involvement of criminal liability for death and destruction resulting from that city's fiery confrontation with the radical group MOVE. The Mayor and his administration were criticized for their "morally reprehensible behavior."

May 6: It was disclosed that one of acting Chicago Mayor Eugene Sawyer's aides, Steve Cokely, had delivered a series of speeches attacking whites, especially Jews.

May 8: Congress begins to take its first step toward approving a system under which Americans who move, to re-register automatically when they fill out a postal change of address form.

May 9: The ABC News primary election exit polls indicated that Jesse Jackson has failed to pull new voters into the party as he did during his first presidential campaign in 1984.

May 15: A team of Democratic Party insiders is assembled by presidential candidate Jesse Jackson to run his campaign at the Democratic National Convention. *The Washington Post* reports that the move was seen as a signal from Jackson that he wanted the convention to be smooth and non-confrontational.

May 16: Rev. Jesse Jackson states in Eugene, Oregon, that he expects to play a powerful role in the selection of the Democratic presidential ticket as well as in writing the party's platform.

May 31: Speaking in the Senate chamber in Trenton, New Jersey, Jesse Jackson says that he has "earned" the right to be considered for the vice presidential nomination and that his progressive campaign planks should be incorporated into the Democratic Party platform.

June 6: Presidential candidate Jesse Jackson all but concedes his 1988 quest for the Democratic nomination for president at the Ward A.M.E. Church in Los Angeles, CA. Jackson begins to move to the next stage of his campaign and outlines how he plans to advance his cause.

June 10: A *Washington Post*-ABC News Poll shows that, although Jesse Jackson is the leading choice for vice president, he would appear to hurt more than help the ticket with key groups of voters that the Democratic party needs in order to win in November.

June 11: Maurice A. Dawkins is the first black ever nominated to statewide office by Virginia Republicans. The 67-year-old Arlington, VA, resident was chosen over two rivals to face former Virginia governor Charles S. Robb in the race for U.S. Senate seat.

July 15: The first black chief of the Miami, FL Police Department, Clarence Dickson, resigns from his position. He is replaced by his assistant, Perry Anderson, who is also black. Dickson, in explaining the reason for his resignation, said that he had been "yelled at and treated in a subservient manner" by city commissioners. He said he was retiring early because he was "frustrated with the games being played" at City Hall.

July 17: Atlanta Mayor Andrew Young is on hand at the airport to greet Gov. Michael Dukakis as he arrives to be nominated for president.

July 19: Coretta Scott King, widow of slain civil rights leader Dr. Martin Luther King, Jr., hosts presidential candidate Gov. Michael Dukakis's visit to the Martin Luther King, Jr. Center in Atlanta during the Democratic National Convention.

July 28: Democratic presidential nominee Michael Dukakis courts supporters of Jesse Jackson in northern New Jersey. Newark Mayor Sharpe James who was Jackson's New Jersey campaign chairman, reacting to Dukakis's efforts, said that the candidate was successful in reaching out to Jackson supporters.

August 1: New York Mayor Edward Koch telephones the Rev. Jesse Jackson to arrange a meeting before the end of the month. Koch had been attempting to make peace after he sharply criticized Jackson during the Presidential primary in New York in April.

August 1: Democratic presidential nominee Michael Dukakis speaks at the National Urban League Conference in Detroit, MI and tells the League that if he is elected president that he would work for better race relations.

August 2: The National Urban League, at its conference in Detroit, Michigan, announces a "Get Out the Vote" campaign to increase black voter turnout in the November 8 general election.

August 3: Rev. Jesse Jackson is keynote speaker at the National Urban League Conference plenary session: "Civil Rights: Approaching a New Decade."

196

August 8: The Center for Constitutional Rights announce plans to file a class action suit challenging the election system of the Town of Hempstead in Nassau County Long Island. The group contends the system excludes minorities from public office.

August 8: Former Representative Barbara Jordan of Texas is released from hospital after nearly drowning in her pool. Her doctor reported her in excellent health and said she could return to normal life soon.

August 11: Lu Palmer, chairman of the Black Independent Political Organization in Chicago says a plan is underway to hold a convention to select a single black candidate to run for mayor in 1989. A new mayor is to be elected to serve the remaining two years in the late Harold Washington's term.

August 17: Coretta Scott King shares box with Barbara Bush, wife of Vice President George Bush, at the Republican National Convention in New Orleans. Republican officials saw this as a sign of better relations between the Republican Party and blacks.

August 20: Los Angeles Mayor Tom Bradley gears for a fifth term in the April 4, 1989, election by reinvigorating his faltering administration. Bradley, a former police officer was the first black elected mayor of a major city in which blacks were a minority.

August 31: Mayor Edward Koch of New York meets with Jesse Jackson in an attempt to bury the political hatchet.

Sept. 29: Baltimore Mayor Kurt L. Schmoke calls for an orderly retreat in the nation's war on drugs during a House Select Committee on Narcotics hearing in Washington.

Sept. 30: The campaign of Maurice A. Dawkins, Virginia's Republican contender for the U.S. Senate, unveils a television commercial which accuses Democrat Charles S. Robb of ''bad judgment'' for attending parties where others allegedly used cocaine.

Sept. 30: Former congresswoman Barbara Jordan (D-Tex.), speaking at the National Press Club in Washington, expressed displeasure at Jesse Jackson for not working hard enough for the Democratic ticket.

Oct. 6: Columnist Carl T. Rowan Sr. criticizes D.C. Mayor Marion Barry for what he called the city's ''malicious, political prosecution'' of him on firearms charges.

Oct. 17:   Three blacks and three whites are candidates in Chicago's special mayoralty election in February to choose a successor to the late Harold Washington. Eugene Sawyer, Chicago's acting mayor is a declared candidate along with black Alderman Danny K. Davis and a third potential candidate, Alderman Timothy C. Evans, began circulating petitions.

Oct. 20:   The Joint Center for Political Studies releases the results of a poll taken in August that showed that blacks generally expressed less support for Democratic nominee Michael Dukakis than they did at the same time four years ago for Walter Mondale. The poll also found great enthusiasm for Jesse Jackson among those blacks surveyed.

Oct. 21:   Democratic presidential nominee Michael Dukakis tells an enthusiastic gathering in a Harlem church that he is on their side. Visit to Harlem came on the heels of polls suggesting that his black support may be a bit soft.

Oct. 26:   A *New York Times*/CBS News Poll shows that a new generation of black voters, for whom the New Deal and even the civil rights legislation of the 1960s are only history lessons, appears less committed than older blacks are to the Democratic Party and the Democratic presidential nominee.

Nov. 8:   Vice President George Bush, the Republican candidate defeats Democratic candidate Governor Michael Dukakis in a hotly contested presidential campaign.

Nov. 8:   Newark, New Jersey City Councilman Donald M. Payne is elected to succeed Democratic Congressman Peter W. Rodino who has represented New Jersey's 10th District for 40 years. Payne becomes the first black representative in New Jersey's history.

Nov. 8:   Republican Maurice A. Dawkins is defeated by former Virginia Governor Charles S. Robb in his bid for the U.S. Senate. Robb is the first Virginia Democrat to be elected to the U.S. Senate in 22 years.

Nov. 15:   John E. Jacob, President and Chief Executive Officer of the National Urban League, speaking at the 32nd Annual Equal Opportunity Day Dinner at New York City's Hilton Hotel calls on President-elect George Bush to convene a meeting with the national black leadership to exchange ideas and get suggestions on personnel and policies.

Nov. 23:   Four blacks in Selma, Alabama, move into primary runoffs in a campaign to elect the first black member to the Dallas County Commission in more than a century. A black has not served on the commission since Reconstruction.

Nov. 27: Manhattan Borough President David N. Dinkins weighs his political options as to whether he will announce his candidacy to run against New York Mayor Edward Koch in next year's election.

Dec. 1: President Ronald Reagan announces plans to nominate national security advisor, Lt. Gen. Colin L. Powell to be chief of the U.S. Forces Command at Fort McPherson, GA, near Atlanta and to promote him to four-star general.

Dec. 5: Rep. William H. Gray III, (D-Pa.) elected Chairman of the House Democratic Caucus and is the first black to hold that post. The post is the fourth ranking position in the Democratic hierarchy.

Dec. 10: Virginia Lt. Governor L. Douglas Wilder prepares to launch his bid for governor with a political apparatus that is built largely outside his Democratic Party's establishment.

Dec. 13: Atlanta Mayor Andrew Young applauds an American decision to initiate contacts with the Palestine Liberation Organization. Young was forced to resign nine years ago as the chief United States delegate to the United Nations for meeting with a representative of the P.L.O.

Dec. 21: Ronald Brown, a former top campaign aide to the Rev. Jesse Jackson's 1988 presidential candidacy is backed by New York Governor Mario Cuomo and New Jersey Senator Bill Bradley to be the new chairman of the Democratic National Committee.

Dec. 25: President-elect George Bush and his wife worship in a black Baptist church in Washington and joined with the choir in singing the Hallelujah chorus from Handel's "Messiah." As Bush left the service at 19th Street Baptist Church, he called it, "a beautiful service, just lovely."

Dec. 29: D.C. Mayor Marion Barry denies using drugs with an acquaintance whom he visited. Speaking to a City Hall news conference, Barry said, "I believe that one is innocent until proven guilty."

Dec. 29: Chicago Alderman Timothy C. Evans drops out of the February Democratic primary for fear of splitting black votes between him and

Acting Mayor Eugene Sawyer. Evans said that he would run as an independent in the general election instead.

Civil Rights

Jan. 12:   A time capsule bearing memorabilia from the life of Dr. Martin Luther King, Jr. is placed in the ground at Western Plaza in downtown Washington. The capsule is not to be opened for a century.

Jan. 12:   Coretta Scott King will not attend a reception at the Embassy of Israel in Washington, which will honor her slain husband, Dr. Martin Luther King, Jr. The executive director of the Arab American Institute said he had written to Mrs. King requesting her not to attend because of "Israel's recent flagrant violations of the human rights of Palestinians in that occupied West Bank and Gaza strip.

Jan. 14:   *The New York Times* reports that as the nation prepares to observe its third holiday for Dr. Martin Luther King, Jr., there are indications that it is establishing its place on the calendar.

Jan. 15:   Memorial services highlight the observance of the birthday of Dr. Martin Luther King, Jr., across the country.

Jan. 30:   The Senate overwhelmingly passes legislation designed to overturn a 1984 Supreme Court decision that restricted the reach of civil rights laws.

Feb. 13:   New York Governor Mario Cuomo proposes the creation of a special civil-rights unit in the State Attorney General's office during an Albany workshop on racial violence.

Feb. 14:   Federal Judge Robert H. Bork, who was a Supreme Court nominee, on his last day on the bench prior to resigning, paraphrases Dr. Martin Luther King, Jr.'s "Free at last, free at last, thank God Almighty, I'm free at last."

Feb. 19:   Civil rights activists greeted Marine Cpl. Lindsey Scott at the Quantico Marine Corps base with pounds on his back after he was found not guilty on charges of attempted murder, rape, sodomy, and abduction. The case had become a crusade for a number of civil rights activists in Prince William County.

Feb. 21:   Lawyers for Boston University ask a judge to order Coretta Scott

King to release tapes of conversations between her husband, Dr. Martin Luther King, Jr., and others recorded secretly by Federal investigators. The school is in a legal fight over an estimated 83,000 documents involving Dr. King which are now held by the university.

Feb. 21: Several district attorneys in New York State express concern about Governor Mario Cuomo's proposal to set up a civil rights unit in the State Attorney General's office. The attorneys feel that the new unit might take over bias investigations that they originate.

March 16: President Ronald Reagan vetoes a major civil rights bill intended to overturn the effects of a Supreme Court decision involving Grove City College in Pennsylvania. The Court had ruled that anti-discrimination provisions governing the use of Federal Aid applied only to specific programs or activities aided by those funds. In the Grove City case, the ruling meant that Federal regulations on sex discrimination did not bind every activity of the private college just because some students got Federal scholarships or loans.

March 20: Five top black leaders are participants in a leadership dialogue at the National Urban League's invitational conference on Manhood and Fatherhood: Adolescent Male Responsibility in Black Families in Atlanta, Georgia. The leaders are John E. Jacob, President and Chief Executive Officer of the National Urban League; Dr. Dorothy I. Height, President of the National Council of Negro Women, Inc.; M. Carl Holman, President of the National Urban Coalition; Dr. Benjamin L. Hooks, Executive Director of the National Association for the Advancement of Colored People; and Dr. Joseph Lowery, President of the Southern Christian Leadership Conference.

March 21: Although a supporter of civil rights legislation, Vice President George Bush supports President Reagan's veto of a major civil rights bill, the Grove City bill, which Congress is expected to override.

March 22: Congress votes to override President Reagan's veto of the Civil Rights Restoration Act with its enactment ending a four-year struggle to overturn the Supreme Court's decision in *Grove City College vs. Bell*, which severely restricted the reach of laws prohibiting recipients of federal aid from discriminating on the basis of sex, race, age, or disability. The vote was 73 to 24.

April 4: In Memphis, Tennessee, a city garbage truck led about 8,000 marchers as they walked 15 blocks from the workers' union hall to the Lorraine Hotel, where Dr. Martin Luther King, Jr., was slain in 1968.

The march was in observance of Dr. King's death in Memphis 20 years ago.

April 10: Specially trained black, Hispanic, and white couples are sent out by the federal government to pretend that they want to buy or rent homes in the first major study of housing discrimination in a decade.

May 5: Civil rights leaders, priests and parishioners greet Bishop Eugene A. Marino in Atlanta as he enters a packed auditorium for his installation as the nation's first black Roman Catholic archbishop.

May 10: Rev. Al Sharpton of Brooklyn, New York, active in racial issues, is arrested in a Queens, New York courthouse for walking out of a Brooklyn court room during a hearing on charges stemming from a civil disobedience demonstration.

June 5: Clarence M. Pendleton Jr., chairman of the U.S. Commission on Civil Rights dies of a heart attack in California.

June 15: A *USA Today* cover story on black mayors attending the National Conference of Black Mayors in Philadelpia shows that the new breed of mayors put economic development and city services ahead of civil rights.

July 15: Three white law enforcement officers, acquitted of violating the civil rights of a black prisoner who, two days after his arrest, died of what prosecutors said was a beating at the hands of the officers.

July 29: Federal Judge Michael B. Mukasey of Federal Court in New York dismisses a civil rights suit brought against the state judiciary by Alton H. Maddox Jr. and an indigent murder suspect whom the lawyer had sought to defend at public expense.

Aug. 10: M. Carl Holman, a poet, editor, scholar, and civil rights leader dies of cancer. At the time of his death, Holman was president of the National Urban Coalition, a position he had held for 20 years.

Aug. 13: U.S. Commission on Civil Rights concurs by a vote of 5 to 1 in President Reagan's selection of William Barclay Allen, a California professor, as agency chairman to succeed the late Clarence M. Pendleton Jr.

Aug. 17: Blacks in Ocean City, Maryland, assert that there is still discrimination in that city and that they do not feel welcome either as tourists or as resort employees, and are threatening action if things do not change.

Aug. 27: A crowd of marchers estimated to be 55,000 marches to the Lincoln Memorial, 25 years after the Dr. Martin Luther King Jr. spoke there in what has been billed as the historic 1963 March on Washington.

Aug. 28: Club carrying police in Chicago keeps groups apart as hooded Ku Klux Klansmen preached white supremacy at rally in the same park where a multiracial group was arriving for a commemoration of the Dr. Martin Luther King, Jr.

Aug. 29: Three white men are indicted by a Queens, New York, grand jury on charges of beating two black women during what was termed a racially motivated argument near Aqueduct Raceway in July.

Sept. 3: The City of Yonkers, New York, faces escalating fines which could lead to bankruptcy after the United States Supreme Court unanimously rejected the city's final appeal to block a court-ordered housing desegregation plan.

Sept. 10: A Superior Court judge in Boston orders a trial to decide whether Boston University must relinquish its collection of the papers of the Dr. Martin Luther King Jr. to his widow.

Sept. 13: The National Association for the Advancement of Colored People appears divided over changes, negotiated by its lawyer, as a means of obtaining City Council approval for a court-ordered housing desegregation plan in Yonkers, New York.

Sept. 13: President Ronald Reagan signs a bill that strengthens enforcement of laws banning housing discrimination stating that the measure had brought America a "step closer to realizing Martin Luther King's dream."

Sept. 30: A Federal District Court jury in Mobile, Alabama, convicts Thomas Reed, President of the Alabama National Association for the Advancement of Colored People for taking $10,000 in exchange for trying to obtain the early release of a convicted murderer from prison.

Oct. 10: The National Board of the N.A.A.C.P., at its meeting in Jackson, Mississippi, plans a nationwide voter drive linked to the murder of Medger Evers, a Mississippi civil rights leader.

Oct. 10: Suzanne Lynn, chief of the New York state Attorney General's civil rights bureau, is among eight staff attorneys pulled from their jobs to do the investigation into the Tawana Brawley case.

Oct. 12: United States Supreme Court hears arguments over whether a federal law enacted in 1866 to help eradicate "the badges of slavery" may be invoked today to sue private citizens accused of discrimination.

Nov. 2: Fourteen black legislators, including the state president of the National Association for the Advancement of Colored People, Thomas Reed, go on trial in Montgomery, Alabama, on misdemeanor trespass charges for trying to remove the Confederate battle flag atop the Capitol building.

Nov. 23: A study by a University of Chicago sociologist finds that because of persistent prejudice by whites, blacks are much more likely to find themselves segregated when they move to the suburbs than other minority groups.

Dec. 1: U.S. District Judge Walter E. Black, Jr., rules in Baltimore that the Town of Thurmont violated the free speech rights of the Ku Klux Klan by imposing unattainable financial charges and a racial non-discrimination pledge as conditions for the white supremacist group to parade in that northern Maryland town.

Dec. 13: President-elect George Bush, in one of a series of meeting he has held with civil rights leaders since the November election, meets for 20 minutes with Coretta Scott King, the widow of Dr. Martin Luther King, Jr., and her son, Marvin.

Dec. 15: Wiley A. Branton, the principal lawyer in the civil rights cases that desegregated the public schools in Little Rock, Arkansas, in 1957 dies of a heart attack at his home in Washington, D.C.

Dec. 19: The National Center for Health Statistics completes its yearly chart of life and death trends. It found for the second consecutive year the life expectancy of blacks in the United States has been cut. This is the only time in the last 100 years that life expectancy for blacks dropped while life expectancy for whites increased.

Dec. 23: Max Robinson, the nation's first black network television anchor eulogized at the Shiloh Baptist Church in Washington by the Rev. Jesse L. Jackson, a close friend of the broadcast journalist. Robinson died December 20 at Howard University Hospital of complications due to AIDS.

Federal Budget

Jan. 7: The Reagan administration, in an effort to minimize squabbles with Congress, drafts a FY 1989 budget that proposes, among other things, a $370 million, or 39 percent, increase in funding for AIDS programs and the elimination of a handful of federal activities.

Jan. 8: White House budget documents disclose that the budget deficit in FY 1989 will rise to $167 billion — $31 billion over the legal target — if the economy performs as private forecasters are predicting.

Feb. 26: New York's Metropolitan Transportation Authority Chairman Robert R. Kiley asserts that New York City's mass transit system is coming back strong but is threatened by Federal budget cuts.

March 23: The Committee for Education Funding, at a news conference in Washington, announces that despite President Reagan's proposed increases in education spending, millions of needy students will not receive critical educational aid if the President's budget is approved.

March 23: The House of Representatives overwhelmingly approves a $1.1 trillion resolution for the coming fiscal year. The plan projects a deficit of $134 billion for the fiscal year beginning Oct. 1, down from the $147.7 billion deficit of the current fiscal year and the deficit of $150.4 billion last year.

April 21: Two well-connected Washington law firms are hired to help persuade Congress to give The Legal Services Corporation less money. The Legal Services program, which has been under attack by the administration since President Reagan took office, is proposing that its budget be slashed from $305 million to $250 million next year. A reduction in the legal services budget is a means of bringing in substantial financial support from other sources.

April 21: The Treasury Department reports that the federal budget deficit is running $4.3 billion below the level of a year ago. The deficit for the first half of FY 1988 was $118.9 billion, compared with $123.2 billion during the same time period last year. The March deficit was $29.1 billion, up from $27.9 billion a year ago.

May 31: The Treasury Department reports total government expenditure for the month at $82.1 billion with total receipts at $59.7 billion.

June 30: The total outlay for the government for the month as reported by the Treasury Department is $89.8 billion with total receipts at $99.3 billion. The June surplus was attributed to taxes which were reported.

July 16: A National League of Cities survey shows that the nation's cities continue to struggle with the loss of federal money, as more local governments scale back services, increase fees and property taxes, and face potential budget shortfalls.

July 20: The Michael Dukakis team successfully presses Jesse Jackson to modify another one of his planks. Instead of doubling the federal education budget, the plank proposes "significantly increasing" school spending.

July 28: The Reagan administration estimates that the Federal deficit for the next budget year would be $140.1 billion, $5.9 billion under the level that, by law, would force automatic across-the-board spending reductions.

Aug. 15: According to the *Associated Press* the Reagan administration experts have made an error in a calculation that cannot be rectified under current law and is preventing Congress from approving as much as $1.2 billion in spending programs for FY 1989.

Sept. 13: In a series on "Campaign '88, The Issues," *Wall Street Journal* reporters Gerald F. Seib and Tim Carrington point out that the real debate in the 1988 presidential campaign is over what to spend the money on. The article points out that Vice President Bush suggests he would devote available dollars first to strategic nuclear programs, both offensive and defensive, while Gov. Dukakis would devote them to nonnuclear, conventional programs.

Sept. 14: Budget analysts and Congressional staff members assert that the government is rapidly approaching the legal spending limit for the fiscal year that begins Oct. 1. This means that only a few hundred million dollars may be available for new drug programs, including increased treatment of addicts, which is far less than Congress wants to devote to the program.

Sept. 22: *The New York Times* reports that as Vice President George Bush campaigns for president, he has proposed five different tax cuts, the most important of which is a much lower rate on capital gains, than $1 trillion a year in taxes in the 1990s and spend more than $1.2 trillion annually.

Sept. 30: Congress, which has had repeated failures to pass a spending bill by the start of a new fiscal year, races the clock in hopes of completing its appropriations work on schedule for the first time in more than a decade.

Oct. 1: President Ronald Reagan signs the last of 13 spending bills for the new Federal fiscal year and praises Congress for completing its work on time. Congress passes the last of the bills just one minute before the start of the new fiscal year.

Oct. 6: The Senate votes unanimously to provide a tax exemption for interest from U.S. Savings Bonds purchased to help defray the costs of higher education. However, it rejects, by a 60 to 33 vote, a proposal to raise taxes on cigarettes, beer, wine and liquor to finance the two-year, $2.6 billion anti-drug-abuse bill.

Oct. 8: The co-chairman of the National Economic Commission, Drew Lewis told the Business Council meeting of chief executives of the nation's largest corporations in Hot Springs, Virginia, that the commission's proposals for reducing the government's budget deficit will be doomed without the support of the next president.

Oct. 16: Republican presidential nominee George Bush refuses to say where he would cut spending to reduce the federal deficit. Bush offered no new details about the deficit beyond his previous campaign speeches.

Oct. 24: At a campaign rally in San Diego, California, Democratic presidential nominee Michael S. Dukakis assails a proposal by Republican presidential nominee George Bush to lower the tax on capital gains. He then points out how the Vice President and his wife could profit from that plan.

Nov. 3: *The Washington Post* reports that members of the National Economic Commission are quarreling openly over spending and tax issues. The Commission was to provide a solution to the federal deficit after the election by devising a package of spending cuts and tax increases acceptable to the White House and Congress.

Nov. 8: The National Economic Commission abandons its December 21 dead line to announce a plan to reduce the federal budget deficit. *The New*

York Times points out that the delay, which could go into late January, March, or September, raises the question as to what influence, if any, the commission will exert.

Nov. 9: *The Washington Post* reports that the looming federal budget deficit threatens President-elect George Bush's hopes of expanding the role of government in such areas as education, child care, and health care for the poor.

Nov. 9: *The New York Times* reports that market experts are not yet convinced that the victory by Vice President George Bush will translate into the policies they consider necessary to reduce the Federal budget deficit and narrow the United States trade deficit further.

Nov. 12: A *Washington Post* poll shows that American voters doubt that President-elect George Bush will manage to keep his campaign promise not to raise taxes and almost eight of 10 people said they would like to see no tax increases in the next four years, but only one in three expects to see that hope fulfilled.

Nov. 28: President Ronald Reagan is expected to recommend in his last budget, that Federal spending plans be prepared for at least two years at a time. If adopted, this recommendation could ease president-elect George Bush's struggles to lower the deficit.

Nov. 29: House Speaker Jim Wright (D-Tex.) warned President-elect George Bush not to expect early negotiations with Congress to reduce the budget deficit next year. Wright calls on Bush to take the first step by quickly laying out a budget blueprint of his own.

Nov. 30: The former chairman of the Federal Reserve, Paul A. Volker, in an appearance before a bipartisan Congressional commission on the deficit, states that the Federal budget deficits threaten to bring recurring turmoil to the stock and currency markets and the kind of recession that would be most difficult to handle. Volker also indicated that he doubted that the deficit could be controlled without raising taxes.

Dec. 1: President-elect George Bush states after a breakfast meeting with Senate Majority Leader, George J. Mitchell (D-Maine) that he will "take the lead" in proposing ways to reduce the federal budget deficit. During his presidential campaign, Bush had frequently blamed Congress for the deficits.

Dec. 9: Federal district Judge Joyce Hens Green temporarily bars the National

Economic Commission which is studying ways to cut the budget deficit from meeting in closed sessions to hear testimony on the state of the economy.

Dec. 11: The Republican co-chairman of the National Economic Commission, Drew Lewis, states on NBC's "Meet the Press" that the government should be able to recover some Medicare payments from the estates of people who die wealthy and that he favors cutting Social Security benefits substantially for retirees with incomes higher than $90,000, and imposing more modest cuts for those who are less well-to-do.

Dec. 18: President Ronald Reagan, in the last budget of his administration proposes reducing the Federal deficit to $92.5 billion, the lowest since 1982, without raising taxes. The FY 1988 budget calls for spending $1.15 trillion, an increase of 4.7 percent over 1988, with revenue of $1.056 trillion, an increase of 8.4 percent.

Affirmative Action

Jan. 6: Officials in Howard County, Maryland, under pressure from their own human rights board and the local NAACP, step up efforts to increase the hiring and promotion of blacks and women in county government.

Jan. 15: Attorney General Edwin Meese III states in Washington that he is "trying to carry out the original intent of the civil rights movement" in proposing to eliminate minority hiring goals for government contractors. Speaking at a news conference on the birthday of Dr. Martin Luther King, Jr., Meese invokes the slain civil rights leader's name in defending his proposal on affirmative action.

Feb. 9: A survey by Richard Clarke, a minority recruiter, in The *Wall Street Journal* reports that 43 percent of black managers believe they have less opportunity now than five years ago to move up the corporate ladder. Clarke's survey notes that many blame their quagmire on the Reagan administration's "retreat" from affirmative action.

March 20: A white supremacist group, the National Alliance, in contending that blacks are intellectually inferior, forces the American Telephone and Telegraph Company (AT&T) into asking shareholders to vote on ending the company's minority hiring program.

March 28: The Justice Department announces that the city of Chicago has agreed to pay more than $9 million in back wages in order to resolve a 15-year-old suit charging that the police department discriminated against minorities and women in hiring and promotions.

March 19: A panel of black journalists meeting at the beginning of a three-day symposium at the New York Hilton Hotel sponsored by the National Association of Black Journalists states that newspapers and broadcasters have failed to recruit enough blacks into the nation's newsrooms. The association also called on newspapers to double the number of black journalists by 1991.

April 15: More than 500 black and white students at Duke University in Durham, North Carolina, stage a rally in support of eight members of the faculty committee who resigned from the committee after other faculty members rejected their recommendation that each department hire at least one black faculty member by 1993. Duke was reported to have 31 black faculty members out of a total of 1,399. Fourteen of the black members are in the university's medical school. More than 35 departments at Duke report no black faculty members.

April 25: The NAACP Legal Defense and Educational Fund newsletter "Equal Justice" reports that the Supreme Court ordered attorneys to submit new briefs in the case involving a black woman from Winston Salem, North Carolina, who sued her employer for damages resulting from racial harassment on the job. The LDF is representing the woman.

May 10: About 50 black law students at Harvard University Law School occupy the dean's outer office demanding increased efforts to recruit faculty members who are women or from minority groups. The students demanded that in the next four years, the school hire at least 20 tenured or tenure-track professors who are women and minority group members.

May 11: Black students at Harvard Law School end a 24-hour occupation of the dean's outer office after the school administration promises to continue to give high priority to hiring faculty members from minority groups. However, law school Dean James Vorenberg said he could not guarantee that specific numbers of minority tenured faculty would be achieved in a specific time.

June 23: The State of Virginia issues an investigative report into the hiring practices at Virginia's social service agencies which discloses a number of instances of racial and sex discrimination, including cases

210

where job applicants were graded on their facial expressions and senses of humor.

June 29: The Supreme Court, in an 8-to-0 ruling makes it easier for women and minorities to prove that they have been discriminated against in hiring or promotions. The Court said that employees may use statistical evidence showing underrepresentation of women or minorities in the workplace.

July 26: *The Washington Post* reports that Prince George's County, for the first time, has met its voluntary goal of awarding about 30 percent of county contracts to minority-owned firms. Minority businesses won nearly 30 percent, or $33 million, of the $111 million in county contracts awarded in the fiscal year that ended June 30.

August 1: The House Government Operations Committee reports that fewer than 200 of the country's 45,000 airline pilots are black and that airlines have done little to promote blacks to other professional and managerial jobs.

Sept. 2: FBI Director William H. Sessions vows to wipe out racism and discrimination at the Federal Bureau of Investigation and approves a new affirmative-action program to hire and promote more minority employees. Sessions announced approval of an affirmative-action plan through 1992 which includes hiring an advertising agency to recruit new minority agents and assigning its most capable staff to serve as recruiters.

Sept. 4: Illinois Attorney George Muñoz, states that affirmative action policies are viewed as sacred cows. Muñoz also says that we would be better off if there were some genetic engineering for the next breed of affirmative action programs. "The kinds that encourage integration and not segregation are what we need," he stated in the *Sun-Times*.

Oct. 5: The Supreme Court begins tackling an affirmative action case involving a challenge to the constitutionality of Richmond, Virginia's set-aside program in the construction industry. The case, *City of Richmond v. J.A. Croson Co.* will likely resolve a number of questions that will affect hundreds of millions of dollars in set-aside contracts in at least two-thirds of the states and 190 cities, and affirmative action programs in general.

Oct. 9: Boston Mayor Raymond L. Flynn begins an investigation into the race and ethnic background of the hundreds of workers hired as members of minority groups over the past decade by the fire, police, and school departments in that city.

Oct. 14:   In an effort to illustrate the expanding number of female, black, Hispanic and Asian managers, New York Mayor Edward Koch asserts that the number of minority group people working for the city of New York has increased 14 percentage points in the last 10 years.

Oct. 15:   Representatives of 21 public hospital community boards in New York City, ask for more stringent affirmative action goals. The reason is that the city has failed to hire and promote enough minority group members at its municipal hospitals.

Oct. 29:   A group of black professors at Harvard University makes an unusual plea to school administrators to begin hiring more black and Hispanic faculty members. According to *The New York Times*, the professors imagine what would happen if all the black professors at the university were killed in a freak explosion. Only then, they say, would they expect the university administration to make a serious effort to recruit black professors.

Nov. 13:   *The Washington Post* reports that the Montgomery County Fire and Rescue Department's recruitment programs to increase the number of women and minorities has increased the number of minorities to 12 percent. In January, seven percent of the department was minority.

Dec. 11:   Eleanor Holmes Norton, professor of law at Georgetown University and former head of the Equal Employment Commission, states: ''The problem with affirmative action is not defining who is a minority but having the statistics — such as how many black accountants are available to run programs fairly.''

Dec. 20:   Jury selection begins in Toledo, Ohio, in the trial of five black ministers charged with disrupting a City Council meeting on June 28 to protest city employment practices as racist.

Education/Desegregation

Jan. 16:   Joe Clark, the tough disciplinary principal of Paterson, New Jersey, Eastside High School turns down a White House job but agrees to act as an unpaid, unofficial adviser to the White House on urban education.

Feb. 10: The Education Department, in an article in *The New York Times*, states that six Southern and border states were still in partial violation of a 17-year-old court order to rid their public colleges of the effects of segregation. The states found to be in partial violation of court-ordered desegregation were Delaware, Florida, Georgia, Missouri, Oklahoma, and Virginia.

Feb. 17: A *New York Times* article on "Colleges seeking ways to keep blacks in school," notes that as colleges and universities struggle to stem the decline in blacks entering college, a major new concern has emerged: how to keep those who are already there.

March 14: The use of standardized tests to help choose teachers, which is a practice that has proliferated in the last decade, comes under heavy attack according to an article on education in *The New York Times*. The tests are being criticized as racially biased, ambiguous, and ineffective in measuring critical teaching skills.

April 1: Dr. John B. Slaughter, chancellor of the University of Maryland at College Park, confirms his resignation and announces that he is going to become president of Occidental College, a small, private college in Los Angeles. Slaughter was the first black top administrator of the century-old campus which is the flagship of Maryland's university system.

April 23: The number of black students going to college in Maryland spurts upward for the first time in five years thereby ending a pattern of dwindling minority enrollment that had worried educators through most of the 1980s.

April 25: A divided Supreme Court in a 5-to-4 ruling decides to review a major 1976 decision prohibiting private schools from discriminating on the basis of race and make it easier for racial minorities to sue for discrimination in housing, education, and a number of other areas.

April 29: The Forrest City High School in Forrest City, Arkansas, holds its first integrated prom in the school's history. Racially segregated dances sponsored by social clubs and individual families had taken the place of traditional proms for 23 years.

May 10: A study by Samuel Yarger, dean of the School of Education at the University of Wisconsin at Milwaukee, called "Teaching Teachers: Facts and Figures" states that, while enrollment in teacher education programs is rising, the vast majority of those students have no intention of working in urban school districts, where the need for new teachers is most critical.

May 24: Acting Superintendent of the District of Columbia school system Andrew Jenkins is named to the superintendent's post that he has sought for seven years. Jenkins began in the D.C. school system in 1961 as a physical education teacher.

June 1: The National Urban League's invitational conference, "Housing Opportunity and Community Development: Meeting the Challenge," begins in Miami, Florida. The conference defined the relationship between community development and fair housing in achieving housing opportunity and addressed such topics as the state of low-income housing.

June 8: The National Assessment of Educational Progress reports that almost half of the 17-year-olds in America cannot perform math problems normally taught in junior high school and that, while performances by blacks and Hispanics remained well below those of whites at all three age levels, minority scores have improved since 1978.

June 11: School board officials in Seattle, Washington, disclose that the number of students bused for desegregation will be cut in half by 1989 under a system that emphasizes integration within certain neighborhoods rather than in individual schools.

June 24: Clark College and Atlanta University vote to merge, which could significantly reshape the academic and financial profile of historically black colleges in Atlanta. The merger of the two institutions will create the largest single member of the consortium of the Atlanta University Center in terms of enrollment and budget.

Aug. 2: New York Schools Chancellor, Dr. Richard R. Green and Dr. Arthur Jefferson, superintendent of Detroit Public Schools are guest speakers during the National Urban League Conference plenary session on "Educating America's Minorities: Public and Private Sector Responsibilities."

Aug. 5: A College Board survey reports that the cost of attending college has outpaced inflation for the eighth straight year, with annual costs breaking $20,000 at the most expensive institutions.

Aug. 5: Figures released by the National Science Foundation show that black students earned only 222, or 1.8 percent, of the 12,480 doctorates awarded to U.S. citizens in graduate science and engineering programs last year. Figures also showed that of 290 doctorates awarded in electrical engineering, none went to black students, and of 242 doctorates in computer and information science, only two went to blacks.

Aug. 16: The 108-year-old Bishop College in Dallas, Texas, which was founded by freed slaves and once the largest black university west of the Mississippi River, closes its doors after 108 years. The school owed $12.6 million to 400 creditors.

Aug. 20: A Federal appellate court panel in Kansas City, Missouri, upholds a district judge's order that imposed a sharp increase in property taxes to help pay the cost of a school desegregation plan.

Aug. 25: Administrative law Judge Steven L. Lefelt rules that New Jersey's system of paying for public education is unconstitutional and discriminates against poor urban school districts. The ruling ended a seven-year legal battle over a lawsuit brought on behalf of 20 school-age children in Camden, Irvington, East Orange, and Jersey City.

Sept. 7: Democratic presidential candidate Michael Dukakis proposes a college loan program that would allow students to pay back their loans over a lifetime through payroll withholding of a small fixed percentage of their income.

Sept. 16: Residents of Hillside, New Jersey, a suburb of Newark and a community of 22,000 and which is 35 percent black and Hispanic, is at odds over a new plan to achieve racial balance in their elementary schools, where more than two thirds of the students are minorities.

Oct. 3: New York City Schools Chancellor Dr. Richard R. Green announces plans to look outside the education field for ideas on reforming the vast education bureaucracy by asking New York's business community to recommend improvements in the system's personnel policies.

Oct. 15: PUSH for Excellence Inc., an educational motivation program founded by Jesse L. Jackson, agrees to pay the federal government $550,000 to settle a long-standing claim over $1.1 million in undocumented expenditures of federal grants and contracts it received in the late 1970s and early 1980s.

Nov. 4: Actor Bill Cosby and his wife, Camille, donate $20 million to Spel-

215

man College in Atlanta, the largest single contribution ever made to a black college and one of the largest donations in recent years to any school. Cosby, in making the donation, said it was intended to spur others to support black learning institutions, which he noted have suffered from serious underfunding in recent years.

Nov. 10: Fifty-one superintendents representing the nation's public school system participate in the National Urban League's National Education Initiative School Superintendents Conference at the Xerox International Center for Training and Management Development in Leesburg, Virginia.

Nov. 21: The National Urban League and Merrill Lynch & Co., Inc., announce a newly established "ScholarshipBuilder" program for 250 inner-city students in the "Class of 2000." The program will benefit 25 first grade children in each of 10 cities with the program being underwritten by the Merrill Lynch Foundation. The Merrill Lynch Foundation will make contributions into a special investment account over the next 16 years to pay for the college education or advanced training of the participating students upon their graduation from high school.

Nov. 23: The local school board in the Bronx, New York, is suspended by New York City Schools Chancellor Dr. Richard R. Green following announcement of a grand jury investigation into complaints that some of its members have used and distributed illegal drugs, stolen school equipment, and extorted money from teachers, principals, and other school employees. Green said that the investigation of the board could prove to be a major test of the city's 18-year-old system of decentralization, under which elected local school boards run elementary and junior high schools.

Dec. 12: A study by the Boston-based National Coalition of Advocates for Students reveals that black students are twice as likely as whites to be suspended from school, physically punished by school authorities, or labeled mentally retarded. The report also showed that only eight percent of black youngsters get placed in gifted and talented school programs, even though they make up 16 percent of the nation's enrollment.

Dec. 16: The Justice Department demands that Maryland's Prince George's County schools stop transferring teachers from one school to another to satisfy racial quotas, stating that the practice is discriminatory.

Dec. 27:   Boston approves a school assignment plan of its own in hopes of salvaging its troubled public school system. The plan comes after 15 years of court-ordered busing that touched off violent opposition and the departure of whites from the city. The plan would allow parents to shop around for a school closer to home, thereby reducing the long bus rides many students endure each day.

Race Relations

Jan. 11:   New York City Mayor Edward Koch attends rededication of Metropolitan AME Church in Harlem and uses the occasion to talk about race relations and urges the congregation to rededicate itself to fighting racism, both black and white in the city.

Jan. 15:   CBS Sports commentator Jimmy (the Greek) Snyder touches off widespread criticism following a televised interview when he said that blacks are better athletes than whites because they have been "bred to be that way," and that "the only thing left for the whites is a couple of coaching jobs."

Jan. 18:   A House panel announces plans to investigate the growing phenomenon of "hate crimes," including the racial incident in Howard Beach, Queens. A series of Congressional hearings is scheduled for March by the Judiciary Committee's Subcommittee on Criminal Justice and will be chaired by Michigan Democratic Congressman John Conyers, Jr.

Jan. 27:   Eleven demonstrators, including the Rev. Al Sharpton of Brooklyn, New York, are arrested at New York's LaGuardia Airport after blocking traffic lanes outside a terminal building in protest of racial injustice in New York City.

Feb. 10:   Civil rights lawyer Alton H. Maddox, Jr., speaking at a Baptist church in Ossining, New York, details how Tawana Brawley, a 16-year-old young black woman from Wappingers Falls, has entered a troubled history of race relations in New York. Brawley has claimed that she was abducted and raped in November 1987 by six white men, including at least one police officer.

Feb. 13:   Black students at the University of Massachusetts in Amherst, Massachusetts, occupy a building to protest alleged racial harassment at the institution. The students began their protest following talks with Chancellor Joseph D. Duffey over a list of demands which included asking for prosecution of five white students accused of attacking two blacks following a dormitory party.

March 4: A week of anti-racism rallies, marches, and forums at Dartmouth College in Hanover, New Hampshire, ends with an open meeting on campus racism. The demonstrations came prior to a disciplinary hearing for four white students accused of harassing a black professor. The harassment charges were made following a classroom confrontation between the students and the professor over an article that the students contributed to Dartmouth Review critical of a music class taught by the professor.

April 12: The Baltimore Orioles becomes the fifth team in baseball history to hire a black manager with Hall of Famer Frank Robinson being named to the post. Robinson had been serving as a special front office assistant for the ball club.

April 13: Black Muslim leader Louis Farrakhan, who has been branded by opponents as racist and anti-semitic, addresses a predominantly black audience of 2,000 people at the University of Pennsylvania. Although Jewish students held a peaceful rally against his views, blacks and whites alike on campus agreed that the university has now opened the way to a new and more constructive period in race relations.

April 14: A black police officer in Anne Arundel County, Maryland, is fired for slapping a man who swore at him and then called the officer a "nigger." The police department's internal affairs division concluded that the officer was guilty of conduct unbecoming to an officer, breaching the officers' code of ethics and failing to promote good public relations.

April 24: College students, administrators, and faculty members from throughout the Northeast gather at Yale University in New Haven, Connecticut, to take stock of race relations at the university, which many find troubling.

May 5: Eugene Antonio Marino becomes the nation's first black Roman Catholic archbishop during ceremonies in Atlanta. Addressing the audience of 4,500 people, Archbishop Marino said that, although his race made his appointment a significant first, he was convinced that it "need not affect the quality of our relationship nor the nature of my service."

May 19: Londell Williams of Washington, Missouri, is indicted by a federal

218

grand jury on a charge of threatening to kill black presidential candidate Jesse Jackson. Williams reportedly said that he was prejudiced "against anything that isn't white."

June 17: A number of prominent black leaders, including Democratic presidential candidate Jesse Jackson, rallies to the defense of Carl T. Rowan. Rowan faces possible criminal charges for shooting a backyard intruder. He called criticism of his actions as racist. The leaders suggested that, if Rowan's intruders had been black, their criminal charges would not have been dismissed, and the black columnist would be faced with significantly less public scorn.

June 28: A *New York Times*/WCBS-TV Poll of New Yorkers finds an overwhelming majority of whites and a solid majority of blacks saying that Tawana Brawley's mother and their advisors have not acted responsibly in the case of the alleged assault on the young woman. The respondents to the poll also viewed New York Governor Mario Cuomo and State Attorney General Robert Abrams favorably and expressed pessimism about race relations.

July 15: Three white law enforcement officers in Hemphill, Texas, are acquitted of violating the civil rights of a black prisoner who, two days after his arrest, died of what prosecutors said was a beating at the hands of the officers. The three face a trial on murder charges in Tyler, Texas, where the prisoner died.

July 15: Three young men from Howard Beach are convicted in State Supreme Court in Kew Gardens, Queens, New York, of misdemeanor riot charges stemming from a racial attack on three black men in that Queens neighborhood. The three were acquitted of felony riot charges stemming from the attack, and a fourth defendant was acquitted of felony and misdemeanor riot charges.

July 17: A black New York City sanitation worker is hospitalized after being attacked by a group of white men on a Bronx, New York, street corner. The incident occurred in a neighborhood where race relations have been difficult over the years and tensions have been running high previous to the attack.

July 28: A group of community leaders in Chicago calls for meetings in churches and synagogues aimed at easing the hostility between blacks and Jews in that city. Relations between blacks and Jews were severely strained since April when it was disclosed that an aide to Acting Mayor Eugene Sawyer had delivered anti-Jewish lectures at the headquarters of the black Nation of Islam from August 1985 to November 1987.

July 31: The National Urban League begins its annual conference in Detroit, Michigan, with President and Chief Executive Officer of the League John E. Jacob calling for racial parity by the year 2000.

Aug. 2: The Congressional Black Caucus calls on Japan to halt all racially derogatory caricatures of black people. During a news conference in Washington with some members of the Japanese-American members of Congress, the caucus urged the country instead to share some of the fruits of its economic boom with U.S. minorities, for example, by awarding them a few Honda and Sony dealerships.

Aug. 6: A civilian review panel in Atlanta reports that the city's police department is divided by racism and failed to follow standard operating procedures in 1987 when it investigated charges that former State Senator Julian Bond was a drug abuser. The report charged that "reciprocal racial problems are still a substantial factor in the Atlanta Police Department."

Aug. 13: Major elements of a lawsuit charging racial harassment that a black agent of the Federal Bureau of Investigation filed against the bureau is dismissed by Federal District Judge Charles R. Richey, in Washington.

Aug. 13: The Thurgood Marshall Law Association, a black lawyers' group in Toledo, Ohio, files a Federal civil rights suit seeking an end to a new police department policy of randomly stopping and questioning black teenagers in a racially mixed neighborhood.

Aug. 14: The United States Army decides that a black woman who was dismissed from her civilian job had been discriminated against by an Asian-American male supervisor and two white male officers.

Aug. 15: The police chief in Toledo, Ohio, yields to pressure from civil rights leaders and rescinds a policy requiring officers to stop black youths at random in a racially mixed neighborhood.

Aug. 28: Police on foot, on horseback, and in unmarked automobiles comes to the rescue of a black man wearing headphones who wandered into a Ku Klux Klan rally in Chicago's Marquette Park. A mob of 500, mostly youths, skinheads, and Klan supporters hurled rocks, bottles, and racial slurs at the man and chased him prior to police intervention.

Sept. 4: The Red Onion Chain of restaurants, based in the Los Angeles suburb of Carson, is ordered to pay a settlement of $15,000 each to 23 people who sued the chain, alleging they were denied service because of their race or ethnicity. The food chain was accused of using dress codes and other excuses to bar minorities from its dining facility.

Sept. 9: Parents of a black teen-ager in Little Rock, Arkansas, who was barred from playing tennis with her high school team at an all-white country club file a civil rights suit in Federal District Court. The suit asks for damages of $2 million.

Oct. 1: A blackface performance by six high school cheerleaders and the student body president in Orange, California, sparks protests from black students. The skits were takeoffs on Stevie Wonder and the Jackson Five.

Oct. 20: The Chicago City Council considers a resolution asking its members to stop using racial, ethnic, and gender-related insults during debates and questioning witnesses during debates and questioning witnesses during council committee meetings.

Oct. 25: Gov. Michael Dukakis'sop aides say there is no organized plan to accuse Vice President Bush's campaign of acerbating racial fears. The charge, angrily denied by the Republicans, revolves around Bush's constant hammering on the case of Willie Horton, a black murderer who escaped from the Massachusetts prison system while on a weekend furlough, raped a white woman in Maryland, and stabbed her fiance.

Oct. 25: The Ku Klux Klan and 12 individuals ordered to pay approximately $1 million to 53 civil rights marchers who were pelted with rocks and bottles during a demonstration in mainly all-white Forsyth County, Georgia. The marchers had gone into the county on Jan. 17, 1987, and were attacked by counter-demonstrators, many of them Klan members or their sympathizers.

Oct. 30: New York Police Department begins investigation into allegations that black police officers in the 113th Precinct in Queens have been subjected to racial slurs and harassment by white officers over the past six months.

Nov. 4: Roy Innis, the national chairman of the Congress of Racial Equality scuttles on the Geraldo Rivera's television talk show with a 20-year-old guest of the program who had insulted him by calling him an "Uncle Tom."

Nov. 27: The Gannett Company institutes a new policy to include people from minority groups in all articles, not just in those relating to racial issues.

Dec. 6: Baseball Commissioner Peter Ueberroth, in his fifth and final report as commissioner, concedes that baseball "must make progress" in hiring blacks as managers and general managers in the major league.

Dec. 19: A group of black leaders, including the Rev. Jesse Jackson and Mayor Richard Hatcher, meeting in Chicago to discuss national goals says that members of its race would prefer to be called African-Americans rather than blacks.

Dec. 19: An internal report on equal opportunity in the Navy discloses racial discord and subtle bias against blacks and Hispanic sailors as well as other minorities in its ranks.

Dec. 30: Just prior to the start of his national television talk show, Arsenio Hall says in a *New York Daily News* article that he doesn't want his show to be a racial platform, although it is clear that he intends to have racial diversity in guests and issues.

NOTES AND
REFERENCES

The Economic Status of Black Americans, *David H. Swinton, Ph.D.*

REFERENCES

Swinton, David H., *"The Economic Status of Blacks 1987"* in Janet Dewart ed., The State of Black America 1988. New York: National Urban League, 1988.

"The Economic Status of The Black Population" in Janet Dewart ed., The State of Black America 1987. New York: National Urban League, 1987.

"The Economic Status of Blacks 1986" in The State of Black America 1988. New York: National Urban League, 1988.

U.S. Department of Commerce, Bureau of the Census, "Money Income and Poverty Status of Families and Persons in the United States: 1987." Washington D.C.: U.S. Government Printing Office, 1988.

Bureau of the Census, "Money Income of Households, Families and Persons in the United States: 1986." Washington D.C.: U.S. Government Printing Office, 1988.

Bureau of the Census, "Household Wealth and Asset Ownership: Washington D.C.": U.S. Government Printing Office, 1986.

Bureau of the Census, "Statistical Abstract of the United States": 1986. Washington D.C.: U.S. Government Printing Office, 1986.

U.S. Department of Labor, Bureau of Labor Statistics, "Employment and Earnings, January and October 1988." Washington D.C.: U.S. Government Printing Office, 1988.

Bureau of Labor Statistics, "Geographic Profile of Employment and Unemployment, 1987." Washington, D.C.: U.S. Government Printing Office, 1988.

Critical Issues for Black Families by the Year 2000, *Robert B. Hill, Ph.D.*

FOOTNOTES

[1] Hill, Robert B., *Economic Policies and Black Progress* (Washington, D.C.: National Urban League Research Department, 1981)

[2] U.S. Bureau of the Census, "Money Income and Poverty Status in United States, *"Current Population Reports,* P-60, No. 161. August, 1988; Robert B. Hill, "The Black Middle Class: Past, Present and Future," *The State of Black American: 1987,* pp. 43-64.

[3] Center on Budget and Policy Priorities, "Still Far From the Dream: Recent Developments in Black Income, Employment and Poverty," Washington, D.C., October 1988.

[4] U.S. Bureau of the Census, "Projections of the Population of the United States, By Age, Sex and Race: 1983 to 2080," *Current Population Reports,* Series P-25, No. 952, May 1984.

[5] U.S. Bureau of the Census, "Projections of the Hispanic Populations," *Current Population Reports,* Series P-25, No. 995, November 1986.

[6] U.S. Bureau of Labor Statistics, "Projections 2000," *BLS Bulletin,* No. 2302, March 1988.

[7] *Ibid,* p. 9.

[8] Hill, Robert B., Economic Policies and Black Progress, *op. cit.*

[9] Center on Budget and Policy Priorities, *op. cit.*

[10] U.S. Bureau of Labor Statisics, *op. cit.*

[11] Hill, Robert B., "The Future of Black Families," *The World and I,* December 1986.

[12] Center on Budget and Policy Priorities, *op. cit.*

[13] U.S. House of Representatives, *Background Material and Data on Programs Within the Jurisdiction of the Committee on Ways and Means,* (U.S. Government Printing Office, March 6, 1987).

225

[14]U.S. Bureau of the Census, "Estimates of Poverty Including the Value of Noncash Benefits: 1987," Technical Paper No. 58, August 1988.

[15]U.S. Department of Education, Office of Educational Research and Improvement, *Youth Indicators: 1988*, Washington, D.C.: August 1988.

[16]Hill, Robert B., "The Impact of Child Support Policies on Black Fathers," Black Family Impact Analysis Program of the Baltimore Urban League, June 1988.

[17]Hill, Robert B., "Building the Future of the Black Family," *American Visions*, Vol. 2, No. 6, December 1987, pp. 16-25.

[18]U.S. Bureau of the Census, "Marital Status and Living Arrangements: March 1987," *Current Population Reports*, P-20, No. 423, April 1988.

[19]Hill, Robert B., *Informal Adoption Among Black Families*(Washington, D.C.: National Urban League Research Department, 1977).

[20]Primm, Beny J., "Drug Use" and "AIDS", *The State of Black America: 1987*(New York: National Urban League, 1987), pp. 145-166.

[21]McGhee, James D., "Running the Gauntlet: Black Men in America," Washington, D.C.: National Urban League Research Department, 1984; Jawanza Kunjufu, *Countering the Conspiracy to Destroy Black Boys, Vol. II.*(Chicago, Ill.: African American Images, 1986).

[22]Wilson, William J., *The Truly Disadvantaged*(Chicago Ill: University of Chicago Press, 1987.

[23]Woodson Robert L. (ed.), *On the Road to Economic Freedom: An Agenda for Black Progress*(Washington, D.C.: Regency Gateway, 1987.

Black Children in America, *Marian Wright Edelman*

FOOTNOTES

[1]U.S. Department of Commerce, Bureau of the Census, *Current Population Reports*, Series P-25, No. 952, "Projections of the Population of the United States, by Age, Sex, and Race: 1983 to 2080" (May 1984), Table 6; and U.S. Department of Commerce, Bureau of the Census, *Current Population Reports*, Series P-25, No. 995, "Projections of the Hispanic Population: 1983 to 2080" (November 1986), Table 2. Calculations by Children's Defense Fund.

[2]*Ibid.*

[3]U.S. Department of Labor, *Workforce 2000: Work and Workers for the 21st Century* (1987), p. 95.

[4]U.S. Department of Commerce, Bureau of the Census, *Current Population Reports*, Series P-60, No. 161, "Money Income and Poverty Status in the United States: 1987 (Advance Data from the March 1988 Current Population Survey)" (August 1988), Table 16; *Monthly Vital Statistics Report*, Vol. 37, No.3, Supplement, "Advance Report of Final Natality Statistics, 1986" (July 12, 1988), Table 30; U.S. Department of Health and Human Services, National Center for Health Statisitics, *Vital Statistics of the United States, Vol. I—Natality*, 1980 (1984), Table 1-46; U.S. Department of Commerce, Bureau of the Census, *Current Population Reports*, Series P-20, No. 423, "Marital Status and Living Arrangements: March 1987" (April 1988), Table 4; U.S. Department of Commerce, Bureau of the Census, *Current Population Reports*, Series P-20, No. 365, "Marital Status and Living Arrangements: March 1980" (October 1981), Table 4; U.S. Department of Labor, Bureau of Labor Statistics, unpublished tabulations from the March 1980 and March 1988 Current Population Survey; *Employment and Earnings*, Vol. 35, No. 1 (January 1988), Table 6; *Employment and Earnings*, Vol. 28, No. 1 (January 1980), Table 5; Anne McDougall Young, "Youth labor force marked turning point in 1982," *Monthly Labor Review*, Vol. 106, No. 8 (August 1983), Table 5; and U.S. Department of Labor, Bureau of Labor Statistics, Press Release USDL 87-227, Table 1. Calculations by Children's Defense Fund.

[5]U.S. Department of Commerce, Bureau of the Census, *Current Population Reports*, Series P-60, No. 161, "Money Income and Poverty Status in the United States: 1987 (Advance Data from the March 1988 Current Population Survey)" (August 1988), Table 16.

[6]*Employment and Earnings*, Vol. 35, No. 1 (January 1988), Tables 49, 50.

[7]U.S. Department of Labor, Bureau of Labor Statistics, unpublished tabulations from the Current Population Survey, 1979 and 1987 annual averages.

[8]U.S. Department of Commerce, Bureau of the Census, *Current Population Reports*, Series P-60, No. 161, "Money Income and Poverty Status in the United States: 1987 (Advance Data from the March 1988 Current Population Survey)" (August 1988), Table 16. Calculations by Children's Defense Fund.

[9]Children's Defense Fund, Adolescent Pregnancy Prevention Clearinghouse Report, *Declining Earnings of Young Men: Their Relation to Poverty, Teen Pregnancy, and Family Formation* (May 1987), p. 11; and Children's Defense Fund, *A Children's Defense Budget, FY 1988* (1987), p. 158. Calculations by Dr. Andrew Sum, Northeastern University, based on data from the Current Population Survey, March 1974 and March 1985.

[10]U.S. Department of Commerce, Bureau of the Census, *Current Population Reports*, Series P-60, No. 98, "Characteristics of the Low-Income Population: 1973" (1975); and U.S. Department of Commerce, Bureau of the Census, *Current Population Reports*, Series P-60, No. 160, "Poverty in the United States: 1986" (1988).

[11]Children's Defense Fund and Center for Labor Market Studies, Northeastern University, Vanishing Dreams: The Growing Economic Plight of America's Young Families (1988), pp. 5-6. Calculations based on data from the Current Population Survey, March 1974 and March 1987.

[12]*Vanishing Dreams*, pp. 46-47.

[13]William Julius Wilson, remarks at Children's Defense Fund National Conference, February 1986, in a session entitled "Teen Pregnancy and Welfare: Part of the Problem or Part of the Solution?" See also William Julius Wilson, *The Truly Disadvantaged: The Inner City, the Underclass, and Public Policy* (Chicago: University of Chicago Press, 1987), pp. 90-92.

[14]U.S. Department of Commerce, Bureau of the Census, *Current Population Reports*, Series P-20, No. 423, "Marital Status and Living Arrangements: March 1987" (April 1988), Table 1.

[15]U.S. Department of Health and Human Services, National Center for Health Statistics, *Vital Statistics of the United States, Vol. I—Natality*, 1970 and 1986 editions (1975, 1988); and *Monthly Vital Statistics Report*, Vol. 37, No. 3, Supplement, "Advance Report of Final Natality Statistics, 1986" (July 12, 1988), Table 19. Calculations by Children's Defense Fund.

[16]Marian Wright Edelman, *Families in Peril: An Agenda for Social Change* (Cambridge: Harvard University Press, 1987), p. 6. Calculations based on data from the Current Population Survey, March 1976 and March 1986.

[17]U.S. Department of Commerce, Bureau of the Census, *Current Population Reports*, Series P-20, No. 387, "Fertility of American Women: June 1982" (April 1984), p. 10. Calculations by Children's Defense Fund.

[18]*Monthly Vital Statistics Report*, Vol. 35, No. 3, Supplement, "Induced Terminations of Pregnancy: 1982 and 1983" (July 14, 1988), Table B, calculations by Children's Defense Fund; and U.S. Department of Labor, Bureau of Labor Statistics, unpublished tabulations from the March 1987 Current Population Survey.

[19]*Monthly Vital Statistics Report*, Vol. 37, No. 3, Supplement, "Advance Report of Final Natality Statistics, 1986" (July 12, 1988), Table 18

[20]U.S. Department of Commerce, Bureau of the Census, *Current Population Reports*, Series P-60, No. 160, "Poverty in the United States: 1986," Table 15; and U.S. Department of Commerce, Bureau of the Census, *Current Population Reports*, Series P-60, No. 161, "Money Income and Poverty Status in the United States: 1987 (Advance Data from the March 1988 Current Population Survey)" (August 1988), Table 16.

[21]U.S. Department of Commerce, Bureau of the Census, *Current Population Reports*, Series P-60, No. 160, "Poverty in the United States: 1986" (1988), Table 15. Calculations by Children's Defense Fund.

[22]*Vanishing Dreams*, p. 49.

[23]Sheldon Danziger and Peter Gottschalk, *How Have Families With Children Been Faring?* prepared for the Joint Economic Committee (November 1985), p. 33.

[24]*Ibid.*, p. 38. Calculations by Children's Defense Fund.

[25]U.S. Department of Labor, Bureau of Labor Statistics, unpublished tabulations from the March 1987 Current Population Survey.

[26]U.S. Department of Commerce, Bureau of Labor Statistics, Press Release USDL 88-431, Tables 1 and 2; and Howard Hayghe, "Rise in mothers' labor force activity includes those with infants," *Monthly Labor Review*, Vol. 109, No. 2 (February 1986), Table 3. Calculations by Children's Defense Fund.

[27]Projection by Children's Defense Fund, based on annual data from the March Current Population Survey for 1970 through 1988.

[28]U.S. Department of Labor, Bureau of Labor Statistics, unpublished data from the March 1987 Current Population Survey. Calculations by Children's Defense Fund.

[29]U.S. Department of Commerce, Bureau of the Census, *Current Population Reports*, Series P-60, No. 161, "Money Income and Poverty Status in the United States: 1987 (Advance Data from the March 1988 Current Population Survey)" (August 1988), Table 18; and Children's Defense Fund, *A Children's Defense Budget, FY 1989* (1987), p. 183. Calculations by Children's Defense Fund.

[30]*Federal Register*, Vol. 53, No. 29 (February 12, 1988), p. 4214. Calculations by Children's Defense Fund.

[31]U.S. Department of Health and Human Services, Family Support Administration, *Characteristics and Financial Circumstances of AFDC Recipients: 1986* (n.d.), Table 11; and U.S. General Accounting Office, *Work and Welfare: Current AFDC Work Programs and Implications for Federal Policy*, GAO/HRD-87-34 (January 1987), Table 5.6.

[32]*Monthly Vital Statistics Report*, Vol. 37, No. 6, Supplement, "Advance Report of Final Mortality Statistics, 1986" (September 30, 1988), Table 13 and *Monthly Vital Statistics Report*, Vol. 37, No. 3, Supplement, "Advance Report of Final Natality Statistics, 1986" (July 12, 1988), Tables 15 and 30. Calculations by Children's Defense Fund.

[33]Children's Defense Fund, *The Health of America's Children: Maternal and Child Health Data Book* (1988), Tables 1.11 and 3.2.

[34]*Monthly Vital Statistics Report*, Vol. 37, No. 6, Supplement, "Advance Report of Final Mortality Statistics, 1986" (September 30, 1988), Table F. Calculations by Children's Defense Fund.

[35]*Monthly Vital Statistics Report*, Vol. 37, No. 3, Supplement, "Advance Report of Final Natality Statistics, 1986" (July 12, 1988), Table 30. Calculations by Children's Defense Fund.

[36]Children's Defense Fund, *The Health of America's Children: Maternal and Child Health Data Book* (1988), Table 2.18D. Calculations by Children's Defense Fund.

[37]Children's Defense Fund, *The Health of America's Children: Maternal and Child Health Data Book* (1988), Table 1.10. Calculations by Children's Defense Fund.

[38]Children's Defense Fund, Adolescent Pregnancy Prevention Clearinghouse Report, *Teens and AIDS: Opportunities for Prevention* (November 1988), pp. 12-13.

[39]National Health Policy Forum, *The Uninsured and Uncompensated Care* (June 1986), Table 1 and Chart 6.

[40]Children's Defense Fund, *A Children's Defense Budget, FY 1988* (1987), pp. 70, 75; and Children's Defense Fund, *A Children's Defense Budget, FY 1989* (1988), p. 74.

[41]U.S. Department of Commerce, Bureau of the Census, unpublished tabulations from the October 1986 Current Population Survey.

[42]*Federal Register*, Vol. 53, No. 29 (February 12, 1988), p. 4214.

[43]Children's Defense Fund, *A Children's Defense Budget, FY 1989* (1988), p. 194.

[44]U.S. Department of Commerce, Bureau of the Census, *Current Population Reports*, Series P-20, No. 426, "School Enrollment—Social and Economic Characteristics of Students: October 1985 and 1984" (April 1988), Table 3. Calculations by Children's Defense Fund.

[45]Committee for Economic Development, *Children in Need* (1987), p. 2.

[46]Children's Defense Fund, Adolescent Pregnancy Prevention Clearinghouse Report, *Preventing Adolescent Pregnancy: What Schools Can Do* (September 1986), p. 5. Based on analysis of the National Longitudinal Survey of Labor Force Behavior Youth Survey by Dr. Andrew Sum, Northeastern University.

228

[47]Children's Defense Fund, *A Call for Action to Make Our Nation Safe for Children: A Briefing Book on the Status of American Children in 1988* (1988), p. 8. Based on analysis of the National Longitudinal Survey of Labor Force Behavior Youth Survey by Dr. Andrew Sum, Northeastern University.

[48]Children's Defense Fund, Adolescent Pregnancy Prevention Clearinghouse Report, *Preventing Adolescent Pregnancy: What Schools Can Do* (September 1986), pp. 4-6. Based on analysis of the National Longitudinal Survey of Labor Force Behavior Youth Survey by Dr. Andrew Sum, Northeastern University.

[49]Congressional Budget Office, *Reducing Poverty Among Children* (May 1985), p. 106; and Children's Defense Fund, *A Children's Defense Budget, FY 1989* (1988), p. 275, calculations by Children's Defense Fund based on U.S. Department of Commerce, Bureau of the Census, *Current Population Reports*, Series P-60, No. 154, "Money Income and Poverty Status in the United States: 1985 (Advance Data from the March 1986 Current Population Survey)" (August 1986), Table 18, and unpublished data from the U.S. Department of Education.

[50]U.S. Department of Commerce, Bureau of the Census, unpublished OEO tabulations from the March 1988 Current Population Survey. Calculations by Children's Defense Fund.

[51]U.S. Department of Labor, Bureau of Labor Statistics, Press Release USDL 88-423, Table 1.

[52]*Vanishing Dreams*, p. 29.

[53]U.S. House of Representatives, Committee on Ways and Means, *Children in Poverty* (May 1985), Table 4.1.

[54]*Employment and Earnings*, Vol. 35, No. 1 (January 1988), Table 6.

[55]Children's Defense Fund, Adolescent Pregnancy Prevention Clearinghouse Report, *Declining Earnings of Young Men: Their Relation to Poverty, Teen Pregnancy, and Family Formation* (May 1987), p. 8. Calculations by Dr. Andrew Sum, Northeastern University based on data from the Current Population Survey, March 1974 and March 1985.

[56]Anne McDougall Young, "Youth labor force marked turning point in 1982," *Monthly Labor Review*, Vol. 106, No. 8 (August 1983), Table 5; and U.S. Department of Labor, Bureau of Labor Statistics, Press Release USDL 87-227, Table 1. Calculations by Children's Defense Fund.

[57]U.S. Department of Commerce, Bureau of the Census, *Current Population Reports*, Series P-60, No. 160, "Poverty in the United States: 1986" (June 1988), Table 9. Calculations by Children's Defense Fund.

[58]U.S. Department of Commerce, Bureau of the Census, *Current Population Reports*, Series P-20, No. 426, "School Enrollment—Social and Economic Characteristics of Students: October 1985 and 1984" (April 1988), Table 13. Calculations by Children's Defense Fund.

[59]The College Board, *Trends in Student Aid: 1980 to 1988* (September 1988), p. 7.

[60]Committee for Economic Development, *Children in Need*, p. 15.

To Make Wrong Right: The Necessary and Proper Aspirations of Fair Housing, *John O. Calmore, J.D.*

FOOTNOTES

[1]Crenshaw, *Race, Reform, and Retrenchment: Transformation and Legitimation in Antidiscrimination Law*, 101 HARV L. REV. 1331, 1387 (1988).

[2]42 U.S.C. 3601

[3]Title VIII and Section 1982, although independent statutory remedies, are complementary at least regarding racial discrimination in housing. Morris & Powe, *Constitutional and Statutory Rights to Open Housing*, 44 WASH. L. REV. 1, 56-83 (1968); Smedley, *A Comparative Analysis of Title VIII and Section 1982*, 22 VAND. L. REV. 459 (1969)[4]Spencer, *Enforcement of Fair Housing Law*, 9 URB. LAW. 514 (1977)

[5]See generally, R. FARLEY & W. ALLEN, THE COLOR LINE AND THE QUALITY OF LIFE IN AMERCIA (1987) [hereinafter THE COLOR LINE] HOUSING DESEGREGATION AND FED-

ERAL POLICY (J. Goering. 1986) [hereinafter HOUSING DESEGREGATION]; and RACE, ETHNICITY, AND MINORITY HOUSING IN THE UNITED STATES (J. Momeni ed. 1986) [hereinafter MINORITY HOUSING].

[6]This is very much a matter of commitment:

"The corrective conception does not tell us exactly what to do. Rather, it insists upon an imagery and locates a source of commitment. The images are rooted in the past—the awful, deliberate wrongs inflicted on black people for so long, the brutal sweep of contunity between past deeds and present life. From that image of wrong comes the commitment to correction, the distinctive dynamic of racial justice. The corrective idea insists that racial justice not be assimilated to other distributive objectives. It affirms that, because of the past, the claims of black Americans are unique and uniquely just. It affirms, at the very least, a way of thinking about racial justice."

Gewirtz, *Choice in the Transition: School Desegregation and the Corrective Ideal*, 86 YALE L. J. 728, 798 (1986).

[7]Lamb, *Equal Housing Opportunity*, in IMPLEMENTATION OF CIVIL RIGHTS POLICY 148 (C. Bullock & C. Lamb eds. 1984).

[8]*Id.*

[9]See, e.g., Days, *Introductory Remarks* ("The Fair Housing Act After Twenty Years" Conference at Yale Law School, March 25, 1988), 6 YALE & POL'Y REV. 332, 333-34 (1988).

[10]Goering *Concluding Remarks*, in HOUSING DESEGREGATION, *supra* note 5, at 333 (fair housing will be "lucky to hold its own for the next decade").

[11]Lake, *Unresolved Themes in the Evolution of Fair Housing, id.* at 317.

[12]See generally W. WILSON, THE TRULY DISADVANTAGED: THE INNER CITY, THE UNDERCLASS, AND PUBLIC POLICY (1987).

[13]Drinan, *Untying the White Noose*, 94 YALE L. J. 435, 440 (1984).

[14]As to the critical nature of the writing, it reflects the words of Harlon Dalton:

"Indeed, I share the concern that we risk undermining ourselves by moving ahead with a positive program before the critique has adequately altered our consciousness. I also recognize the utility and even necessity of delegitimation. I am convinced, however, that the movement can and must proceed on two tracks simultaneously. Despite the risk of replicating the tried and untrue path, we must create even as we reenvision. In my view, negative critique and positive program are, or at least can be symbiotic; the former launches the latter and keeps it on course, whereas the later saves the former from petulance and self-parody."

Dalton, *The Clouded Prism*, 22 HARV. C.R.-C.L.L. REV. 435, 436 n. 4 (1987)

[15]INSTITUTE FOR POLICY STUDIES' WORKING GROUP ON HOUSING, A PROGRESSIVE HOUSING PROGRAM FOR AMERICA 8-12 (1987).

[16]REPORT OF THE PRESIDENT'S COMMISSION ON HOUSING XXVII (1982).

[17]JOINT CENTER FOR HOUSING STUDIES OF HARVARD UNIVERSITY, THE STATE OF THE NATION'S HOUSING 1988, 1 (1988).

[18]Moore, *Lost in America; Low-Rent Housing*, L.A. Times, June 12, 1988, 5, at 4, col.1.

[19]*Editor's Introduction*, in CRITICAL PERSPECTIVES ON HOUSING xi-ix (R. Bratt, C. Hartman, & A. Meyerson eds. 1986) [hereinafter CRITICAL PERSPECTIVES].

[20]HOUSING IN AMERICA: PROBLEMS AND PERSPECTIVES 1 (R. Montgomery & D. Mandelker eds. 2d ed. 1979) [hereinafter HOUSING IN AMERICA].

[21]Achtenberg & Marcuse, *Toward the Decommodification of Housing*, in CRITICAL PERSPECTIVES, *supra note* 19, at 474.

[22]*Editor's Introduction, id* at xi.

[23]R. Montgomery & D. Mandelker, *supra* note 20, at 73.

[24]R. Bratt et al., *supra* note 19, at xi.

[25]*Id.*

[26]*Id.*

[27]*Id.*

[28]*Id.*

[29]Simons, *Toward a New National Housing Policy*, 6 YALES L. & POL'Y REV. 259 268-70 (1988) (The author served as Assistant Secretary for Housing of the Dept. of Housing and Urban Development (HUD) from 1971-1981). See also McDougall, *Affordable Housing for the 1990's*, 20 U. OF MICH. J. OF L. REFORM 727 (1988).

[30]In 1981, the ratio was increased to 30 percent through the Omnibus Reconciliation Act, now codified at 42 U.S.C. & 1437A (A) (1).

[31]R. Bratt et al. *supra* note 20, at xiv.

[32]At the extreme, the scenario increasingly leads to homelessness. See generally HOMELESSNESS IN AMERICA (M.E. Hombs & M. Snyder eds. 1982). See also *Current Topic, Homelessness: Halting the Race to the Bottom*, 3 YALE L. POL'Y REV. 551, 552 (1985).

[33]NATIONAL HOUSING TASK FORCE, A DECENT PLACE TO LIVE 8 (1988). See also, Hinds, *Owning a Home Recedes as an Achievable Dream*, N.Y. Times, Sept. 13, 1987, 12, at 15.

[34]Bates, *Money to Buy First House Often Tough to Find*, L.A. Times, July 16, 1988, 4, at 14.

[35]*Id.*

[36]R. Bratt et al., *supra* note 19, at xiv.

[37]*Id.*

[38]*Id* at xv.

[39]Pettigrew, *New Patterns of Racism: The Different Worlds of 1984 and 1964*, 37 RUTGERS L. REV. 673, 676 (1985).

[40]Swinton, *Economic Status of Blacks 1987*, in THE STATE OF BLACK AMERICA 1988 137 (J. Dewart ed. 1988).

[41]See generally Malveaux, *The Economic Statuses of Black Families*, in BLACK FAMILIES 133 (H. McAdoo ed. 2d ed. 1988).

[42]Pettigrew, *supra* note 39, at 685-86.

[43]Tidwell, *Black Wealth: Facts and Fiction*, in THE STATE OF BLACK AMERICA 1988 193 (J. Dewart ed. 1988).

[44]See, e.g., Bullard, *Blacks and the American Dream of Housing*, in MINORITY HOUSING, *supra* note 5, at 63 ("[D]iscrimination... continue[s] to deny a substantial segment of the American society a basic form of wealth accumulation and investment through home ownership").

[45]R. Bratt et al, *supra* note 19, at xiv-xv.

[46]*Id.* at xiii.

[47]*Id.*

[48]According to Montgomery and Mandelker:

"Filtering refers to the apparently systematic tendency of both houses and household to sequentially exist in or occupy different submarkets. In the most common version, it refers to the situation in which households of successively lower incomes will sequentially occupy or filter through a dwelling or neighborhood from the relatively well-to-do original owners to the welfare recipients who last occupy the units before final abandonment. Seen the other way around the dwelling in question has filtered down into ever lower price and lower quality submarkets until it drops from the market entirely.

Actually, filtering often denotes both trickle-down and trickle-up processes. It is an omnibus concept applied to several distinct processes. Housing filters downs in quality, and, as it does, so it filters down through the spectrum of household incomes moving from the richer to the poorer. Paralleling this there is a filtering of prices and values, the process of depreciation with advancing age. Filtering implies the constant flow of people through the housing stock. When a person buys a new house it usually means he moves out of an older one. One move leads to another. A species of musical chairs game ensues as people circulate or filter through housing. The rules of this game are among the imputed laws of housing market dynamics."

HOUSING IN AMERICA, *supra* note 20, at 161.

[49]Downs, *Are Subsidies the Best Answers for Housing Low and Moderate Income Households*, in HOUSING AND COMMUNITY DEVELOPMENT 122 (D. Mandelker et al. eds. 1981).

[50]*Id.* See also Wolfman, *Tax Expenditures: From Idea to Ideology* (Book Review), 99 HARV. L. REV. 491 (1985). For a critique of homeowner deductions, see Dolbeare, *How the Income Tax System Subsidizes Housing for the Affluent*, in CRITICAL PERSPECTIVES, *supra* note 19, at 264. In 1987, the federal government spent approximately $70 billion on housing, including tax expenditures, housing program budgets, and housing assistance benefits. As Simons points out, "Of this amount, almost 75% was spent to promote homeownership—three times the amount spent on all subsidized and rental housing programs combined." Simons, *supra* note 29, at 284 n. 72.

[51]Checkoway, *Large Builders, Federal Housing Programs, and Postwar Suburbanization*, in CRITICAL PERSPECTIVE, *supra* note 19, at 119.

[52]D. Mandelker et al., *supra* note 49, at 361.

[53]*Id.*

[54]*Id.*

[55]Sander, *Individual Rights and Demographic Realities: The Problems of Fair Housing*, 82 NW. U.L. REV. 874, 887 (1988).

[56]Downs, *supra* note 49, at 123.

[57]*Id.*

[58]R. Montgomery & D. Mandelker, *supra* note 20, at 203.

[59]Mc Dougall, *supra* note 29, at 755 and 761.

[60]15 HOUS. & DEVEL. REP. 600 (Jan. 11, 1988).

[61]*Id.*

[62]McDougal, *supra* note 29, at 759. For a federal housing policy overview, see Fernslere, Tuttle, Kessler, Kogan, Simons & Walsh, *Historical Perspectives, Current Trends and Future Roles in Housing and Community Development*, 16 URB. LAW. 683, 687-90 (1984); Nolon, *Reexamining Federal Housing Programs in a Time of Austerity: The Trend Toward Block Grants and Housing Allowances*, 14 URB. LAW. 249, 253-57 (1982). See also Bender, *Fenderal Budget Cuts in Housing: Is There No Place Like a Decent Home?*, 10 J. LEGIS. 457, 457-67 (1983). On rental versus home ownership in federal policy, see Hoeflich & Malloy, *The Shattered Dream of American Housing Policy — The Need for Reform*, 26 B.C.L. REV. 655, 657-59 (1985).

[63]THE PRESIDENT'S COMMISSION ON HOUSING, INTERIM REPORT 3 (1980).

[64]Nolon *supra* note 62, at 250.

[65]Bender, *supra* note 62, at 457-67.

[66]See generally, Hartmen, *Housing Policies Under the Reagan Administration*, in CRITICAL PERSPECTIVES, *supra* note 19, at 362.

[67]*Id.*

[68]As summarized by the National Housing Law Project in Berkeley:

"HUD has been encouraging the demolition or sale of public housing projects, including sales to tenants, by having the governing rules loosened, by issuing policy statements in favor of local effort to demolish or sell projects and, finally, by creating financial pressures on housing authorities to sell or demolish. Similarly, with the private programs, HUD has encouraged legislative changes loosening the grounds for allowing prepayment of the mortgages, has taken no steps to prevent Section 8 landlords from deciding not to renew their project-based Housing Assistance Payments (HAP)contracts, and has pursued property disposition policies that eliminate the federal government's commitment to subsidize projects in the future."

NATIONAL HOUSING LAW PROJECT, HUD HOUSING PROGRAMS: TENANTS RIGHTS 1/2 (Supp. 1985) (hereinafter HUD HOUSING PROGRAMS).

[69]Pub. L. No. 100-242, [S.825 101 stat. 181] (1987).

[70]Simons, *supra* note 29, at 275.

[71]As Simons states:

"Recent proposals have been made to sell of the federal government's public housing inventory either to tenants or private owners, or to demolish troubled public housing projects. Advocates of such action argue that the federal government is incapable of managing public housing. Such proposals immediately threaten thousands of units of low-income housing and future generations of needy families would be deprived of this permanent source of affordable housing."

Id. at 272. See also note, *New Developments Concerning the Demolition and Disposition of Public Housing Units* 18 HOUS. L. BULL. 91 (Sept. - Oct. 1988).

[72]See Pennsylvania v. Lynn, 501 F. 2d 848 (D.C. Cir. 1974).

[73]McDougal, *supra* note 29, at 745-48.

[74]See NATIONAL HOUSING LAW PROJECT, *supra* note 68, Chap. 15.

[75]See respectively, Section 181 and Section 201-235.

[76]Note, *Major Threats Imperil Subsidized Projects*, 16 HOUS. L. BULL. 1 (July - Aug. 1986).

[77]Lehman, *Low-Income Housing Stock Bottom Out*, U.S. REAL ESTATE WEEK 16 (Sept. 7, 1987).

[78]*Id.*

[79]*Id.*

[80]National Housing Law Project, *Summary of the 1987 Federal Housing Legislation*, 21 CLEAR-INGHOUSE REV. 1183, 1190 (1988).

[81]Simons, *supra* note 29, at 271.

[82]15 HOUS. & DEVEL. REP 738 (Feb. 22, 1988).

[83]*Id.*

[84]*Id.* at 914-15 (April 18, 1988).

[85]*Id.*

[86]Hartman, *supra* note 66, at 369-74.

[87]As the National Housing Law Project stated:

"Any voucher program which is adopted must be an entitlement program, must not be the sole federal housing program, cannot be a replacement for existing public housing and Section 8 projects, must be a supplement to, not a replacement for income maintenance programs, must include provisions guaranteeing tenants' right [as a result of much litigation over the years, public housing tenants have a range of rights generally not available to private-market tenants under most states' landlord-tenant laws] and must be distributed fairly."

Id. at 373.

[88]See generally, Abbott, *Housing Policy, Housing Codes and Tenant Remedies: An Integration*, 56, B.U.L. REV. 1 (1976).

[89]Pettigrew, *supra* note 39, at 676.

[90]See generally Bratt, *Public Housing: The Controversy and Contribution*, in CRITICAL PER-SPECTIVES, *supra* 19, at 335.

[91]Celis, *Public-Housing Units Are Rapidly Decaying, Causing Many to Close*, The Wall St., Dec. 15, 1, at 1, Col. 1.

[92]*Id.*

[93]42 U.S.C. 5301 et. seq.

[94]*Id.* at 5301(d)(4).

[95]See generally De Leon and Le Gates, *Community Development Block Grants: Redistributive Effects and Equity Issues*, 9 URB. LAW 364 (1977); Fernsler, Tuttle, Kessler, Kogan, Simons &

Walsh, *Historical Perspectives, Current Trends and Future Roles in Housing and Community Development*, 16 URB. LAW 683 (1984).

[96]D. BELL, RACE, RACISM AND AMERICAN LAW 544-45 (2d ed. 1980).

[97]McGee, *Urban Renewal in the Crucible of Judicial Review*, 56 VA. L. REV. 826, 874 (1970).

[98]NATIONAL HOUSING LAW PROJECT, HUD HOUSING PROGRAMS: TENANTS RIGHTS 119 (1981).

[99]LeGates & Hartman, *Displacement* 16, 15 CLEARINGHOUSE REV. 207 (1981).

[100]Hopper & Hamberg, *The Making of America's Homeless: From Skid Row to New Poor, 1945-84*, in CRITICAL PERSPECTIVE, *supra* note 19, at 13.

[101]HOUSE COMMITTEE ON GOV'T OPERATIONS, THE FEDERAL RESPONSE TO THE HOMELESS CRISIS, H.R. REP. NO. 47, 99th Cong. 1st Sess. 7 (1985).

[102]*Id.*

[103]16 HOUS & DEVEL. REP. 612 (Nov. 28, 1988).

[104]*Id.* See also Crenshaw, *supra* note 1, at 1384 n. 199:

> "The racial character of rationalization that legitimate poverty is exemplified by advocates who seek to educate the American public about the severity of the homelessness problem by revealing that many of the new homeless are white. This does not necessarily indicate that advocates prefer whites over Blacks; instead, it is an acknowledgment that such a problem can easily be disregarded as the result of personal failure if its victims are Black. The vast number of white homeless, however, raises the inescapable inference that something is amiss within American' economic structure."

[105]*supra* note 19, at xvi - xvii

[106]National Housing Law Project, *supra* note 80, at 1197.

[107]*Id.* at 1197-98.

[108]D. NEWMAN, N. AMIDEL, B. CARTER, D. DAY, W. KRUVANT, & J RUSSELL, PROTEST, POLITICS, AND PROSPERITY: BLACK AMERICANS AND WHITE INSTITUTIONS, 1940-75, 138-39 (1978).

[109]See generally Lake, *The Fair Housing Act in a Discriminatory Market: The Persisting Dilemma*, AM. PLAN. A.J., Jan. 1981, at 48; Belton, *Burdens of Pleading and Proof in Discrimination Cases: Toward a Theory of Procedural Justice*, 34 VAND. L. REV. 1205 (1981). Two excellent books on fair housing are J. Kushner, FAIR HOUSING: DISCRIMINATION REAL ESTATE, COMMUNITY DEVELOPMENTS AND REVITALIZATION (1983) and R. Schwemm, HOUSING DISCRIMINATION LAW (1983).

[110]Note, *Discriminatory Housing Markets, Racial Unconscionability, and Section 1988: The Contract Buyers League Case*, 80 YALE L. J. 516, 561 (1971).

[111]See, e.g., Smith v. Anchor Bldg. Corp., 536 F.2d 231 (8th Cir. 1976).

[112]See Note, *Justifying a Discriminatory Effect Under the Fair Housing Act: A Search for the Proper Standard*, 27 U.C.L.A. L. REV. 398 (1979).

[113]See, e.g., Schwemm, *Discriminatory Effect Cases Under Title VIII*, 27 TRENDS IN HOUSEING 3 (June-July 1988).

[114]See, e.g, Pearce, *A Sheltered Crisis: The State of Fair Housing Opportunity in the Eighties*, in U.S. COMM'N ON CIVIL RIGHTS, A SHELTERED CRISIS: THE STATE OF FAIR HOUSING IN THE EIGHTIES 143 (1983) [hereinafter A SHELTERED CRISIS].

[115]Tidwell, *Housing Discrimination: A New Technology*, id. at 159.

[116]*Id.* at 160.

[117]*Id.*

[118]Note, *Discriminatory Housing Markets*, *supra* note 110, at 561.

[119]*Id.*

[120]*Id.* See, e.g., U.S. v. City of Parma, Ohio 494 F. Supp. 1049, 1055-65 (N.D. Ohio 1979).

[121]Note, *Discriminatory Housing Markets*, *supra* note 110, at 561.

[122]Hall v. Werthan Bag Corp., 251 F. Supp. 184, 186 (M.D. Tenn. 1966) *Accord*, Oatis V. Zellerback Corp., 398 F. 2d 496, 499 (5th ir. 1968)

[123]Welch, *Removing Discriminatory Barriers: Basing Disparate Treatment Analysis on Motive Rather than Intent*, 60 S. CAL. L. REV. 733, 744 (1985).

[124]Brest, *The Supreme Court, 1975 Term - Foreword: In Defense of the Antidiscrimination Principle*, 90 HARV. L. REV. 1, 7-8 (1976). The worst example, perhaps, is seen in the area of capital punishment, devaluing black victims. See, e.g., Kennedy, *McClesky v. Kemp; Race, Capital Punishment, and the Supreme Court* 101 HARV L. REV. 1388, 1391-94 (1988).

[125]Brest, *supra* note 124, at 8.

[126]Ely, *The Wages of Crying Wolf: A Comment on Roe v. Wade*, 82 YALE L. J. 920, 934 n. 85 (1973). See also Lawrence, *The Id, the Ego, and Equal Protection: Reckoning with Unconscious Racism*, 39 STAN. L. REV. 317, 337-39, 343-44 (1987).

[127]Welch, *supra* note 123, at 746. Closely associated with stereotyping is the process of stigmatization, which provides social meaning to racial segregation. As Lawrence explains:

> "Stigmatization is the process by which the dominant group in society differentiates itself from others by setting them apart, treating them as less than fully human, denying them acceptance by the organized community, and excluding them from participating in that community as equals....

> Stigmatizing actions harm the individual in two ways: They inflict psychological injury by assaulting a person's self-respect and human dignity, and they brand the individual with a sign that signals her inferior status to others and designates her as an outcase. The stigma theory recognizes the importance of both self-esteem and the respect of others for participating in society's benefits and responsibilities.

> [R]acial stigma is self-perpetuating. Labeling blacks as inferior denies them access to societal opportunities; as a result, inadequate educational preparation, proverty of experience, and insufficient basic necessities limit their ability to contribute to society, and the prophecy of their inferiority is fulfilled. Furthermore, separate incidents of racial stigmatization do not inflict isolated injuries but are part of a mutually reinforcing and pervasive pattern of stigmatizing actions that cumulate to compose an injurious whole that is greater than the sum of its parts."

Lawrence, *supra* note 126, at 350-51.

[128]Brest, *supra* note 124, at 31.

[129]Schnapper, *Perpetuation of Past Discrimination*, 96 HARV L. REV. 828 (1983).

[130]*Id.* at 840.

[131]Welch, *supra* note 123, at 747.

[132]Schnapper, *supra* note 129, at 840.

[133]Welch, *supra* note 123, at 776.

[134]L. TRIBE, CONSTITUTIONAL CHOICES 241 (1985).

[135]R. FARLEY & W. ALLEN, *supra* note 5, at 140. Discrimination and segregation are intertwined but separate phenomena. The latter has proven to be less amenable to fair housing's reach in terms of both rights and remedies. While the interconnectedness between discrimination and segregation if often well-analyzed in education controversies, it is generally not so in housing controversies.

[136]One commentator states, however:

> "The Fair Housing Act of 1968 directly attacked only discrimination. So did nearly all state and local fair housing laws. These laws focused on individual and institutional behavior and sought to prevent specific acts of discrimination from taking place. Whether those who enacted these laws may have assumed or hoped that integration would follow when discrimination declined is a difficult question. But they clearly did not imagine that a successful attack on discrimination would require strategies geared towards group dynamics as well as individual behavior. To argue, as ultimately one must, that segregation (and thus dis-

crimination) can often be eliminated only by shaping collective behavior is to step outside the mainstream of our legal traditions.''
Sander, *supra* note 55, at 903.

[137]The analysis is further complicated by expanding intraracial social stratification within the black community, manifesting itself in spatial separation. See, e.g, Bernstein, *20 Years After the Kerner Report: Three Societies, All Separate*, N.Y. Times, Feb. 29, 1988, at B8, col. 2 and Lauter & May, *A Saga of Triumph, a Return to Poverty: Black Middle Class Has Grown but Poor Mutliply*, L.A. Times, April 2, 1988, 1, at 16, col. 1. See generally, Calmore, *Exploring the Significance of Race and Class in Representing the Black Poor*, 61 ORE. L. REV. 201 (1982)

[138]But see Section IV *infra*.

[139]But see K. BUMILLER, THE CIVIL RIGHTS SOCIETY 1-22 (1988) J. BLOOM, CLASS, RACE, AND THE CIVIL RIGHTS MOVEMENT 214-224 (1987); and THE CIVIL RIGHTS MOVEMENT IN AMERICA 127-155 (1986) (detailing the limits of the civil rights movement generally to attain material equality).

[140]R. FARLEY & W. Allen, *supra* note 5, at 141-43.

[141]Galster, *More than Skin Deep: The Effect of Housing Discrimination on the Extent and Pattern of Racial Residential Segregation in the United States*, in HOUSING DESEGREGATION, *supra* note 5, at 119.

[142]Darden, *Population Growth and Spatial Distribution*, in A SHELTERED CRISIS, *supra* note 114, at 9-10.

[143]M. DANIELSON, THE POLITICS OF EXCLUSION (1976), in G. FRUG, LOCAL GOVERNMENT LAW 406 (1988).

[144]*Id.*

[145]P. MULLER, THE OUTER CITY: GEOGRAPHICAL CONSEQUENCES OF THE ORGANIZATION OF THE SUBURBS (1976), in HOUSING IN AMERICA, *supra* note 20, at 371-72.

[146]*Id.* at 372.

[147]Orfield, *Minorities and Suburbanization*, in CRITICAL PERSPECTIVE, *supra* note 19, at 223.

[148]*Id.* at 225.

[149]Sander, *supra* note 55, at 887.

[150]*Id.* at 884.

[151]R. FARLEY & W. ALLEN, *supra* note 5, at 144.

[152]*Id.* at 142-43.

[153]*Id.* at 148.

[154]*Id.* at 145.

[155]*Id.*

[156]*Id.* at 146

[157]Sander *supra* note 55, at 885-86.

[158]Swinton, *supra* note 55, at 131-38.

[159]Tidwell, *supra* note 115, at 195.

[160]R. FARLEY & W. ALLEN, *supra* note 5, at 144-45.

[161]*Id.* at 145

[162]Firebach & Davis, *Trends in Antiblack Prejudice, 1972-1984: Region and Cohort Effects*, 94 AM. J. SOC. 251, 258-59 (1988).

[163]*Id.* at 251-52, 267. Pettigrew, however, distinguishes traditional antiblack prejudice from its present form, describing the latter as follows:

"Modern antiblack prejudice is characterized by the following six features: (1) rejection of gross stereotypes and blatant discrimination; (2) normative compliance without internalization of new behavioral norms of racial acceptance; (3) emotional ambivalence toward black people that stems from early childhood socialization and a sense that blacks are curretnly violating traditional American values; (4) indirect "micro-aggressions' against blacks which is expressed in avoidance of face-to-face interaction with blacks and opposition to racial change for ostensibly nonracial reasons; (5) a sense of subjective threat from racial chance, and· (6) individualistic conceptions of how opportunity and social stratification operate in American society."

Pettigrew, *supra* note 39, at 687.

[164]Fireback & Davis, *supra* note 162, at 253. See also H. SCHUMMAN, C STEEH, & L. BOBO, RACIAL ATTITUDES IN AMERICA: TRENDS AND INTERPRETATIONS 134 (1985).

[165]Fireback & Davis, *supra* note 162, at 253.

[166]Shumman & Bobo, *Survey-based Experiments on White Racial Attitudes Toward Residential Integration*, 94 AM.J. SOC. 273, 274 (1988).

[167]*Id.* at 275.

[168]Dovidio & Gaertner, *Prejudice, Discrimination, and Racism: Historical Trends and Contemporary Approaches*, in PREJUDICE, DISCRIMINATION, AND RACISM 1-34 (J. Dovidio & S. Gaertner eds. 1986).

[169]Sears, *Symbolic Racism*, ELIMINATING RACISM: MEANS AND CONTROVERIES 53 (P. Katz & D. Taylor eds. 1988). See also Kinder, *The Continuing American Dilemma: White Resistance to Racial Chance 40 Years after Myrdal*, 42 J. SOC. ISSUES 152 (1986).

[170]Jackman & Muha, *Education and Intergroup Attitudes: Moral Enlightenment, Superficial Democratic Commitment, or Ideological Refinement?* 49 AM. SOC. REV.751 (1984).

[171]Silverman, *Subsidizing Tolerance for Open Communities*, 1977 WIS L. REV. 375, 429-471.

[172]R. FARLEY & W. ALLEN, *supra* note 5, at 151-52.

[173]Silverman, *supra* note 171, at 468.

[174]Shumman & Bobo, *supra* note 166, at 295-96.

[175]*Id.* at 296.

[176]R. FARLEY & W. ALLEN, *supra* note 5, at 154.

[177]*Id.*

[178]*Id.*

[179]Muth, *The Causes of Housing Segregation*, in U.S. COMM'N ON CIVIL RIGHTS, 1 ISSUES IN HOUSING DISCRIMINATION 8-9 (1985).

[180]Note, *Benign Steering and Benign Quotas: The Validity of Race Conscious Governmental Policies to Promote Residential Integration*, 93 HARV L. REV. 938, 944-45 (1980).

[181]*Id.* at 939.

[182]See generally Goering, *Neighborhood Tipping and Racial Transition: A Review of Social Science Evidence*, 44 J. AM INST. PLANNERS 68 (1978); Ackerman, *Integration for Subsidized Housing and the Question of Racial Occupancy Controls*, 26 STAN. L. REV. 245 (1974).

[183]Polikoff, *Sustainable Integration or Inevitable Resegregation: The Troubling Questions*, in HOUSING DESEGREGATION, *supra* note 5, at 45; Mariano *Nation's Policy in Integration at Crossroads*, Washington Post, July 21, 1984, at E3, Col. 1.

[184]Orfield, *The Movement for Housing Integration: Rationale and the Nature of the Challenge*, in HOUSING DESEGREGATION, *supra* note 5, at 18.

[185]Barrick Realty, Inc. v. City of Gary 491 F. 2d 161, 164065 (7th Cir. 1974). See also, the important case of Otero v. New York City Housing Auth., 484 F.2d 1122, 1125 26 (2d Cir. 1973).

[186]Burney v. Hous. Auth. of Beaver, 551 F. Supp. 746, 769 (W.D. Pa. 1982). See also, United States v. Starret City Assocs., 660 F Supp. 668 (E.P.N.Y. 1987), aff'd., 840 F.2d 1096 (2d Cir. 1988). See also *U.S. Supreme Court Lets Stand Two Appellate Court Rulings on Housing Bias*, 16 HOUS & DEVEL. REP. 560-61 (Nov. 14, 1988) (According to William Bradford Reynolds, assistant atty. general for the civil rights division of the Justice Dept., although the Supreme Court refused to review the case and it sets no national precedent, it "sends a strong signal" that racial quotas used to support integration maintenance are illegal).

[187]Leigh & McGhee, *A Minority Perspective on Residential Racial Integration*, in HOUSING DESEGREGATION, *supra* note 5, at 39.

[188]R. FARLEY & W. ALLEN, *supra* note 5, at 152.

[189]Muth, *supra* note 179, at 12-13.

[190]Silverman, *supra* note 171, at 491.

[191]Sander, *supra* note 55, at 928-30.

[192]Silverman, *supra* note 171, at 471.

[193]See R SCHWEMM, *supra* note 109, at 227-300.

[194]*Id.* at 230-31.

[195]24 C.F.R. 115.6(e)(1)(1987), *amended* 53 Fed. Reg. 260, 6964 (1988). See also Calmore, *North Carolina's Retreat from Fair Housing: A Critical Examination of North Carolina Human Relations Council v. Weaver Realty Co*, 16 N.C. CENT. L. J.154 (1987) (arguing that Title VIII and the North Carolina Fair Housing Law are not "substantially equivalent").

[196]Waldrop, *Enforcement of the Fair Housing Act: What Role Should the Federal Government Play*, 74 KY. L.J. 201, 225 (1985-86).

[197]Kushner, *An Unfinished Agenda: The Federal Fair Housing Enforcement Effort*, 6 YALE L. & POL'Y REV. 348 (1988).

[198]Note, *The Legality of Race-Conscious Access Quotas Under the Fair Housing Act of 1968*, 9 CARDOZO L. REV. 1053, 1054 n. 54 (1988).

[199]As stated by Professor Schwemm:

> "This limitation is significant. It was inserted into section 810 as a result of the famous "Dirksen Compromise." In the original version of the bill proposed by Senator Mondale, HUD could issue 'cease and desist' and other affirmative orders. Senator Dirksen's support, which was needed to pass the bill, was gained in exchange for abandoning these powers and replacing them with merely 'conference, conciliation, and persuasion powers.' The Dirksen Compromise has resulted in an agency procedure that provides for absolutely no sanctions against a recalcitrant defendant. In its first review of this statute, the Supreme Court concluded that 'HUD has no power of enforcement."

> Schwemm, *Private Enforcement and the Fair Housing Act*, 6 YALE L. & POL'Y REVIEW 375,377 (1988).

[200]*Id.* 379-81. This is evidenced by the fact that federal court decisions involving housing discrimination number approximately 400; about 20 reported cases a year, or less than two per month whereas reported decisions on employment discrimination run 5 to 10 times that number, *Id.*

[201]Pub. Law 100-430 [H.R. 1158]; 102 STAT. 1619-1639. See generally, National Housing Law Project, *Summary of Fair Housing Amendments*, 18 HOUS. L. BULL.100 (Sept./Oct. 1988); Schwemm, *The Fair Housing Amendments Act: Legislative History*, 27 TRENDS IN HOUSING 1 (Aug. - Sept. 1988).

[202]See 804 and 805(a) of the new Act. Before amended Title VIII banned discrimination on the grounds of race, color religion, national origin and, since 1974, sex. See 42 U.S.C. 3604.

[203]See 810 and 812.

[204]812(g)(3).

[205]814(d).

[206]808(b).

[207]Golubock, *Housing Discrimination Against Families with Children: A Growing Problem of Exclusionary Practices*, in A SHELTERED CRISIS, *supra* note 114, at 129-131.

[208]Marshall, *Women with Children in Today's Housing Market*, *id.* at 110-113; Packer, *Discrimination Against Hispanic Women in Housing*, *id.* at 114-127.

[209]736 F.2d 983 (4th Cir. 1984) (all adult housing policy had a racially disparate impact on blacks and, if not justified as business necessity, it violates Title VIII). In California, the state Fair Employment and Housing Commission ruled that occupancy limits may not be used to try to keep children out of

rental units in California, declaring a restriction of one occupant per bedroom to discriminate against families with children. California law already had prohibited discrimination against families with children, but landlords had used occupancy limits as a subterfuge. Billiter, *Ruling May Help Ex-GI in Allegation of Housing Bias*, L.A. Times (Orange County Edition), Nov. 29, 1988 2, at 1 co. 1.

[210]See Calmore, *Proving Housing Discrimination: Intent vs. Effect and the Continuing Search for the Proper Touchstone*, in ISSUES IN HOUSING DISCRIMINATION, *supra* note, at 77. See also Huntington Branch NAACP v. Huntington U.S., affirming the appellate decision at 844 F.2d 926 (2d Cir. 1988) (Supreme Court upholding a discriminatory impact standard's application, but not resolving which test is the proper one for proving discrimination. See *U.S. Supreme Court Lets Stand Two Appellate Court Rulings on Housing Bias*, *supra* note 186, at 561.

[211]National Housing Law Project, *supra* note 201, at 100. See also Selig, *The Justice Department and Racially Exclusionary Municipal Practices: Creative Ventures in Fair Housing Act Enforcement*, 17 U.C. DAVIS L. REV. 445, 486, n. 193 (1984) ("Civil Rights Division attorneys were not permitted to argue for the application of an effects test in the post-trial briefs filed in the Reagan administration.").

[212]CONG. REC. 12449 (daily ed. Sept. 14, 1988).

[213]Bell, *Foreward: The Civil Rights Chronicles*, 99 HARV L. REV. 4, 5-13 (1985). Bell deems it a myth "that racial justice can be realized without [white people] sacrificing the material and psychological rewards of racial domination." *Id.* at 13. Bell's chronicles are expanded in D. BELL, AND WE ARE NOT SAVED: THE ELUSIVE QUEST FOR RACIAL JUSTICE (1987). As far back as 1981 it was reported that most whites believed that "equal opportunity" already existed. Orfied, *supra* note 184, at 27.

[214]Calmore, *National Housing Policies and Black America: Trends, Issues, and Implications*, in THE STATE OF BLACK AMERICA 1986, 138-140 (J. Williams ed. 1986). See also Calmore, *Exploring the Significance of Race and Class in Representing the Black Poor*, 61 ORE L. REV. 201, 237-44 (1982).

[215]Phillips & Agelasto, *Housing and Central Cities: The Conservation Approach*, 4 ECOLOGY L. Q. 797, 880 (1975).

[216]Plessy v. Ferguson, 163 U.S. 537 (1896) ("separate but equal" railway carriages were non unconstitutionaly discriminatory).

[217]Harold Cruse is simply right in saying:

> "Even without arguing the comparative assessments of the minority group status of blacks versus the status of other minorities, the impact of these minorities on contemporary civil rights processes makes it obligatory to reassess the former separate-but-equal doctrine. A reexamination is require not in the light of Plessy or even Brown, but in the light of actual racial and ethnic pluralism as an American reality. Philosophically, 'separate but equal' is, in the normative sense, 'unequal' only if in social practice it is the governing intent to make separateness politically, economically, and socially unequal, which of course makes such practices immoral. Thus separateness, which is not immoral, became segregation, which is immoral because it was not the intent to make separate equal. However, because it was not within the putative intent or within the economic and political capability of the state of Louisiana in 1896 to make separate facilities equal, this does not ipso facto absolve the state of some future obligation, under changed conditions, to render separate equal when, and if, it becomes feasible to do so. The Brown decision, in effect, absolved the state(s) of that obligation as a consequence of a legal analysis that separateness is inherently to mean inferior. Intrinsically, it means no such thing. Legally imposed segregation was what rendered separateness implicity inferior. Remove the legal sanctions of imposed segregation, and separateness has the potential of achieving equality in its own right.

H. CRUSE, PLURAL BUT EQUAL 67 (1987).

[218]The term "noneconomic liberalism" refers to pursuing constitutional legalism instead of economic empowerment. *Id.* at 372-73.

[219]L. TRIBE, AMERICAN CONSTITUTIONAL LAW 1515-16 (2d ed. 1988).

[220]Horwitz, *Right*, 23 HARV. G. R. C. L. L. REV. 393. 404 (1988).

[221]This is no easy task. Alan Freeman has characterized the development of antidiscrimination law "as not the linear reformist progress celebrated by liberals, but instead as a process of containing

and stabilizing the aspiration of the opressed through tokenism and formal gestures which actually enhance the material lives of few." Freeman, *Racism, Rights and the Quest for Equality of Opportunity: A Critical Legal Eassay*, 23 HARV. C. R. - C. L. L. REV. 295, 296 (1988). But see Crenshaw, *supra* note 1, at 1385: "Black people can afford neither to resign themselves to, nor to attack frontially, the legitimacy and incoherence of the dominant ideology....On the other hand, delegitimating race consciousness would be directly to Black needs, and this strategy will sometimes require the pragmatic use of liberal ideology."

[222] 223. B. MOORE, INJUSTICE: THE SOCIAL BASES OF OBEDIENCE AND REVOLT (1978).

[224] 23 HARV. C.R. - C.L.L. REV. 415 (1988).

[225] *Id.* at 418

[226] *Id.* at 430

[227] As Derrick Bell puts it:

"while the abandonment of overtly discriminatory policies has lowered racial barriers for some talented and skilled blacks seeking access to opportunity and advancement, their upward mobility is deemed the 'final proof' that racism is dead. This ......, however, underrates the achievement of those who have moved ahead and denies even societal sympathy to those whose opportunities are less promising today than they were twenty-five years ago."

Bell, *supra* note 213, at 12.

[228] Calmore, *Redefining Our Housing Priorities: Is Fair Housing Obscuring the Need for Low-Income Housing Assitance?*, PONT OF VIEW 38 (WINTER 1987)

[229] *Id.*

[230] *Id.*

[231] See Calmore, *Fair Housing v. Fair Housing: The Problems with Providing Increased Housing Opportunities Through Spatial Deconcentration*, 14 CLEARINGHOUSE REV. 7 (1980).

[232] Comment, *supra* note 24, at 417.

[233] *Id.*

[234] *Id.*

[235] *Id.* at 447.

[236] *Id.* at 481.

[237] See M. DEUTSCH, DISTRIBUTIVE JUSTICE 46-63 (1985).

[238] KERNER COMMISSION, REPORT OF THE NATIONAL ADVISORY COMMISSION ON CIVIL DISORDERS 406 (Bantum ed. 1968).

[239] See Kotlowitz, *Racial Gulf: Blacks' Hopes Raised by '68 Kerner Report Are Mainly Unfilled*, Wall St. J., Feb. 26, 1988, at 1, col. 1.

[240] KERNER COMMISSION, *supra* note 240, at 407.

[241] *Id.*

[242] Gewirtz, *supra* note 6, at 798.

[243] H. Cruse, *Supra* note 217.

[244] L. TRIBE, *supra* note 219, at 1521.

[245] Kushner, *Apartheid in America: An Historical and Legal Analysis of Contemporary Racial Residential Segregation in the United States*, 22 HOW. L. J. 547 (1979).

[246] J. KUSHNER, APARTHEID IN AMERICA i (1980.

[247] *id.*

[248] Schnapper, *supra* note 129, at 858.

[249] Boyd, *Kemp, Picked as Chief of H.U.D., Pledges to Combat Homelessness*, N.Y. Times, Dec. 20, 1988, at A1, cols. 1-2.

[250] *Id.* Indeed it may help all of us to recall the words of President Johnson, upon signing the Civil Rights Act of 1964:

"I want to take this occasion to talk to you about what the law means to every American. We believe that all men are created equal. Yet many are denied equal treatment. We believe that all men have certain unalienable rights. Yet many Americans do not enjoy these rights. We believe that all men are entitled to the blessings of liberty. Yet millions are being deprived of those blessings—not because of their own failures, but because of the color of their skin . . . But it cannot continue. Our Constitution, the foundation of our republic, forbids it. Morality forbids it. And the law I will sign tonight forbids it. Its purpose is to promote a more abiding commitment to freedom, a more constant pursuit of justice, and a deeper respect for human dignity. We will achieve these goals because most Americans are law-abiding citizens who want to do what is right."

Address of President Lyndon Johnson, Washington, D.C. (July 2, 1964), quoted in C. WHALEN & B. WHALEN, THE LONGEST DEBATE: A LEGISLATIVE HISTORY OF THE 1964 CIVIL RIGHTS ACT 227-28 (1985).

[251] Boyd, *supra* note 249.

[252] R. FARLEY & W. ALLEN, *supra* note 5, at 419.

On Parity and Political Empowerment, *Charles V. Hamilton, Ph.D.*

FOOTNOTES

[1] *The New York Times*, November 9, 1988.

[2] Underlines added.

[3] Anthony Lewis, "The Dirty Little Secret," *The New York Times*, October 20, 1988. p. A27. See also: Harry A. McPherson, "How Race Destroyed the Democrats' Coalition," *The New York Times*, October 28, 1988. p. A.35. That writer concluded: "Race — in the narrow political sense, meaning attitudes toward the participation of blacks in society — has always been a highly charged issue, whether or not explicitly raised in a campaign. . . . The consequences of slavery endure. Racism is still the most debilitating virus in the American system. It should be addressed directly and indirectly, in schools and on the job. But, another great attack on its consequences will require political consensus, or, at least, majorities, and those will not be obtained from defensive people who resent being adressed as racists. Practical ends and restrained language will be needed in composing the next liberal agenda."

[4] *The State of Black America 1988* (New York: National Urban League, January, 1988. p. 157.)

[5] *The State of Black America*, Ibid., p. 157.

[6] The New York Times/CBS News Poll. November 21, 1988. p. B16.

[7] Raymond E. Wolfinger and Steven J. Rosenstone, *Who Votes?* (New Haven: Yale University Press. 1980).

[8] Kleppner, Paul, *Who Voted? The Dynamics of Electoral Turnout, 1970-1980*, (New York: Praeger Publishers, 1982).

[9] Joint Center for Political Studies, *Black Elected Officials: A National Roster* (Washington, D.C.: Joint Center for Political Studies, 1985).

[10] Engstrom, Richard L., and McDonald, Micahel D., "The Election of blacks to City Council: Clarifying the impact of electoral arrangements on the seats/population relationship," *American Political Science Review*, Vol. 75, June 1981. 344-354. See also: "The Election of blacks to Southern City Councils: The dominant impact of electoral arrangements." Chapter 13 in *Blacks in Southern Politics*, eds., Lawrence W. Moreland, Robert P. Steed, and Tod A. Baker (New York: Praeger. 1987).

[11] Conyers, James E. and Walter Wallace, *Black Elected Officials: A Study of Black Americans Holding Governmental Office*, (New York: Russell Sage Foundation. 1976.) p. 31.

[12] The New York Times/CBS News Poll Post-Election Survey. November 10-16, 1988.

[13] Media General/Associated Press Poll. June 22-July 3, 1988. *The Polling Report*, Vol. 4. No. 16. August 22, 1988.

The New York Times/CBS News Poll. Late October Survey. October 21-24, 1988.

Black Higher Education: Crisis and Promise, *Reginald Wilson, Ph.D.*

FOOTNOTES

[1]The American Council on Education and The Education Commission of the States, *One-Third of A Nation*. Washington: The American Council on Education, May 23, 1988.

[2]The American Council on Education, *Seventh Annual Status Report on Minorities in Higher Education*, 1988.

[3]*The Chronicle of Higher Education*, "Placement Test Aids Minority Students," December 14, 1988.

[4]*Status Report*, op. cit., p. 11.

[5]*Status Report*, Ibid, p. 9.

[6]*Status Report*, Ibid, p. 10.

[7]This argument is developed in various places in the Seventh Annual Status Report.

[8]*Status Report*, p. 13.

[9]Holly Hexter, *Joining Forces: The Military's Impact on College Enrollments* (American Council on Education), October, 1988.

[10]Ibid, p. 13.

[11]Study commissioned by the Association of Independent Colleges and Schools (unpublished), 1987.

[12]*Status Report*, op. cit., p. 11.

[13]Ibid, Table 13.

[14]Cited in Reginald Wilson, "Past Methods of Affirmative Action," paper read at Conference on Race and Education (unpublished), Yale University, October 15, 1988, p. 12.

[15]Ibid, p. 12.

[16]Reginald Wilson and Sara Melendez, "Strategies for Developing Minority Leadership," in Madeleine F. Green (ed.), *Leaders for a New Era*. (New York: American Council on Education (Macmillan Publishing Company), 1988, p. 126.

Valuing Diversity: The Myth and The Challenge, *Price M. Cobbs, M.D.*

BIBLIOGRAPHY

Cobbs, Price M. and William Grier. 1988. *Black Rage*. Basic Books, Inc.

Cobbs, Price M. and William Grier. 1971. *The Jesus Bag*. McGraw-Hill.

Cobbs, Price M. Critical Perspectives On The Psychology of Race. The State of Black America 1988. National Urban League, Inc.

Copeland, Lennie. *Valuing Diversity, Part 1: Making the Most of Cultural Differences at the Workplace*. Personnel, June, 1988

Cuomo, Mario M. *The American* Dream and The Politics of Inclusion Psychology Today, July, 1986

DuBois, W.E.B. *The Souls of Black Folks — Essays and Sketches*, A. C. McClurg and Company, Chicago, Illinois, 1903.

Foster, Badi G., Jackson, Gerald, Cross, William E., Jackson,

Bailey and Hardiman, Rita. *Workforce Diversity and Business*. Training and Development Journal, April, 1988.

Graves, Earl. *Corporate Tragedies*. Black Enterprise Magazine, March, 1984.

Harragan, Betty L. 1977. *Games Mother Never Taught You*. New York: Rawson Associates.

Harris, Philip R., and Robert T. Moran. 1979. *Managing Cultural Differences*. Gulf Publishing Company.

Hennig, Margaret and Ann Jardim. 1977. *The Managerial Women*.

New York: Anchor Press/Doubleday.

Kanter, Rosabeth. 1977. *Men and Women of the Corporation*. Basic Books.

Kerr, Clark and Jerome N. Rosow, eds. 1979. *Work in America: The Decade Ahead*. Van Nostrand Reinhold Company.

McLeon, Beverly. *The Oriental Express*. Psychology Today, July, 1988.

Opportunity 2000. *Creative Affirmative Action Strategies For a Changing Workforce*. Hudson Institute, September, 1988.

Polsby, Nelson W. *Prospects for Pluralism*. Society, January-February, 1985.

Robson, Britt. *Corporate Cultures*. Black Enterprise Magazine, March, 1984.

Sargent, Alice G., ed. 1977. *Beyond Sex Roles*. San Francisco West Publishing Co.

Shipper, Frances C. and Frank M. *Beyond EEO: Toward Pluralism*. Business Horizons, June, 1987

Terry, Robert. *The White Male Club: Biology and Power*. New York: Harper and Row, 1978.

Leonard, George. *Walking on the Edge of the World*. Houghton Mifflin Company, 1988.

Workforce 2000. *Work and Workers for the 21st Century*. Hudson Institute, Inc., June, 1987.

Drugs in the African American Community: A Clear and Present Danger, *Wade Nobles, Ph.D. and Lawford L. Goddard, Ph.D.*

BIBLIOGRAPHY

Barnes, C., Melanin: The Chemical Key to Black Greatness. Black Greatness Series, Vol 1 (082486). Houston, Texas. 1988.

Goddard, L. L. The impact of substance abuse on the Black community: A position paper, commissioned by the Sinkler-Miller Medical Association. Unpublished manuscript, 1988.

Heckler, M. M., Report of the Secretary's Task Force on Black and Minority Health. Volume I: Executive Summary. U. S. Department of Health and Human Services, Washington, D. C. U. S. Government Printing Office, August, 1985.

Heckler, M. M., Report of the Secretary's Task Force on Black and Minority Health. Volume VII: Chemical Dependency and Diabetes. U. S. Department of Health and Human Services, Washington, D.C.: U. S. Government Printing Office, August, 1985.

Herrington, L. H. The White House Conference for a Drug-free America, Final Report, June, 1988.

Katner, H. P. and Pankey, G. A., Evidence for a Euro-American origin of human immunodeficiency virus (HIV). Journal of National Medical Association, 79, pp. 1068-1082, 1987.

Lipscomb, W.R., "Black Driniking Practices Study" Source, Inc. Berkeley, California, 1981.

National Center for Health Statistics: Health, United States, 1987. DHHS Pub. No. (PHS) 88-1232. Public Health Service. Washington, D.C.: U. S. Government Printing Office, March, 1988.

National Institute of Drug Abuse: National Trends in Drug Use and Related Factors Among American High School Students and Young Adults, 1975-1986. U. S. DHHS Pub. No. (ADM) 87-1535, Public Health Service. Washington, D.C.: U. S. Government Printing Office, 1987.

National Institute of Drug Abuse: National Household Survey on Drug Abuse: Population Estimates 1985. U.S. DHHS Pub. No. (ADM) 87 1539, Public Health Service Washington, D.C.: U. S. Government Printing Office, 1987.

National Institute of Drug Abuse: National Survey of Drug Abuse, Main Findings 1982. U. S. DHHS Pub. No. (ADM) 83-1263, Public Health Service. Washington, D.C.: U. S. Government Printing Office, 1983.

National Institute of Drug Abuse: Statistical Series, Series 1, No. 6, Annual Data, 1986. Data from the Drug Abuse Warning Network (DAWN). U. S. DHHS Pub. No. (ADM) 87-1530, Public Health Service. Washington, D.C.: U. S. Government Printing Office, 1987.

Nobles, W. W., Goddard L. L., Cavil, W. E., and George, P. Y., "A Clear and Present Danger: The Effects of Drugs and Drug Trafficking on the Mental Health of Black Children and Families in Oakland," Final Report. Alameda County Health Care Services Agency. Oakland, California, 1987.

Williams, M., *"Blacks and Alcoholism: Issues in the 80's,"* Alcohol and Research World, Vol. 6 No. 4, 1982.

Acknowledgments

The National Urban League acknowledges with sincere appreciation the contributions of the authors of the various papers appearing in this publication; Johnnie Griffin, technical editor; Michele R. Long, proofreading assistant; and the special contributions of NUL staff, including Ernie Johnston, Jr., B. Maxwell Stamper, Farida Syed, Faith Williams, Ollie Wadler, and Denise Wright of the Public Relations and Communications Department; Washington Operations; the Research Department; and the Program Departments. We also acknowledge the research assistance of the Schomburg Center for Research in Black Culture.

Order Blank

National Urban League Publications
500 East 62nd Street
New York, N.Y. 10021

	Per Copy	Number of Copies	Total
The State of Black America 1989	$19.00	_____	_____
Recent Volumes in series:			
The State of Black America 1988	$18.00	_____	_____
The State of Black America 1987	$18.00	_____	_____
The State of Black America 1986	$18.00	_____	_____
The State of Black America 1985	$17.00	_____	_____
Postage & handling: Individual volumes——$1.50 each		_____	_____
	Amount enclosed	_____	

"The Promise" Lithograph

Limited edition, numbered lithograph of "The Promise" by Hughie Lee Smith, signed by the artist. "The Promise" is the second in the Great Artists series created for the National Urban League through a donation from the House of Seagram. Proceeds benefit the National Urban League.

Unframed lithograph 29″ × 21″. Full color. $1,000 each, includes postage and handling.

For information and to order, contact:

National Urban League, Inc.
Office of Development
500 East 62nd Street
New York, New York 10021

Please make checks or money orders payable to:
National Urban League, Inc.